IN PRAISE OF VEGETABLES

In Praise

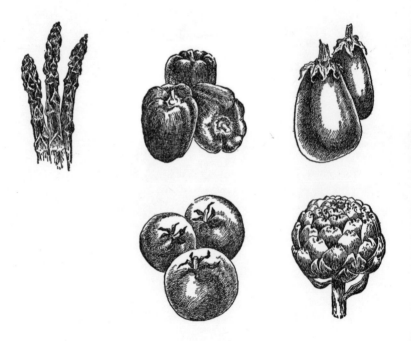

# of Vegetables

Luise Light

CHARLES SCRIBNER'S SONS
New York

*I dedicate this book to my husband,
Jack, for his practical aid, inspiration,
wise counsel and gustatory discernment.*

Preface

A book, like a house, is conceived and constructed according to a master architectural plan, element by element. This book would not have been possible without the help of those named below who provided the superstructure on which this book was built.

My thanks go to those who gave moral and practical aid, provided recipe and food ideas, volunteered useful information and suggested source material. My gratitude to all friends and house guests who tested and tasted my culinary creations.

To those whose encouragement and positive attitudes spurred me to complete this work, my sincere appreciation.

Mr. & Mrs. Meyer Landes, Mr. & Mrs. Rose Light, Mrs. Martha Light, Mrs. Evelyn Dorfman, Mr. Albert Rudolph, Mrs. Rae Rudolph, Mrs. Ruth Markowitz, Mrs. Sonia Landes, Mrs. Paul Winchell, Edith Montlack, Mrs. Elizabeth Boeke, Lalli, Mr. Steve Addis, Mrs. Gilda Ekelchik, Mrs. Mimi Turque, Louie Cheney Becker, Tibbi Duboys, Dilip Mehta, Laurie J. Wilson, Mr. Han, Mrs. Loretta Koppen, Mrs. Judith Weintraub, Marie & Pat of Fantasia Beauty Parlor, Mr. & Mrs. Harry Preisler, Mrs. Bertha Glaberman, Mrs. Vera Albergo, Joseph of Joseph's Oriental Grocery, Mrs. Rogers of the Akron Restaurant, Mr. & Mrs. Weiser and Mr. & Mrs. Gottshall of The Glockenspiel Restaurant, The Mennonite Ladies of Lancaster County, Dr. Frank Celenza and Dr. Max Siegal.

Special thanks go to Mrs. Cathy Porcaro for the excellent job of deciphering and typing my notes.

—LUISE LIGHT

vii

Contents

Preface   *vii*
Introduction   *xi*
Glossary of Cooking Terms   *xix*

PART ONE

Chapter 1
FROM THE MARKET TO THE POT   3

What to Shop For   3
Keeping Your Vegetables Fresh   12
Basic Preparations and Definitions   13

Chapter 2
THE ART OF SEASONING   18

Vegetables in Many Languages   22
Herb and Spice Guide   29
Other Flavorings and Seasonings   32
Vegetable Seasoning Guide   36

PART TWO

Chapter 3
SAUCES—YOUR ACE IN THE HOLE   45

Hot Sauces for Hot Vegetables   46
Some Unusual Hot Sauces for Vegetables   52
Cold Sauces for Hot or Cold Vegetables   56

Chapter 4
THE ADVENTURE OF SALAD MAKING   59

    Preparing Raw Salads   60
    My Favorite Salad Dressings and Marinades   62
    Favorite Salads in My House   66

Chapter 5
A SOUP FOR ALL SEASONS   78

    Definitions   81
    The Stock-Pot   82
    Hot Soups   84
    Cold Soups   96

Chapter 6
CASSEROLES FOR CAREFREE LIVING   99

Chapter 7
LEFTOVERS REDRESSED   111

Chapter 8
THE VEGETABLE LOVER'S DIET   118

    Vegetable Recipes for Dieters   129
    Adapting Recipes to Reducing Diets   141

PART THREE

Chapter 9
INDIVIDUAL VEGETABLE RECIPES   145

Introduction

As a child I hated vegetables. Potatoes, tomatoes, peas, corn and an occasional lettuce leaf were my absolute limit. I can remember my mother valiantly trying to tempt me with steamy platters of asparagus, beets, cauliflower and the like. In the interest of good nutrition, she tried everything the market offered. They were presented boiled, stewed, and baked. Occasionally, they were sauced or mashed. Once in a blue moon, they were fried. A bright confetti of chopped vegetables always garnished these nutritionally sound plates. Still, I passed them by. As my mother watched the products of her work cool into a wilted heap on the table, she would inevitably cry out, "but they're good for you, dear!" That was the clincher. By the inexorable logic of childhood, anything that was good for you just had to taste awful.

By the time I reached dating age I had outgrown baby fat and grown into chubbiness. Tired of hearing about girl friends' social whirls and having none of my own to relate, I was determined to slim down and get popular. I visited my family physician for advice. He weighed me in, shook his head, and handed me a printed diet list. I scanned it quickly. "Have you got any others," I asked naïvely? He glowered, "What's wrong with this one?" "It's mostly vegetables," I explained. "So?" he chided. I replied quite coolly, "I don't eat vegetables." His answer made me feel like a criminal. "Well, you darn well better learn to eat them and like them if you want to lose weight. The trouble with you and the rest of the young people today is that you eat all the junk that's sold and ignore the good, healthful foods." Feeling very much like a martyr to the cause, I resolved to give his diet a try. I handed the list to my mother. For lunch that day I was served one quarter of a head of lettuce, three slices of tomato, one half of a cup of boiled green beans, some meat and a fruit. One bite of lettuce, a few slices of tomato, and one rather limp green bean was what I managed to down. Dinner's vegetable allotment was celery and carrot stalks, plain boiled cabbage, and three tablespoons of peas. After four days of near famine I decided it was far better to feast alone than to starve surrounded by beaux.

At college, I managed to win some degree of popularity despite my aversion to greens. Of course, college dates were more sophisticated than high school ones. I was escorted to the theatre as well as to movie houses and to fashionable foreign restaurants in place of neighborhood snack joints. Everywhere we dined vegetables reared their (to me) unlovely heads. The forms varied. Now they were called Eggplant Parmigiano, Caesar Salad, Broccoli Hollandaise, Snow Peas with Bamboo Shoots and Mushrooms, Artichoke Vinaigrette. Most of them looked appealing. Some even smelled divine. Yet, in deference to torments of the past, I could never bring myself to taste them. My escorts made comments. A few really put themselves out to break down my (anti-vegetable) resolve. I became the victim of the syllogistic approach: I enjoyed well-prepared foods from the most exotic to the more mundane, vegetables hold a place of honor in all international cuisines; therefore, I would love them if I tried them. I was the butt of statistics. I learned the percentage of the earth's population for whom vegetables comprise the major portion of their diet, the average lifespan of a vegetarian as opposed to a non-vegetable-eater, and the proven salutary effects of greens on meat eaters. I developed a standard defense. "Vegetables all taste the same: bland! Greens are for rabbits! Vegetables are food for livestock! They're just not worth the trouble!" My dates must have thought I was crazy. But this craziness didn't seem to dampen my social schedule. On the contrary, I was more and more popular. Young men vied for the opportunity to bring me face to face with vegetables.

America is a bountiful land. With a multi-vitamin capsule swallowed faithfully each morning it is quite possible to survive, even to flourish on foods other than vegetables. There are fruits, dairy products, meats, fish, poultry, breadstuffs, condiments and sweets to choose from; an infinite variety of non-vegetable products with which to titillate one's palate. As long as I remained home in the United States I was safe within my prejudice.

Shortly after college, an opportunity to study abroad presented itself. I always had a yen for travel, and after attending a college in my home town, I was eager for the chance to be on my own. I would have to learn a language only vaguely familiar to me and the way of life, I knew, would be quite different from my own. But these things seemed challenges rather than obstacles.

Armed with a modest living allowance and a few portable conveniences of life, I arrived in Israel. I was greeted by a sun-bright Mediterranean country uniquely combining the industry of the West with the sounds and colors of the Levant. Bewitched by the aromas of jasmine, oleander and blossoming citrus trees that filled the air those first Fall months, I set about digging in. Friends were made quickly. The Israelis are an open-hearted people and proud to show off their country to strangers. I was invited to share their homes, their food, and their recreations. Learning to share the love they bore for their homeland was easy.

Part of my new-made friends' program for getting me to know and understand their country was the thorough-going exploration of the town that was to be my home for the year, Jerusalem. "It is a special city," they would tell me. "It is like no other in Israel. You will feel it, an atmosphere of scholarship, of wisdom, of dignity; Jerusalem is the queen of cities." There was a magical feeling about the town, a serenity that seemed as ancient as the massive granite slabs with which most of the houses had been built. (By special ordinance, all of the city's houses had to be made of stone.) The newer part of town had great tree-lined avenues and fortress-like buildings set back from the street. But it was the old city of winding, cobbled streets, yellowed and crumbling houses built around courts Arab-fashion, shop stalls as dark and deep and cool as caves (where the most ancient of European and Oriental Jewish tradition melted into a common living present), that captivated me.

I was looking for a cot for my newly acquired apartment. I'd been sent to the "old market" in the "old town." I had no idea where it was. I asked for directions as I walked. After an hour's hike, I found myself in Shuk Yehuda, an open-air market as old in tradition as the city itself. Everything from furniture to windowpanes to shoes and foodstuffs was for sale. Pots, yard-goods, rugs, clothing, the entire assortment of goods for sale, dangled and flapped from overhead railings like banners at a street fiesta. Street after street was lined with merchandise stalls and flimsy-framed shops. It looked like a Stateside carnival, except that here the merchants wore kefiyahs and called out their wares in a high, nasal melody. Old men sat cross-legged between doorjambs of shops puffing rhythmically at nargillas (water-pipes) and fondling strings of yellow beads. Hoary women swathed in black sat in long solemn rows, their backs against the shop walls, asking for alms from passerbys or simply dreaming with eyes shut and smiling, silent lips. At the market stalls, Bukharian women in brightly patterned pantaloons and kerchiefed heads contested elbow to elbow with modern Israeli housewives in neat print dresses. The odors of open sacks of spices, brine cheese, olives of all varieties, rosewater-flavored sweets, and baking bread made one dizzy. At an open-air bakery, I watched a young man throw a ball of dough into the air and spin it out into pancake thinness. He was making Hibis, the traditional flatbread of the Middle East. My quest for a cot was forgotten. The hallucinatory pageant of the ancient Levant had me in thrall.

Hours later, I was still wandering down market streets, my eyes feasting on crates of fruit and vegetables so fabulously sized and colored I couldn't believe they were real. I passed a modest-looking restaurant named "The Workman's Cafe." The rich food smells emanating from it made me wake to the fact that after a three-hour trek through the Shuk I was famished. It was half-past noon and the sun was fierce overhead. It was time for cover.

True to its name, the entire clientele of the cafe were men in greasy work clothes. They sat at rough, raw wood tables on long benches eight abreast. The men ate quickly, hungrily, without conversations. I asked the waiter for a menu. He recited it, pointing to three big iron tubs on a counter before the kitchen: Hummous, meatballs in red sauce or okra with veal in red sauce, orange or lemon drink. I chose houmous, a chickpea appetizer ground to a paste with sesame seed dressing, lemon juice and condiments. It was served with hot Arab breads, a plate of green and black olives, and another of pickled turnips. It must have been a combination of my hunger, the wholesomeness of the atmosphere and the strangeness I felt in the place but I cleared my plate, leaving not an olive or a pickled turnip. I was still hungry. A huge, steamy bowl of okra and veal in sauce appeared before me. I watched my neighbors dunk their bread into the sauce and scoop up the veal chunks and okra pieces with it. I did the same. For all the French, Italian, Chinese and assorted other exotic restaurants I had been feasted in at home, nowhere had food tasted as good to me. Then I realized . . . vegetables . . . it had been almost entirely vegetables.

I took to doing most of my shopping in the old market. There were no supermarkets in Jerusalem at the time. Although every street had at least one combination vegetable-grocery market, in the Shuk prices were considerably lower, the produce better and the fun incalculable. Twice a week, before my morning classes, I walked the mile or more to the old part of town. Each succeeding time I passed the rows of fresh farm produce, ripe, huge, unblemished, looking for all the world like painted wax imitations because they were so perfect, my resolve weakened another notch. Peppers of every color and shape, green squash, purple and white turnips, cabbage, celery, kohlrabi, okra, cauliflower, rhubarb, strings of onions and garlic all saw their way into my kitchen before the year was up. Meat was scarce. Veal abounded but it was tough and lacked flavor. Chicken was available but it wasn't my favorite dish. Fish was expensive. Under these circumstances I was forced to rely on vegetables to fill out my diet. University friends and myself took turns in creating original vegetable dishes using the most limited ingredients. These limitations were heightened by the fact that we had only single kerosene burners or double gas burners to work with and no ovens. But our cooking limitations seemed to sharpen our culinary zeal. It was too expensive for students to eat in good restaurants. For those of us who loved good food there was no alternative. We had to make it ourselves.

Traveling home at year's end, I did some sightseeing in Greece and Italy. My new-found interest in food preparations led me to explore styles of cookery as well as ancient ruins and historical or artistic landmarks. The variety of preparations I met with reinforced what I already knew: vegetables could be fabulous.

Some time after my return home, I met my husband-to-be. He shared the majority of my interests, among them, love of food. His bachelor travels had included gastronomic tours of Spain, Italy, France, Belgium, Yugoslavia, Switzerland and Japan. It wasn't till after we were married that I discovered we had still another characteristic in common, a childhood aversion to vegetables. I undertook a two-year course of indoctrination. I prepared every variety of vegetable on the market in the widest gamut of cooking styles. Of course, now, he too is a vegetable lover. As a matter of fact, I wrote this book at his insistence. He hopes I will have the same effect on my readers as I had on him.

From soups and salads to side dishes, entrees, and desserts, vegetables are the undisputed favorites of my kitchen. Recipes drawn from Oriental, Mid-Eastern, European and regional American cuisines, as well as my own variations on these themes, never fail to delight and surprise my family and friends. The surprise is due, I'm convinced, to the fact that vegetables are often a neglected food in our country. Even in fine restaurants, you are more likely to be disappointed in the vegetable dishes than in any others. It always amazes me that these foods which generally require less time in preparation than others and present so many possibilities for cooking adventure should be treated so poorly.

I offer this book to the discriminating home cook who wishes the vegetable segments of her dinners to be as enticing as the rest, to calorie-conscious families for whom a reliance on vegetables can mean keeping the "count" down and the appetite sated, to time-conscious wives and mothers like myself who want to serve well but with a minimum of time and effort expended, and to the budget-minded to whom I hope to prove that to be a gourmet of vegetables does not require an inflated pocketbook.

Post-Script — In writing this book I have tried to present dishes for modern American tastes. Whenever possible, I have moderated the richness of recipes, relying on the good taste of seasonings and spices in foods rather than heavy cream and oil sauces for flavor.

All recipes serve 4–6 persons unless otherwise specified.

Glossary of Cooking Terms

BAKE — To cook in dry heat such as in the oven.

BASTE — To moisten roasting foods with fat or liquid while cooking.

BATTER — Combination of flour, liquids, eggs, etc. loose enough to be poured.

BEAT — To mix by stirring vigorously and repeatedly with an appropriate utensil.

BLANCH — To place raw foods in boiling water for 1–5 minutes.

BLEND — To mix 2 or more ingredients together until smooth.

BOIL — To cook foods at boiling point; bubbles continually rising and breaking on the surface.

BOILING POINT — The temperature at which liquids boil.

BOUILLON — A clear, light broth made from meat, poultry or vegetables.

BOUILLON CUBES — Commercially-made concentrated form of bouillon meant to be mixed with boiling water.

BRAISE — To brown foods in fat, add small amount of liquid, cover and simmer over low heat.

BROIL — To cook directly over or under open heat or fire.

BRUSH — 1. To coat foods lightly with adhering liquid such as egg or fat. 2. To scrub vegetables clean under water with a vegetable brush.

CASSEROLE — To place foods in an oven-proof dish for baking and later serving in the pot.

CHILL — To allow foods to cool thoroughly in the refrigerator, but not to freeze them.

CHOP — To cut into small bits.

COAT — To cover surface of foods with flour, crumbs, cream, etc.

COMBINE — To mix together 2 or more ingredients and blend well.

CONSOMME — A clear, concentrated broth made from meat, poultry or vegetables.

CREAM — To beat ingredients smooth such as butter and flour.

CRISP — To firm vegetables by dipping in or holding under cold water briefly.

CROQUETTE — A small pancake of chopped meats, poultry, seafood or vegetables bound with flour or crumbs and eggs.

CROUSTADE — A hollowed-out, toasted bread crust, round or patty shell used to hold creamed foods.

CRUSH — To grind dry herbs between the fingers.

CUBE — To cut into bite-size square pieces.

CURRY — Any dish made with East Indian spices such as mustard seed, turmeric, cumin, etc. Also, a commercial preparation of ground spices from the East.

DICE — To cut into tiny cubes.

DISSOLVE — To melt or make liquid.

DOT — To speckle food surface with bits of food such as butter, cheese, etc.

DREDGE — To coat food lightly with dry ingredients such as flour or bread crumbs.

DRIPPINGS — The fats and juices that drain from baking or roasting foods.

DUST — To sprinkle food surfaces lightly.

ENTREE — Main course.

FLOUR — To coat food with light film of flour or crumbs.

FOLD IN — To combine ingredients such as stiff egg whites and whipped cream gently, with a minimum of mixing, so as not to lose their airiness.

FRY — To cook in moderate amount of fat or oil on top of the range.

DEEP FRY — To cook in enough boiling hot oil to thoroughly immerse cooking food.

GARNISH — To decorate with chopped bits such as parsley, pimiento, olives, etc.

GRATE — To grind or shred food by rubbing on a grater.

GRIND — To chop food finely by putting it through a food mill or grinder.

GUMBO — A stew that thickens itself with the addition of tomatoes and okra.

HORS D'OEUVRES — Bite-size cocktail snacks or appetizers served hot or cold before or between meals.

JULIENNE — Vegetables or any other foods cut into match-stick-like strips.

MARINADE — Oil and acid (such as vinegar or lemon juice) mixture used to flavor and tenderize foods soaked in it. Herbs, spices and condiments can be added to it for flavoring purposes.

MARINATE — To soak in a marinade.

MELT — To dissolve over heat.

MINCE — To chop or cut into miniscule pieces or bits.

MIX — To combine ingredients evenly by beating or stirring.

MSG — Monosodium glutamate. Added to cooking foods to enhance their natural flavors.

PAN-BROIL — To cook foods in a hot, lightly greased skillet.

PAN-FRY — To cook in a skillet with a small amount of hot fat.

PARBOIL — To put food into vigorously boiling water and cook till half-tender.

PAR-COOK — Same as parboil.

PARE — To trim or cut away rind of skin or fruits and vegetables.

POACH — To cook slowly over simmering water in a double boiler type arrangement or to simmer slowly in hot water.

PREHEAT — To heat oven at desired temperature for 5 or more minutes before introducing foods to be cooked into it.

PURÉE — A thin paste of cooked foods. To purée is to rub cooked foods through a sieve or to liquify them in a blender.

ROAST — To cook in dry heat such as an oven's.

ROUX — A mixture of melted fat and flour browned over heat. Used to thicken stews, soups and sauces.

SAUTÉ — To fry quickly, turning frequently, in a small amount of fat.

SCALD — To heat liquids (such as milk) to just below the boiling point.

SCORE — To cut deep gashes in the surface of foods before baking or roasting for the purpose of even cooking and deep penetration of flavoring ingredients.

SEAR — To brown foods quickly in a skillet over intense heat.

SHRED — To cut food into thin, narrow strips.

SIFT — To strain dry ingredients through a sieve.

SIMMER — To cook foods gently, below boiling point.

SOAK — To place hard or stale foods in liquid to absorb and soften.

STALK — A branch of a vegetable or fruit-producing plant.

STEAM — To cook on a steamer rack in a covered pot over boiling water or in the top part of a double boiler.

STEEP — To soak in boiling water to extract or infuse flavor.

STEM END — Side of fruit or vegetable which is naturally attached to plant.

STEW — To simmer or boil slowly in a small amount of liquid.

STIR — Same as mix.

STIR-FRY — To sauté quickly, stirring constantly to prevent scorching and uneven cooking.

STOCK — Water in which meat, fish, poultry or vegetables have been cooked.

STUFF — To fill a hollowed cavity in food to be cooked with well-seasoned ingredients.

TABASCO — Commercially produced hot pepper sauce.

TOAST — To brown on or under direct heat.

TOSS — To mix gently, with a light hand.

WHIP — To beat vigorously in order to incorporate air and make ingredients frothy.

Part One

1

From the Market to the Pot

WHAT TO SHOP FOR

Always buy the best quality vegetables you can find. The best stay fresh longer and can be prepared with the least waste. That may sound like expensive advice. It isn't. The only bargain in vegetables are vegetables bought in season. (You can find out which are in season by watching for information in the food section of your daily newspaper.) Portion by portion, you'll find vegetables cheaper than any other food on the market of equal nutritional value.

Price is not always an indicator of what's best on the market. Try to judge quality for yourself by these general rules. Choose the brightest, richest colored produce. Select clean-looking vegetables over sandy, gritty or dirt-covered ones. Over-all firmness is a sign of vegetable good health. Crispness is a hallmark of freshness. Avoid vegetables that are wilted, wrinkled, discolored

3

or blemished. If a vegetable appears soft or tough, better not buy it. When in doubt, ask your vegetable dealer's advice. He's an expert. You'll find him happy to guide your selection.

The biggest is not necessarily the best. Sometimes, overlarge fruits and vegetables look glamorous but have sacrificed flavor to get that way. Quantity buying, too, can leave quality on the short end. Purchase only what you can adequately store and use in a short period of time. Many vegetables are highly perishable and even under home refrigeration will spoil after a few days. For the sake of flavor, nutrition, and appearance, it's always better to buy fresh. Of course, it probably isn't convenient for you to shop every day. Twice a week at the produce market should keep your vegetables fresh and tasty under normal conditions.

If you are buying pre-packed fresh goods, make sure you're getting fair value, that is, the full stated measure. Weigh the package, if you're in doubt. Short weights are rare but they have been known to happen. Also, be sure the quality of your packaged produce is uniform throughout. What's at the bottom should look as good as what's on top.

There are more kinds of vegetables available in our country today than ever before. For each kind sold there are numerous government-regulated qualities. It's a hard job for today's home-maker to keep them all in mind. To guide you in your selections, I have provided the following list of vegetables commonly available with a description of what they should look like at their peak.

ARTICHOKES — The type we are most familiar with is called the globe artichoke. It is the flower bud of a thistle plant grown in certain parts of California. It is a highly perishable food. Brown mottling appears with age or injury to the leaves. The best are tight, plump buds that are heavy for their size. The shape should be globular (as the name suggests), and the leaves should be large, fresh, and fleshy. A uniform green color is a reliable indicator of freshness. Size has no relation to flavor or quality.

ASPARAGUS — Young, slender, firm stalks with closed, compact tips are the best. All the green part should be tender and edible after cooking. The white part should be cut away, but may be saved for flavoring soups or stews. It is a fairly perishable vegetable. Once cut, it ages fast. Wilted asparagus have opened tips which may be discolored, and tough, leathery stalks.

LIMA BEANS — Large and small limas are sold in the market, usually in their shells. The small limas have the most delicate flavor. The large ones are more starchy and are particularly good in soups, stews and casserole dishes. The pods of fresh limas are well-filled, clean, and of bright appearance. Limas will be tough and poor in flavor if the shells look dry, shriveled, yellowed or dark-spotted. If you buy them shelled, look for plump, unwrinkled, green or greenish white beans.

SNAP BEANS — The most popular are green and wax (or yellow) beans. The best grade beans are of a clean, firm appearance, free of scars, and well-shaped. Snap one in two (if your dealer allows) to check crispness. Most beans in a lot should be of uniform size. Young beans are relatively stringless. Stringiness develops with over-maturity. Beans that have large seeds within may be tough and fibrous.

BEETS — Leaves should be fresh-looking, deep green in color, and free of wet areas of decay. Medium-size beets have the best flavor. They should be firm and smooth and without soft spots.

BROCCOLI — The sprouts should be fresh, clean and compactly clustered. Color should be deep green. No yellow should appear in the buds. Stalks should be green throughout, tender but firm. Broccoli shows age by a woody toughness at the base of the stalks and discoloration in the buds.

BRUSSELS SPROUTS — These are miniature cabbages. Good quality sprouts are firm, compact heads with delicate green color.

CABBAGE — There are many varieties available on the market; pointed or early cabbage, Danish, domestic, Savoy, and red cabbage. Heads should be firm and heavy for their size. Stems should be cut close to the heads and few of the outer (wrapper) leaves should remain. Wormy and yellowing cabbages should be avoided. Over-ripe cabbages will have outer leaves widespread from the base. These may be very strong in flavor and coarse in texture.

CARROTS — Young and mature carrots appear on the market. The young carrots are smaller and thinner in size, more tender, milder in flavor and brightly colored. Mature carrots are usually longer, fatter, stronger in flavor and less sweet than the others. They are particularly suited to flavoring soups, stews and casseroles.

CAULIFLOWER — It is a delicate vegetable, easily bruised or injured. For that reason, it is often pre-packed in cellophane or paper before it goes to market. Good quality heads are white or creamy white in color and have clean-looking, compact flower curds. They should have a coat of fresh green leaves remaining around the base to protect against injury. Size of heads does not affect quality. Avoid discoloration or spotting on the flowers as well as wide-spread buds and bruised heads.

CELERY — The two most popular varieties sold in this country are green Pascal celery and golden (or blanched) celery. You may also purchase celery hearts. (These are bunches that have been stripped of their outer, less tender stalks.) The best grade celery is clean, crisp, of medium length and thickness with stalks that are compactly bunched. Stay away from bunches that have rounded, spread apart stems and stalks that are either wilted or too hard. (These may be used for flavoring.) It's wise to avoid discolored celery.

SWISS CHARD — This is a green from a beet-like plant. It has a distinct and delicate flavor. Leaves should be tender but crisp, free from insect bites and wet areas of decay. As in other greens, avoid wilted stems. (See *Greens.*)

CHICORY, ENDIVE *and* ESCAROLE — These are three types of related greens that may be used fresh in salads or cooked. Chicory may be recognized by its broad-leaved, upright, spreading head. So-called Belgian or French endive is actually blanched chicory. In its blanched condition, leaves should be folded onto each other tightly, forming a compact elongated head. Endive is known by its distinctive, narrow curly leaves. Escarole is broader-leaved, and both of the latter share a flat, spreading leaf formation. Look for brightness of color, cleanness, and freshness in heads. (See *Greens.*)

CORN — Sweet and fresh corn are the two varieties most familiar to us. Sweet corn is a more mature, yellow and white (mostly yellow) kerneled vegetable. Fresh corn is whiter, with smaller, less starchy kernels. It loses flavor quickly and is at its best shortly after picking. The best corn has bright, plump, milky kernels. Husks should be of fresh green color with golden tassels which appear neither strawlike and dry nor dark with wet rot. Stay away from pale, dry-looking husks and shrivelled or soft, underdeveloped kernels. Corn of this type will be flavorless.

CUCUMBERS — Good quality cucumbers will be firm, fresh, deep green in color, well-shaped, seeds within should be immature. Avoid withered or shrivelled vegetables, or over-ripe ones with dull or yellowed skins and a puffy appearance. Watch out for water-soaked areas and sunken, irregular spots. These indicate decay.

EGGPLANT — These should have a uniform, dark purple color, be firm, heavy in relation to their size, and free of scars and cuts. Stay away from vegetables with wormholes and dark brown areas of decay visible on the surface.

GARLIC — Heads should have plump, firm cloves visible on the surface. The outer membrane should be intact and dry. Avoid soft or spongy garlic, surface mold, dry or wet areas of decay, and shrunken or shrivelled cloves.

GREENS — (Spinach, beet tops, kale, turnip tops, collards, leafy broccoli, chard, water cress, dandelion greens, mustard greens, sorrel, chicory, endive, and escarole are included under this heading.) The best greens are fresh, tender, and brightly colored. Stay away from leaves that show insect damage. Coarse stems may indicate overmaturity. Dry or yellowed leaves, excessive dirt, poorly developed plants, greens with dark wet spots, or a wilted appearance should be avoided.

LETTUCE — There are three categories of lettuce familiar to us; *Crisp heads*, such as Iceberg lettuce with large, solid heads and crisp, fringed leaves, *Butterheads*, like Bibb, Big Boston, and White Boston which are smaller, rosette-like, with smooth, tender, light-colored leaves, and *Cos heads*, the Romaine types of lettuce, recognizable by a tall cylindrical shape, deep green color and thick-textured leaves. All of the above should be relatively clean, free of rusty-colored areas of decay, and trimmed of most outer, covering leaves. Discolorations and water-soaked spots should be avoided.

MUSHROOMS — This vegetable, as you probably know, is a member of the fungus family. The only type of edible mushroom grown commercially in our country is white to cream white in color and, generally, $\frac{3}{4}$ to three inches in diameter. Make sure they are over-all white when you buy them and of a clean appearance. Avoid mushrooms with split caps, pit marks, discolorations, and wilting. The area between the cap and the stem, known as the gill, should be light in color. Brown or black gills are a sign of aging.

OKRA — This vegetable is the immature seed pod of the hibiscus plant. They should be green or white green in color, two to four inches in length, fresh-looking, tender and of clean appearance. Okra should snap easily when broken. If they seem wilted, discolored or of a dull, dry appearance, avoid them.

DRY ONIONS — There are numerous types of dry onions familiar to our markets. *Bermuda* onions are "sweet" or mild-flavored, usually, large-sized and flat at bottom and top. *Spanish* onions and *Italian Red* onions are also mild-flavored but globular in shape. Sweet onions are particularly good in salads and dressings. The most familiar onion to us all is the Globe or *Late Crop* onion. It is globular in shape, generally, of medium size, and has a strong flavor which makes it particularly good cooked alone or with other foods. (Some of the strong flavor gets "cooked out.") It comes to market in a range of colors: yellow, white, red or brown. *Boiler* onions are the small white variety sometimes known as Pearl onions. These are excellent in cooked dishes and may be left whole. Look for onions that are bright and of a clean appearance. They should be firm, well-shaped, and dry-skinned.

Avoid onions with sprouts as these may have a woody center (called seed stem). Stay away from misshapen ones or those with splits, double bulbs, and mottle-necks. Moisture at the neck of the onion is a sign of decay.

GREEN ONIONS, LEEKS, *and* SHALLOTS — *Green onions* are actually immature onions. *Shallots* are tiny onion bulbs which grow in bunches. (They look like grape clusters in brown skins.) *Leeks* are extra-large scallion-type plants. All of these types, but particularly the latter, are prized for their mild, delicate flavor. The scallion-like plants should have fresh-looking green tops, medium-sized necks, with the white part showing at least two inches up from the root. They should be young, crisp and tender. Avoid yellowed, wilted, or discolored tops. (Use the criteria for onions, above, in the selection of shallots.)

PARSLEY — The best known varieties are plain (flat-leaf or Italian) parsley and *curly-leaf* parsley. Good quality parsley is fresh, deep-green colored, free of grit and wilted or yellowing leaves. A slight amount of wilting can be eliminated by bathing the greens under fresh, cold, running water. This treatment will not help seriously wilted greens, however.

PARSNIPS — The best are white to cream in color, smooth-skinned, firm to the touch, well-shaped, and small to medium in size. (Like young carrots.) Stay away from soft or flabby parsnips, shrivelled roots, as well as large, coarse-textured ones. The latter are likely to be tough and woody.

PEAS — High grade green peas are young, tender and sweet. Pods should be fresh looking, of uniform size, and light green in color. Look for well-filled pods that are velvety to the touch. Immature peas have flat, dark green pods, and sometimes, a wilted appearance. Swollen, overly pale, or grey-flecked pods should be avoided as these are likely to contain over-mature peas which are less flavorful and tough. Stay away from pods with dark, wet areas of decay and yellowing.

PEPPERS — The two kinds of peppers known to us are called *Bell* or *sweet peppers* and *hot* or *chili peppers*. Bell peppers may be sold in a variety of colors ranging from the deepest dark green to green and red, all red and even red with yellow. Actually, most peppers are picked for market when they are deep dark green and have a strong, pungent flavor. As they ripen, they turn bright red and sweeten in taste. Shapes of sweet peppers vary widely but this does not affect quality in any way. Good peppers (of any type or color) are fresh and bright looking, thick-fleshed, and firm to the touch (although red peppers are likely to be less firm than deep green ones). Avoid shrivelled, limp, soft, or dull lusterless peppers. Injured peppers will decay quickly and therefore, they too, should be avoided. Stay away from peppers with dark, soft spots, water-soaked areas and bleached or blackened parts.

POTATOES — *New* or *Early* potatoes are small, delicate and less starchy than the familiar *Late* or *Mature-crop* potatoes. Either type may be round and white, long and white, russet or red in color. Medium-size *Mature-crop* potatoes are likely to be the best cooking. These, like tiny new potatoes, are good prepared in any fashion. Long, flat *Idaho* potatoes are recommended for baking only. They vary in size from medium to extra-large. The best potatoes of any type are firm, smooth-skinned and well-shaped. Avoid wilted, leathery or discolored potatoes. "Sunburned" potatoes that have large green areas visible on the skin should be avoided, as well. Sprouted, shrivelled or spongy feeling potatoes should not be purchased.

RADISHES — Elongated, large white radishes and the smaller, round, red-skinned radishes are best known in this country. Look for freshness of leaves, a firm skin (bruises or cuts to the vegetable are not necessarily harmful), a clean unwrinkled surface. Radishes should be well-formed, tender, crisp and mild-flavored. Stay away from vegetables that are pithy, spongy, or show signs of age or decay.

RHUBARB — This vegetable comes to market twice a year. Early in the season *Forced* or *hothouse* rhubarb is available. It is light pink to pale red in color with yellowish-green, undeveloped looking leaves. *Field* rhubarb appears in late spring and lasts till early summer. It is a dark, rich red in color, and has deep green

leaves. The best quality is fresh, firm, crisp, tender and bright looking. Stalks should not be too thin. Young stems with immature leaves have the best flavor. Avoid rhubarb with wilted stems, flabby stalks, overlarge or poorly colored stalks.

SPINACH — Leaves should be clean, fresh, and tender-looking with a rich green color. Avoid yellowed, discolored, wilted or bruised leaves. Decay appears in wet, slimy areas. (See *Greens*.)

SQUASH — There are many varieties on the market during a year. In color, they range from pale cream to green-black; they may be green-striped, light green, bluish green, or orange. Shapes are as various as color, from the bulbous-ended, crook-necked *Butternut* type to the thin elongated *Zucchini*. Squash can be divided into two seasonal groups. *Winter Squash* have hard, thick rinds, are heavy in relation to their size, feel solid and hard to the touch. *Summer Squash* have thin, tender skins, a crisp, firm feeling (although they are not so hard as winter varieties), and should be free of cuts and bruises. Avoid squash with water-soaked areas of decay, a shrivelled or wilted appearance.

SWEET POTATOES — There are two varieties marketed. *Yams* are deep orange-brown in color, plump-bellied in shape. When cooked, they are the most moist and sweet, with a deep orange-colored flesh. *Regular* "sweets" are light orange-brown in skin color and somewhat more elongated in appearance than the former. They are drier, less sweet, and pale orange or light yellow fleshed when cooked. The best are clean, smooth-skinned, well-shaped, and firm and bright looking. Stay away from misshapen sweets, ones with growths showing, or cracked or worm-holed vegetables. Dampness on the surface is an indicator of decay. Avoid shrivelled, discolored, bruised or injured sweet potatoes.

TOMATOES — They range in size from baby cherry tomatoes to giant beefsteaks. The best are vine-ripened, well-formed, plump, uniformly red in color, free of cuts or bruises, neither over-ripe and soft nor too firm and under-ripe. Avoid vegetables with damages, wormholes, unhealed growth cracks, puffiness or soft decaying areas.

TURNIPS — *Early* turnips are small and tender, usually sold in bunches with the top leaves still on. *Late crop* turnips are larger, more mature. *Rutabagas* are large, elongated turnips with yellow flesh. The best turnips are heavy in relation to size, smooth-skinned, firm to the touch. Top leaves should be fresh, green colored. Shrivelled or soft turnips are likely to be tough after cooking. Large, overgrown turnips, light in relation to size, are likely to be tough, woody and over-strong in flavor.

WATER CRESS — (See *Greens.*)

🖾 KEEPING YOUR VEGETABLES FRESH

The general rule for all vegetables is: the fresher the better. You can keep most vegetables fresh for two or three days under refrigeration. Certain vegetables need to be safeguarded against moisture evaporation. Others do well in a cool storage bin outside of the refrigerator. Still others need room temperature and a maximum of air circulation. For the purposes of home storage, vegetables can be divided into three categories.

PERISHABLES — Asparagus, salad greens, tomatoes, corn, cucumbers, radishes, green peppers, green onions are the most highly perishable vegetables. All will do well if washed quickly, dried gently, placed in plastic bags and kept in the crisper bin of your refrigerator. Salad greens should be washed quickly under cold running water and handled as little as possible when dried. Corn should be cleaned and husked before storing and used as close to purchase time as possible. Leave these vegetables whole, neither cut nor torn till use. Discard over-ripe, bruised, damaged or partially rotted vegetables before storing. Asparagus may be trimmed before being bagged in plastic.

SEMI-PERISHABLES — Green and wax beans, broccoli, cabbage, Brussels sprouts, peas in pods, lima beans, cauliflower, celery are somewhat less fragile than the above. Excessive dirt may be removed by washing and then these vegetables may be placed in plastic bags or other covered containers and stored on a

refrigerator shelf. Store peas and beans whole in their pods. Use green peas and beans as soon after purchasing as possible.

STAPLES — Eggplant, winter squash, dry onions, carrots, beets, rutabagas, parsnips, turnips, potatoes are the hardiest in terms of storage. Onions do well at room temperature where the air can circulate around them. (A wicker or wire basket is a good container.) Keep these away from high humidity and heat. It is not necessary to wash these vegetables. (Their outer coverings protect them.) Put squash, potatoes and onions where it is dry and not too hot. Eggplant, carrots, beets, rutabagas, parsnips and turnips need a cool, moist atmosphere. If you do not have a sufficiently cool place to store them outside of the refrigerator, put them in.

BASIC PREPARATIONS AND DEFINITIONS

There are numerous methods of preparing vegetables that require no recipe and the minimum amount of preparation time. If you find it difficult or tedious to follow a recipe, these are for you. You may find your family's favorite vegetables lend themselves to one or all of the following methods. Experiment and find out. Let your tastebuds be your guide.

BAKING

Place vegetables in a pan, with suitable fat beneath to insure against sticking, and cook over a fire either open in the oven or covered on the range. Some vegetables may need to be dotted with fat to keep from drying out in preparation. This method takes a good deal of time and is suitable to root vegetables such as carrots, potatoes, onions, etc., in particular. Eggplant may be baked in its skin this way for later dressing up.

BOILING

Vegetables, either whole and in their skins (if the skins are thin and tender), or pared and cut into serving pieces, may be cooked in boiling liquid till tender. To save on vitamins, use as little liquid as possible. Just enough to protect the pan's bottom from scorching is sufficient. The cooking liquid may be water, juice, milk or bouillon. It is suggested that salt and pepper be added *after* cooking but you may want to flavor the liquid with a bay leaf or other seasonings, herbs or spices. Bring the liquid to a rolling boil, that is, to a steady rate of bubbling, add the vegetables, bring to a boil once more, cover the pan, and cook until tender. Remove the vegetables from the liquid in the pot promptly. Remember that food continues to cook in hot liquids even after you turn off the heat under them. Add salt, pepper, any other seasonings you like, butter or oil if you wish, and serve. A boiling guide to vegetables follows:

VEGETABLE	BOILING TIME*:
Asparagus — whole	10–20 minutes
tips only	5–15
Beans — limas	20–25
snap or wax	15–30
Beets — small, whole	30–40
large, whole	45–90
sliced or diced	15–25
Broccoli — flowers only	10–15
flowers and heavy stalks	
whole	15–25
Brussels sprouts	10–20
Carrots — small, whole	15–20
large, whole	20–30
sliced or diced	10–20
Cauliflower — separated into	
flowerettes	8–15
whole	15–20
Celery — cut into serving pieces	15–18
Corn-on-the-cob	5–15
Greens	10–15
Kohlrabi — diced or sliced	20–25
Okra	10–15
Onions	15–30

* Time of preparation varies with the size of vegetables, quality of heat and kind of cooking liquid.

VEGETABLE	BOILING TIME[*]:
Parsnips — whole	20–40
cut	10–20
Peas	8–20
Potatoes — whole (medium sized)	25–40
quartered	20–25
diced	10–15
Rhubarb — cubed	10–15
Rutabagas — cut up	20–30
Spinach	3–10
Squash — summer, sliced	10–20
winter, cut up	15–20
Sweet potatoes — whole	25–35
Tomatoes — cut into wedges or cubes	7–15
Turnips — cut up	10–20
whole	20–30

BRAISING

Vegetables are either cut or left whole, as you expect to serve them. First, sauté (see *Frying*) vegetables in butter or oil until lightly browned. Next, cook vegetables in stock or bouillon along with other flavoring foods such as meats or meat bones, poultry or other vegetables.

BROILING

Coat vegetable to be broiled with a small quantity of fat and whatever seasonings you desire. Place under heat at a moderate temperature. Watch and test for doneness with a fork. Vegetables that require long cooking must be partially cooked by some other method first.

FRYING

There are two ways that vegetables may be fried: sautéed in a shallow frying pan or deep-fried in a deep skillet. Sautéeing means fast cooking in just enough hot fat to cover the bottom of the pan or to partially cover the vegetable. Quick-cooking vegetables may be cooked until brown by sautéeing. Longer cooking vegetables may be partially cooked by sautéeing and finished by some other method. Or, you may partially cook foods by one method and finish the cooking in the sauté pan. Keep the heat moderate under your sauté pan if you are using butter for fat. It burns and smokes easily. Deep frying requires a deep pan of oil in which you immerse the vegetables to be fried. It's a good idea to use a wire or mesh basket or strainer to keep your vegetables in while deep frying (unless they are batter-coated). Use corn or peanut oil for this type of preparation, as it will not smoke.

PAN-COOKING

Melt one or two tablespoons of fat in a heavy, wide skillet. Add one inch of boiling water. Bring liquid to a boil. Add the vegetables, and cover the pan. Reduce the heat and simmer the vegetables until tender. Test with a fork for the right degree of doneness. It's a good idea to shake the pan from time to time to insure even cooking.

POACHING

Cook vegetables in a shallow pan in hot liquid, which is just barely bubbling, until tender. Remove with slotted spoon or spatula.

ROASTING

Cook vegetables in the oven in an open pan which contains fatty liquids. Spoon this liquid over the vegetables from time to time during the cooking. (This process is called basting.)

SIMMERING

Cook vegetables in a liquid which has been brought to just below boiling. The liquid will be slightly hotter for simmering, bubbling occasionally, than it would be for poaching.

STEAMING

Vegetables are placed on a perforated rack (either a French steamer tray, a Chinese bamboo steamer basket or a wire or mesh basket) which rests above the water level in a covered pot. The water is brought to a boil and the vegetables cook in the steam that is produced. This is a slower method than ordinary boiling but it is considered the most nutritious way of preparing vegetables as the vitamins in the food are not boiled out in the cooking water.

STEWING

Vegetables are cooked in a heavy-duty pot either in the stove or on top of the range. Very little liquid is required; add a small quantity of liquid or use only that which the vegetables themselves produce in the cooking process. This process preserves the whole vegetable pieces.

2

The Art of Seasoning

What comes to mind when someone mentions seasoning? Salt and pepper? What else? In my mother's kitchen seasoning meant the addition of salt, pepper, paprika, and occasionally, garlic or onion, dill or pickling spice. Lemon juice was sometimes used for flavoring. Cinnamon or ginger might be added to a sweet dish. There it ended. Of course, the ubiquitous catsup bottle and mustard pot were available at dinner. It was only years later I learned that the art of seasoning is multifold and various and that there is a great assortment of seasoning agents easily obtainable in this country. In fact, it's my recent experience that the array of spices, herbs and condiments met with in the average super-market is so large as to scare off all but the most intrepid explorer of food tastes. What do you do with bay leaves, marjoram, basil, thyme, nutmeg, aniseed, fennel, etc., I can hear you ask your-self, as you turn from the spice racks, shrugging. Buying spices does require a knowledge of what to do with them. It's not always practical to have a spice guide handy on the occasions of shopping expeditions. Most homemakers avoid the issue, therefore, settling for those flavorings familiar to them through long experience. For those of you who are spice and herb avoiders, I have an experiment to suggest. But first, let me convince you that seasonings have an important place in the kitchens of vegetable cooks.

In their natural state, that is, picked, cooked and served the same day, vegetables have rich enough flavor not to require additives other than salt and pepper. Few of us are that lucky. We live in urban or suburban centers. By the time produce reaches our table it has been picked, stored, packed, shipped, uncrated, displayed, and handled. This process may take days or weeks. In certain seasons, vegetables may come to us from months in cold storage. Flavor is a highly perishable commodity. It is lost minute by minute after the picking. I don't suggest that our vegetables are tasteless. That they are muted in taste is without question. It is up to us as individual cooks to help our vegetables along. If we must eat a balanced diet, as nutritionists suggest, we might as well enjoy it.

Let us suppose that you are expert at preparing vegetables. Your salads are bright and crisp looking. Your cooked greens are tender, neither water-soaked nor cooked out of color. Your white and yellow vegetables come to the table soft but shapely, never mushy unless you intended them that way. Yet, however well you manage to prepare them, your family avoids vegetables like the plague. They seem to eat everything on the table but vegetables. It's a familiar refrain. I've heard it over and over from friends, neighbors and relatives. Vegetable-phobia is a disease that knows no ethnic or social bounds. If your family has been struck, don't despair. There is a treatment that may effect a cure. It worked for me.

From the beginning of our marriage, my husband and I shared the love of good food. His adventurous palate far outran mine in the restaurants we visited during courting days. You can imagine my surprise, after our marriage, when I discovered that my husband was a vegetable loather. Dish after dish of succulent

cooked produce was passed by. It hurt me. Because I loved vegetables I gave them tender loving care in preparation. Something
would have to be done.

I decided that the way to transform my husband from a
loather to a lover was by making vegetable eating a grand adventure. They would have appeal to palate and eye. They would
have to taste entirely different than they had in my husband's
childhood home, where he had first developed his aversion. Vegetables would have to be fun.

Every dinner included one carefully worked out vegetable
recipe, either soup, salad or entree. Sometimes I went to extrava-
gant lengths to think up vegetable desserts which tasted as good
as any other sweet. Borrowing from what I had learned of international cuisine, flavorings, methods of preparations and taste
combinations, I simplified, substituted American ingredients for
unobtainable alien ones, used convenience foods where I could
to save on cooking time, and ended up with a dish less exotic
than the original, but certainly not run of the mill. I started to
explore spices and herbs.

The first herbs used in my kitchen were chervil, tarragon and
rosemary, as I recall. I developed a passion for tarragon in those
early days. It got so that when I brought a dish to the table, my
husband would sniff, savor and exclaim: "What, no tarragon?"
Realizing I had overdone it, I introduced new herbs to my
kitchen. My husband was suspicious of these, at first. Undaunted,
I helped myself to brimming portions of the foods I had prepared, and ate them with gusto. Before long he weakened and
tried them too. It gave me courage to experiment with types of
vegetables and preparations totally new to me. In the process,
vegetables I had shunned from childhood became palatable.

One day, we dined out in a well-known country inn. The
dining-room was lovely. The menu seemed bountiful. The service
was just right. We settled down to what we hoped would be a
gastronomic experience. The appetizer arrived prettily garnished.
My husband tasted and made a dour face. "It seems to be missing
something," he advised me. The dish was fresh-tasting but bland.
The soup, the salad and the side dish vegetables were the same.
After the dessert, my husband leaned across the table, took my

hand, and looking earnestly in my eyes, asked: "why can't they learn to prepare vegetables the way you do?" I knew then that my treatment was a success.

You, too, can make vegetables an eating adventure in your home. Spices and herbs can help you do it. Your family will be wary, at first. The main thing is for you to have a positive attitude. No one who genuinely likes food can long resist a dish that someone near and dear to them thinks delicious. Seasoned food has a way of growing on you. Mashed potatoes and green peas *au naturel* have no excitement in them. Add to these a herb or spice or condiment and they are transformed. It will only take moments out of your day to season vegetables in new ways.

Leftovers are the bane of housewives. Personally, I don't like to eat the same food two days in succession. But what can you do with yesterday's green beans, beets, asparagus, squash, etc.? The green beans won't be recognized a day later marinated in dilled French dressing. The beets will seem all new with sugar, vinegar, and onion added. The squash can only be improved served mashed, spiced and baked as squash pie. For the budget-minded, seasonings are a boon.

If you are a family of weight-watchers, as we are, seasonings can be a secret weapon. Spices and herbs contain no calories. Most commercial condiments have few. You can actually feel full faster eating a well-spiced dish than enjoying a bland one. You will eat less yet feel satisfied. Experiment for yourself and see if it doesn't work for you.

I'm not suggesting that my readers make a dash for the supermarket and buy out the herb and condiment section. Most housewives, myself included, take exception to recipes that call for rare or unusual spices fated to be used once in cooking and never again. They only take up useful pantry room. Buy the condiments you think you will like and use again and again. Select ones that many recipes call for in common. Spices and herbs should be bought in small quantities and, ideally, should be used up and replaced often. They lose potency with age. Start small. Choose three on four standbys, for a start. Use them till you feel you know their attributes, one at a time, and in moderation. When you feel your family has come to accept their existence, splurge on one or two more. Once in a while, say every six months or so, or when you're in an exotic mood, buy a really "way out" spice for your larder, tumeric or cumin, for examples. Use them when you're all out of ideas of what to make for dinner and all the vegetables in your vegetable bin look tired and ordinary to you.

Add ground spices and herbs just before serving, while the food is still hot but no longer on the fire. They have a tendency to "burn out" their flavor and give a bitter taste when cooked with foods. Commercially packaged condiments usually carry suggestions of foods they can be used with. The lists are limited. If you feel daring and have an urge to add a certain something to asparagus . . . go ahead. You can safely count on $\frac{1}{4}$ of a teaspoon of a herb or spice to flavor four to six average portions. Dried whole leaf herbs should be crushed between the fingers before use. Whole dried berries such as nutmeg, juniper and pepper can be used whole in cooking or ground and added at the end of cooking. Fresh herbs are better flavored than dried, but harder to come by. Dried herbs are better than none.

At the end of this chapter is a list of herbs, spices and other seasoning agents with which to dress up your vegetables. On page 36 you will find my suggestions of vegetables to match with these. Personal preference is the best guide. Don't be afraid to play your own matching game. The amounts of condiments suggested here are for dishes that serve 4–6 persons.

✍ VEGETABLES IN MANY LANGUAGES

THE CHINESE WAY

3 *tbs. corn or peanut oil*
1 *clove garlic, diced*
1 *tsp. fresh ginger, chopped, or $\frac{1}{2}$ tsp. ground ginger*
4 *cups cleaned, trimmed greens or 2 cups any other vegetable*
$\frac{1}{4}$ *cup broth (chicken, beef or vegetable, as preferred)*
   Dash MSG

1 *tbs. dry Sherry*
   Salt to taste
1 *tsp. cornstarch mixed with 1 tsp. water*

Heat the oil in a heavy-bottomed pan along with the garlic and ginger* (if fresh ginger is used). When hot, add the vegetable, broth and MSG. Bring to a boil, reduce heat and simmer vegetable until tender. (Cooking time will depend on vegetable selection.) In the final moments of cooking, add the Sherry, salt and cornstarch mixture to which some of the hot broth has been added. After adding the cornstarch, stir constantly until it is well mixed in. Serve. Soya sauce may be added at the table, if desired.

   Suitable Vegetables: Artichoke hearts, asparagus, green beans, broccoli, Brussels sprouts, cabbage, carrots, celery, corn, cucumbers, eggplant, greens, lettuce, mushrooms, onions, peas, peppers, potatoes, squash, tomatoes.

THE CREOLE WAY

2 *cups vegetables in bite-sized pieces*
½ *cup bacon, beef fry or sausage meat, diced or chopped*
1 *onion, chopped*
1 *red or green pepper, chopped*
1 *tsp. parsley, minced*
¼ *cup meat broth (or hot water, if preferred)*
½ *tsp. chili powder*
¼ *tsp. allspice*
   Salt and pepper
2 *tbs. olive oil or animal fat*

Brown diced meat and onion in hot oil in heavy-bottomed pan. Add pepper and simmer until it softens. Pour in vegetable, broth and seasonings. Bring to a boil, lower heat and simmer, covered, until vegetable is tender. Serves 6–8.

   Suitable Vegetables: Asparagus, snap beans, lima beans, broccoli, Brussels sprouts, cabbage, carrots, cauliflower, celery, corn

---

* If ground ginger is used, disregard instructions for fresh ginger and add powder in the final cooking moments along with Sherry.

(off the cob), cucumbers, eggplant, greens, kohlrabi, lentils, mushrooms, okra, turnips, rutabagas, peas, potatoes, squash (summer and winter), tomatoes.

THE FRENCH WAY

2 *cups firm, steamed*   1 *cup hot milk*
   vegetables   *Salt and pepper*
2 *tbs. flour*   *Dash Tabasco or cayenne*
2 *tbs. butter*   *pepper*

Drain vegetables and keep warm. Melt the butter in the top part of a double boiler. Add the flour and stir until mixture is well blended and begins to bubble. Add the hot milk slowly, stirring all the while. When sauce is thick and creamy, season to taste. You may add ¼ tsp. of your favorite herb or spice (mustard powder, crushed tarragon, etc.), if you desire. For a cheese flavor, add to mixture ½ cup of grated American, Cheddar or Swiss cheese and stir until cheese melts and blends. Pour over vegetables in serving dish and bring to the table. Serves 6–8.

Suitable Vegetables: Almost all vegetables lend themselves admirably to this preparation.

THE HUNGARIAN WAY

2 *cups cooked vegetables,*   2 *tbs. bread crumbs*
   diced or sliced   ½ *pint dairy sour cream*
3 *tbs. oil or fat*   *Salt and pepper*
1 *tbs. onion, minced*

Drain cooked vegetables well. Fry onion in 1 tbs. oil or fat. Add vegetable, salt and pepper and sour cream. Remove from heat. Grease a baking pan and dredge with bread crumbs. Pour vegetable mixture into pan. Sprinkle top with crumbs, dot with remaining oil or fat and garnish with paprika. Bake in hot oven (400°) until brown on top. Serve.

Suitable Vegetables: Asparagus, snap beans, beets, broccoli, Brussels sprouts, carrots, cauliflower, celery, eggplant, kohlrabi,

mushrooms, parsnips (omit onion, add cinnamon and sugar before serving), turnips (omit onion, add cinnamon and sugar before serving), peas, potatoes, rhubarb (omit onion, treat like parsnips), winter squash (may be treated like other vegetables or like parsnips), zucchini (need not be pre-cooked).

THE INDIAN WAY

2 tbs. light oil
¼ tsp. mustard seed
2 cups vegetables, in bite-size pieces
Hot water

½ tsp. curry and chili powder, combined
Dash of paprika
Salt to taste

Heat the oil in a heavy-bottomed skillet. When hot, add the mustard seed. When the seeds begin to jump in the pan, add 2 cups of your favorite vegetable or vegetable combination and enough hot water to cover them. Bring the mixture to a boil. Reduce the heat, cover the pan, and simmer for fifteen to twenty minutes. Add the curry and chili powders, paprika and salt. Stir until well blended and pour into a serving dish. The consistency of the vegetables should be quite soft but chunks of vegetables should be visible. Serve with grated, unsweetened coconut, chopped peanuts, chutney, and hard-boiled eggs chopped or quartered.

23 Good combinations*:

1. Fried onions, tomatoes, cut asparagus.
2. Green beans, mushrooms, potatoes.
3. Fried tomatoes, green beans, turnips.
4. Chopped broccoli and green peas.
5. Cabbage, potato and tomato.
6. Carrots, winter squash and peas.
7. Fried onions and cauliflower.
8. Celery, corn and okra.

* There are endless possibilities. Try your own combinations. You may use unthawed frozen vegetables or fresh ones. Canned vegetables may be used as well, but the result will be more mushy.

9. Fried onions, corn, green beans and mushrooms.
10. Eggplant and green peas.
11. Fried onions, eggplant and potatoes.
12. Eggplant and tomatoes.
13. Fried onions and mixed chopped greens.
14. Mixed or single chopped greens, mushrooms and potatoes.
15. Fried onions, lentils and tomatoes.
16. Mushrooms, turnips and green peas.
17. Okra and tomatoes.
18. Fried onions, green peppers and tomatoes.
19. Fried onions, green peppers and potatoes.
20. Summer squash, eggplant and potatoes.
21. Summer squash, cauliflower and tomatoes.
22. Winter squash, sweet potato and potato.
23. Winter squash, turnip and sweet potatoes.

THE ITALIAN WAY

2 *cups firm-cooked vegetables, diced*
3 *tbs. olive oil*
1 *small onion, minced*
1 *clove garlic, minced*
  Salt and pepper
1 *tbs. fresh or dry parsley, chopped*
  Grated Italian (Parmesan or Romano) cheese (opt.)

Drain vegetables. (Quick-cooking vegetables such as spinach do not have to be pre-cooked.) Heat the oil in a skillet along with onion and garlic. When onion becomes transparent, add the vegetable. Season with salt and pepper, cover and cook over low heat until quite soft. (Time will depend on choice of vegetable.) Add chopped parsley in final moments of cooking. Serve with grated Italian cheese, if desired.

Suitable Vegetables: Artichoke hearts, asparagus, snap beans, lima beans, broccoli, Brussels sprouts, carrots, cauliflower, celery, corn, eggplant, greens, lentils, mushrooms, green peas, green peppers, potatoes, spinach, summer squash, tomatoes.

THE MIDDLE-EASTERN WAY

2 *cups cooked vegetables,*
　diced
3 *tbs. olive oil*
1 *tbs. pine nuts*

1 *tbs. currants (opt.)*
¼ *tsp. allspice (opt.)*
　Salt to taste
　Juice of 1 lemon

Heat oil in skillet. Add drained, cooked vegetable, pine nuts and currants. Heat and stir till currants are plumped and vegetable is lightly browned. Remove from heat. Add allspice, salt, and lemon juice. Serve.

Suitable Vegetables: Artichoke hearts, asparagus, green beans, beets, broccoli, Brussels sprouts, cabbage, carrots, cauliflower (omit nuts and currants), celery, eggplant, greens, mushrooms, onions, turnips, parsnips, rutabagas, green peas, green peppers, potatoes, rhubarb, squash, tomatoes.

THE PENNSYLVANIA DUTCH WAY

2 *cups firm-cooked*
　vegetables, diced
2 *slices bacon, or beef fry,*
　minced
¼ *cup cooking liquid from*
　vegetables
½ *cup sugar*

¼ *cup vinegar*
¼ *tsp. salt*
2 *tbs. onion, chopped*
1 *tbs. celery, chopped*
1 *tbs. salad oil*
1 *tsp. cornstarch and 1 tsp.*
　water, mixed

Fry bacon or beef fry in hot skillet until brown. Add sugar, cooking liquid and vinegar and cook until sugar dissolves. Add cooked vegetable and salt and simmer, uncovered, for approximately 15 minutes, stirring from time to time so vegetable does not stick. At end of cooking, add cornstarch mixed with water and blend into mixture. Cook for an additional few minutes. Add celery and onion just before serving. Serves 6–8.

Suitable Vegetables: Same as for Creole recipe.

THE SPANISH WAY

2 *cups vegetables, cut into serving pieces*
2 *onions, chopped*
2 *garlic cloves, minced*
¼ *cup olive oil*
2 *tbs. tomato paste or 1 fresh tomato, diced*
1 *tsp. parsley, minced*
¼ *cup meat broth (beef or chicken)*
2 *tbs. slivered almonds*
¼ *tsp. cumin (seeds or powdered)*
   Salt and pepper, paprika

Cook onions and garlic in hot oil. When onions are soft and transparent, add vegetable, tomato paste, and broth. Simmer, covered, until vegetable is tender. In final moments of cooking, add cumin, almonds, parsley, salt, pepper and paprika. Serves 6–8.

   Suitable Vegetables: Same as for Creole recipe.

Herb and Spice Guide

HERB OR SPICE	AMOUNT	DESCRIPTION
Allspice	$\frac{1}{4}$ tsp. ground	Dried berry of pimento tree. Flavor compares to a combination of cinnamon, nutmeg and cloves
Anise	$\frac{1}{4}$ tsp. ground	Dried seeds of a celery-like plant. Mild, licorice flavor.
Basil	$\frac{1}{4}$ tsp. crushed	Fresh or dried leaves and stems of basil plant. Sweet, slightly pungent flavor.
Bay leaf	1 leaf cooked with food, or $\frac{1}{4}$ tsp. ground added at end of cooking	Dried leaf of laurel tree. Aromatic, mild flavor.
Caraway	$\frac{1}{4}$ tsp. ground or whole	Dried seeds of plant indigenous to Holland and North America. Fragrant, strong, tart, mintish flavor.
Cardamom	$\frac{1}{4}$ tsp. ground	Seeds of a plant belonging to ginger family. Mild, aromatic, exotic flavor.
Cayenne	1 or 2 dashes	Ground, small, hot red peppers. Fiery flavor.
Celery seed	$\frac{1}{4}$ tsp.	Dried seed of celery plant. Celery flavor.
Chervil	$\frac{1}{4}$ tsp. crushed	Fresh or dried leaves of chervil plant. Mild, parsley-like flavor.
Chili powder	$\frac{1}{4}$ tsp.	Ground chili peppers and blended spices. Usually includes garlic, oregano, salt and cumin.
Cinnamon	$\frac{1}{4}$ tsp. or more to taste	Dried bark of cinnamon tree. Aromatic, sweetish flavor.

Herb and Spice Guide (Continued)

HERB OR SPICE	AMOUNT	DESCRIPTION
Clove	¼ tsp.	Nail-shaped flower bud of clove tree. Sweet, pungent flavor.
Coriander	¼ tsp. ground	Dried seeds of Eastern plant. Pungent, aromatic.
Cumin	¼ tsp. ground	Dried seeds. Light and spicy flavor.
Curry powder	¼ tsp.	East Indian blend of spices including: celery seed, coriander, cumin, ginger and turmeric.
Dill	¼ tsp. minced or ground	Fresh or dried leaves or dried seed. Leaves are stronger in flavor. Somewhat like caraway-mint combination, fresh flavored.
Fennel	¼ tsp. crushed or ground	Dried seeds of plant. Fragrant and sweet. Faint anise flavor.
Garlic	½ to 1 clove, crushed, minced or powdered	Fruit of garlic plant. Spicy taste, strong, odoriferous.
Ginger	¼ tsp. minced or ground	Roots of a tuberous plant. Spicy, peppery flavor.
Marjoram	¼ tsp. crushed	Member of the mint family. Aromatic, slightly bitter flavor.
Mint	¼ tsp. crushed	Dried or fresh leaves. Aromatic, cool to the palate.
Mustard	¼ tsp. seeds or powder	Dried seeds of mustard plant. Hot, spicy taste.
Nutmeg	1 dash to ¼ tsp., to taste	Dry kernel of nutmeg fruit. Sweetish, spicy flavor.

HERB OR SPICE	AMOUNT	DESCRIPTION
Oregano	¼ tsp. crushed	Fresh or dry leaves. Flavor close to marjoram but more pungent.
Paprika	1 dash to ¼ tsp.	Ground sweet red peppers. Domestic paprika is mild, sweet, somewhat peppery. Imported is hotter.
Parsley	1 tsp. or more to taste	Italian-style parsley is fresh-tasting, somewhat minty in flavor. Domestic is milder, better as a garnish. Blends flavors in dishes to which it is added.
Pepper	1 dash or more to taste, or two or three berries cooked with food	Dried berry of vine plant. Hot, spicy flavor.
Pickling spice	1 tbs. in cheesecloth bag during cooking	Combination of whole spices: hot peppers, black pepper, bay leaf, juniper berries, dill and fennel seed.
Poppy seed	¼ tsp. toasted	Tiny, dried seeds of Dutch poppy plant. Toasted, they have a nut-like flavor.
Poultry seasoning	¼ tsp.	Ground mixture of sage, oregano, ginger, rosemary, thyme, pepper and celery seed. Mildly spicy and aromatic.
Rosemary	¼ tsp. crushed	Leaf of an evergreen shrub. Fresh, sweet, pine-needle flavor.
Sage	¼ tsp. crushed or ground	Dried leaf of a shrub in the mint family. Mild, somewhat musky flavor, slightly bitter.
Savory	¼ tsp.	Tiny, dried leaves of plant relating to mint. Delicate, aromatic flavor.

Herb and Spice Guide (Continued)

HERB OR SPICE	AMOUNT	DESCRIPTION
Sesame seeds	1 tbs. toasted	Seeds of an East Indian plant. Nut-like flavor.
Tarragon	¼ tsp. crushed	Dried leaves of plant. Slightly anise-flavored.
Thyme	¼ tsp. crushed or ground	Dried leaves of plant. Aromatic, pungent flavor.
Turmeric	1 dash to ¼ tsp., to taste	Ground, dried root of plant in ginger family. Bright yellow in color. Richly aromatic, peppery in taste.

Other Flavorings and Seasonings

SEASONING	AMOUNT	WHEN TO ADD	COMMENTS
Toasted almonds	1 to 2 tbs.	Just before serving	Imparts nutty flavor.
Anchovies	3 to 4 strips, chopped	Just before serving	Very salty, oily taste.
Fried or broiled bacon	3 to 4 strips, minced	Just before serving	Smoky, meat flavor.
Ground peanuts or cashews	1 to 2 tbs., to taste	Just before serving	Smooth, nut flavor.
Grated cheese	2 tbs.	While still hot, before serving	Use Italian grating cheese, American, Cheddar or Swiss. Each lends its own flavor.

SEASONING	AMOUNT	WHEN TO ADD	COMMENTS
Melted cheese	2 or 3 thin slices	After cooking, place vegetable with cheese over it under broiler for moments	Same as above. Instead of Italian grating cheese, use Mozzarella.
Diced cooked chestnuts	¼ cup	Final moments of cooking	Gives nut-like flavor.
Chicken or pork fat	2 tbs., diced	Sauté vegetable in fat to begin cooking process	Imparts meaty, nut-like oily taste.
Chives	2 tbs., chopped	Final cooking moments or just before serving	Similar to scallion greens but more delicate.
Toasted coconut	2 tbs., shredded	Just before serving	Nutty flavor.
Sweet or dairy sour cream	2 tbs.	When heat is turned off but food is still in pot	Rich buttery taste, mildly sweet or sour.
Fried croutons	¼ cup	Just before serving	Crunchy taste, similar to above.
Buttered crumbs	2 tbs.	After cooking, sprinkle on top of food and brown a moment under broiler	Buttery, nut-like flavor.
Sliced or diced frankfurters or sausage.	¼ cup	Cook with food	Meaty flavor.
Minced ham	¼ cup	Add before serving or cook with food, as desired	Delicate, smoky flavor.
Honey or molasses	2 tbs.	Can be cooked with food or added before serving	Sweetens, makes food mildly fragrant.

Other Flavorings and Seasonings (Continued)

SEASONING	AMOUNT	WHEN TO ADD	COMMENTS
Horse-radish	1 to 2 tbs.	Grate on before serving	Makes food tangy and spicy.
Lemon or orange rind	1 tsp. or rind of 1 lemon and $\frac{1}{2}$ orange, or juice, $\frac{1}{2}$ lemon or orange	Grate on before serving	Imparts fruit flavor. Tart, fruit taste.
Lemon or orange juice		Before serving	
Marshmallows	2 tbs., diced	Add after cooking and brown under broiler	Sweet, nutty flavor.
Monosodium glutumate	$\frac{1}{4}$ tsp.	Add after cooking and brown under broiler	Sweetish flavor, enriches natural flavors.
Chopped or sliced cooked mushrooms	$\frac{1}{4}$ cup	Final moments of cooking	Delicate, nut flavor.
Prepared mustard	1 tbs.	Before serving	Peppery, tart flavor.
Chopped nuts of any kind	2 tbs.	Final moments of cooking	Add their own flavors.
Chopped olives	2 tbs.	Before serving	Tart, vinegary taste.
Fried onion	$\frac{1}{4}$ cup	Final moments	Nutty flavor.
Grated or minced onion	1 tbs.	Final moments of cooking or before serving. Former will be milder tasting	Slightly sharp taste.
Pickle relish	1 to 2 tbs, to taste	Before serving	Gives sweet, vinegary flavor.

SEASONING	AMOUNT	WHEN TO ADD	COMMENTS
Diced, roasted pimiento	2 to 3 tbs.	Before serving	Gives pungent, oily flavor. Enhances look of greens, yellow and white vegetables.
Salad oil or butter	2 tbs.	Either before cooking for sautéing foods or after for softening and blending foods	Somewhat nutty, fried flavor if used for sautéing.
Chopped scallions	2 tbs.	Final moments of cooking or just before serving as for onions	Combination onion and parsley-like flavor.
Soya sauce	1 tbs.	Final moments of cooking	Salty, Oriental flavor.
Tabasco	Few drops	Before serving	Hot pepper taste.
Vinegar and sugar	2 tbs. 1 tsp. or more to taste	With cooking water	Sweet-sour flavor.
Wines & liquors: Sherry, Marsala, dry Vermouth, red or white wine, brandy or gin	1 tbs. or more to taste	After cooking, while still in pot	Flavor of beverage added.
Worcestershire sauce	1 tsp. or more to taste	Before serving	Slightly sweet, spicy flavor.
Yoghurt	2 tbs.	After cooking, while still in pot	Tart, creamy flavor.

Vegetable Seasoning Guide

For information on how to prepare and when to add these condiments, see above.

VEGETABLE	HERBS AND SPICES SUGGESTED	OTHER SEASONINGS
Artichoke hearts	Basil, chive, coriander, curry, dill, fennel, garlic, ginger, marjoram, mustard, oregano, sage, savory, thyme, turmeric.	Almonds, bacon, cheese, cream, crumbs, croutons, lemon, olives, onion, pimiento, oil or butter, yoghurt, red wine.
Asparagus	Basil, caraway, celery seed, chervil, chili powder, chives, curry, dill, fennel, garlic, ginger, marjoram, nutmeg, oregano, sage, savory, tarragon, thyme.	Anchovies, bacon, cheese, cream, crumbs, croutons, lemon, mushrooms, mustard, nuts, onion, pimiento, oil or butter, sausage, scallions, soya sauce, vinegar and sugar, yoghurt, Worcestershire.
Snap beans	Anise, basil, caraway, celery seed, chervil, chili powder, chives, coriander, curry, dill, fennel, garlic, ginger, marjoram, mint, mustard, nutmeg, oregano, rosemary, sage, savory, thyme.	Almonds, bacon, cheese, chestnuts, animal fat, coconut, cream, croutons, sausage, ham, honey, horse-radish, lemon, mushrooms, mustard, nuts, olives, onion, pimiento, oil or butter, scallions, soya, vinegar and sugar, yoghurt, Worcestershire.
Beets	Allspice, anise, basil, caraway, celery seed, chervil, cinnamon, chili powder, chives, cloves, coriander, curry, cumin, dill, fennel, ginger, marjoram, mint, mustard, nutmeg, poppy seed, sage, tarragon.	Cheese, coconut, cream, crumbs, croutons, sausage, honey, horse-radish, lemon and orange, marshmallows, mustard, nuts, onion, relish, oil or butter, vinegar and sugar, yoghurt, Sherry, Marsala.

VEGETABLE	HERBS AND SPICES SUGGESTED	OTHER SEASONINGS
Broccoli	Basil, celery seed, chili powder, curry, garlic, ginger, marjoram, mustard, oregano, sage, savory, thyme.	Almonds, anchovies, bacon, cheese, chestnuts, animal fat, cream, crumbs, sausage, ham, horse-radish, lemon, mushrooms, nuts, pimiento, oil or butter, scallions, soya, vinegar and sugar, yoghurt, Sherry, Marsala, dry Vermouth, gin, Worcestershire.
Brussels sprouts	Basil, celery seed, cinnamon, curry, cumin, fennel, garlic, ginger, marjoram, mustard, nutmeg, oregano, sage, tarragon, thyme.	Bacon, nuts, cheese, chestnuts, cream, crumbs, croutons, sausage, lemon, mustard, onion, pimiento, oil or butter, soya, yoghurt, Sherry.
Cabbage	Anise, basil, bay leaf, caraway, celery seed, cinnamon, cloves, curry, cumin, garlic, mustard, nutmeg, oregano, poppy seed, rosemary, sage, savory, thyme.	Bacon, cheese, animal fat, cream, crumbs, croutons, sausage, lemon, mustard, onion, pimiento, oil or butter, soya, yoghurt, Sherry.
Carrots	Allspice, anise, basil, caraway, celery seed, chervil, cinnamon, chili powder, chives, cloves, coriander, curry, cumin, dill, fennel, ginger, marjoram, mint, mustard, nutmeg, oregano, poppy seed, poultry seasoning, rosemary, savory, tarragon, thyme.	Almonds, nuts, cheese, chestnuts, animal fat, coconut, cream, croutons, crumbs, sausage, ham, honey, lemon and orange, marshmallows, mushrooms, mustard, onion, pimiento, oil or butter, scallions, sugar, Sherry, Marsala, brandy.

Vegetable Seasoning Guide (Continued)

VEGETABLE	HERBS AND SPICES SUGGESTED	OTHER SEASONINGS
Cauliflower	Anise, basil, caraway, chili powder, chives, coriander, curry, cumin, dill, fennel, garlic, ginger, marjoram, mustard, nutmeg, rosemary, sage, savory, thyme, turmeric.	Anchovies, cheese, animal fat, cream, crumbs, sausage, ham, lemon, mustard, onion, pimiento, oil or butter, scallions, vinegar and sugar.
Celery	Anise, basil, bay leaf, caraway, chervil, chili powder, chives, curry, cumin, dill, fennel, garlic, ginger, marjoram, mustard, nutmeg, oregano, poppy seed, poultry seasoning, savory, tarragon, thyme.	Almonds, bacon, cheese, chestnuts, animal fat, cream, croutons, crumbs, sausage, ham, lemon, mushrooms, mustard, nuts, olives, onion, pimiento, oil or butter, soya, vinegar and sugar, Sherry, white wine, Worcestershire, yoghurt.
Corn	Allspice, anise, basil, celery seed, chervil, cinnamon, chili powder, chives, cloves, coriander, curry, cumin, dill, fennel, ginger, marjoram, mustard, nutmeg, oregano, rosemary, sage, savory, tarragon, thyme.	Bacon, cheese, coconut, cream, croutons, crumbs, sausage, ham, honey, mushrooms, mustard, olives, onion, relish, bell peppers, pimiento, oil or butter, scallions, Sherry, or Worcestershire.
Cucumbers	Allspice, basil, celery seed, chives, dill, mint, mustard, oregano, tarragon, thyme.	Anchovies, bacon, cheese, animal fat, cream, croutons, crumbs, sausage, lemon, mushrooms, onion, soya, vinegar and sugar, yoghurt.

VEGETABLE	HERBS AND SPICES SUGGESTED	OTHER SEASONINGS
Eggplant	Allspice, basil, celery seed, chili powder, coriander, curry, cumin, fennel, garlic, ginger, marjoram, mustard, nutmeg, oregano, sage, tarragon, thyme.	Anchovies, bacon, cheese, animal fat, cream, croutons, crumbs, sausage, lemon, mushrooms, onion, soya, vinegar and sugar, yoghurt.
Greens	Allspice, anise, basil, celery seed, chervil, coriander, curry, cumin, fennel, garlic, ginger, marjoram, nutmeg, oregano, rosemary, sage, savory, tarragon, thyme.	Almonds, anchovies, bacon, nuts, cheese, chestnuts, animal fat, coconut, cream, croutons, crumbs, sausage, ham, horseradish, lemon, mushrooms, onion, pimiento, oil or butter, scallions, soya, Sherry, Worcestershire, yoghurt.
Kohlrabi	Allspice, caraway, chervil, cinnamon, coriander, curry, fennel, garlic, ginger, marjoram, mustard, nutmeg, poppy seed, rosemary, savory, thyme.	Bacon, cheese, cream, croutons, crumbs, sausage, ham, lemon, mushrooms, olives, onion, oil or butter, Sherry, brandy, yoghurt.
Leeks	Anise, bay leaf, celery seed, chervil, dill, fennel, ginger, marjoram, mint, mustard, nutmeg, rosemary, sage, tarragon, thyme.	Almonds, bacon, nuts, cheese, chestnuts, animal fat, cream, croutons, sausage, ham, lemon, mushrooms, mustard, pimiento, oil or butter, vinegar and sugar, Sherry, Vermouth (dry), yoghurt.
Lettuce	Anise, basil, caraway, celery seed, chervil, chives, dill, garlic, mint, mustard, nutmeg, oregano, rosemary, sage, savory, tarragon, thyme.	Almonds, anchovies, bacon, nuts, cheese, coconut, cream, croutons, crumbs, honey, lemon, orange, mustard, olives, onion, relish, pimiento, oil or butter, scallions, vinegar and sugar, Sherry, gin, yoghurt.

Vegetable Seasoning Guide *(Continued)*

VEGETABLE	HERBS AND SPICES SUGGESTED	OTHER SEASONINGS
Mushrooms	Allspice, anise, basil, bay leaf, celery seed, chervil, chili powder, coriander, curry, cumin, fennel, garlic, ginger, marjoram, mustard, nutmeg, oregano, rosemary, sage, savory, tarragon, thyme.	Almonds, bacon, nuts, cheese, animal fat, coconut, cream, croutons, crumbs, sausage, ham, lemon, mustard, onion, oil or butter, scallions, soya, vinegar and sugar, Sherry, Marsala, brandy, red wine, Vermouth (dry), yoghurt.
Okra	Chili powder, curry, garlic, ginger, mustard, oregano, savory, thyme.	Bacon, cheese, animal fat, cream, croutons, sausage, ham, onion, pimiento, oil or butter, yoghurt.
Onions	Allspice, anise, bay leaf, chervil, cinnamon, chili powder, cloves, coriander, curry, cumin, dill, fennel, garlic, ginger, marjoram, mustard, nutmeg, oregano, poppy seed, sage, savory, tarragon, thyme.	Almonds, bacon, nuts, cheese, animal fat, coconut, cream, croutons, crumbs, sausage, ham, honey, lemon, mushrooms, mustard, olives, pimiento, oil and butter, soya, vinegar and sugar, Sherry, Marsala, brandy, gin, yoghurt.
Parsnips	Allspice, celery seed, cinnamon, clove, curry, cumin, garlic, ginger, mustard, nutmeg, tarragon.	Bacon, cheese, animal fat, cream, croutons, crumbs, sausage, ham, honey, lemon, pimiento, oil or butter, vinegar and sugar, Sherry, brandy, yoghurt.

VEGETABLE	HERBS AND SPICES SUGGESTED	OTHER SEASONINGS
Peas	Allspice, anise, basil, celery seed, chervil, chili powder, chives, coriander, curry, cumin, dill, fennel, garlic, ginger, marjoram, mint, mustard, nutmeg, oregano, rosemary, sage, savory, tarragon, thyme.	Almonds, anchovies, bacon, nuts, cheese, chestnuts, coconut, cream, croutons, crumbs, animal fat, sausage, ham, honey, lemon, mushrooms, mustard, olives, onion, pimiento, oil or butter, scallions, soya, vinegar and sugar, Sherry, yoghurt.
Peppers	Bay leaf, chili powder, curry, dill, fennel, garlic, ginger, mustard, oregano, sage, thyme.	Anchovies, bacon, cheese, animal fat, cream, crumbs, croutons, sausage, lemon, mushrooms, onion, pimiento, oil or butter, scallions, soya, vinegar and sugar, Worcestershire, yoghurt.
Potatoes	Allspice, anise, celery seed, chervil, chili powder, chives, coriander, curry, cumin, dill, fennel, garlic, ginger, marjoram, mint, mustard, nutmeg, oregano, poppy seed, poultry seasoning, rosemary, sage, tarragon, thyme.	Anchovies, bacon, nuts, cheese, animal fat, cream, croutons, crumbs, sausage, horse-radish, lemon, orange, mushrooms, mustard, olives, onion, pimiento, oil or butter, scallions, vinegar and sugar, Worcestershire, yoghurt.
Rhubarb	Allspice, anise, cinnamon, clove, coriander, curry, cumin, ginger, mint, nutmeg, rosemary, savory.	Coconut, cream, honey, orange, marshmallow, oil or butter, Sherry, Marsala, brandy, rum, yoghurt.

Vegetable Seasoning Guide (Continued)

VEGETABLE	HERBS AND SPICES SUGGESTED	OTHER SEASONINGS
Summer squash	Basil, celery seed, cinnamon, chili powder, coriander, curry, dill, fennel, garlic, ginger, marjoram, mint, oregano, rosemary, sage, tarragon, thyme.	Bacon, cheese, animal fat, cream, croutons, crumbs, sausage, lemon, mushrooms, onion, pimiento, oil or butter, soya, vinegar and sugar, Sherry, yoghurt.
Sweet potatoes	Allspice, anise, cinnamon, clove, coriander, curry, cumin, ginger, nutmeg, rosemary, savory.	Almonds, bacon, nuts, cheese, animal fat, coconut, cream, crumbs, sausage, ham, honey, lemon, orange, marshmallows, mustard, onion, oil or butter, Sherry, brandy, rum, fruit, yoghurt.
Tomatoes	Basil, bay leaf, celery seed, chervil, chili powder, chives, curry, cumin, dill, garlic, ginger, marjoram, mint, mustard, oregano, rosemary, sage, tarragon, thyme.	Anchovies, bacon, cheese, animal fat, cream, croutons, crumbs, sausage, ham, lemon, mushrooms, olives, onion, oil or butter, scallions, vinegar and sugar, yoghurt.
Turnips and Rutabagas	(Same as parsnips.)	(Same as parsnips.)
Winter squash	(Same as sweet potatoes.)	(Same as sweet potatoes.)

Part Two

3

Sauces–Your Ace in the Hole

As you scan this book it will probably dawn on you that there are a multitude of methods you may use in the preparation of vegetables. Some of these are simple, requiring little time and few additions, other methods are complex, requiring more time, more ingredients and more effort. Certain styles of preparation may appeal to you as appropriate for company dinners. A goodly number of recipes will recommend themselves as everyday family fare. Whatever your needs, whichever style or method suits your purpose, sauces are your ace in the hole.

If company suddenly descends on you and there's no time for elaborate, fussy cooking, yet you feel your dinner must be memorable, you can rely on a sauce to turn the trick. When the family is home early or you are late to start your dinner, or when you've come back from a day's or week's outing famished and too tired for the intricacies of kitchen duty, a sauce is in order. If you're like me, there's at least one Sunday in each month when you come home late after a long day's visit to family or friends, starved because you've traveled through the supper hour, and faced with the exhausting prospect of cooking and serving dinner, getting the children to bed, the day's paraphernalia put away and the dishes washed. At those times, I whip out my favorite saucepan, churn up a sauce with convenient ingredients, toss in the previous day's leftovers and voilà—dinner! It always meets with approval in my house.

Sauces are good for more times than when you're in a hurry. It is a fact that the finest international cuisines are based on sauce cookery. The French are famous for them, the Chinese are masters of them. It is said that you can judge a chef by his sauces. It is not my intention to initiate you into the secrets of the Grand Saucier. His work is elaborate, requiring multitudes of ingredients and procedures, at its best. For us home cooks, shortcuts are necessary. We must rely on available ingredients. We need foolproof cooking methods which guarantee us good results. Still, with very little extra effort expended, with a modicum of courage and a measure of enterprise, you too can be famous for your sauces.

Certain sauces are classic, the backbone of international cookery. Choose a white or brown sauce, add a few imaginative ingredients and you have a truly original and glamorous result. Of course, these classics may be used as is. Whether you wish to dress them up or serve them plain, it is good to have them at your fingertips.

HOT SAUCES FOR HOT VEGETABLES

CLASSIC WHITE SAUCE

THICK	MEDIUM	THIN
3 tbs. butter or fat	2 tbs. butter or fat	1 tbs. butter or fat
3 or 4 tbs. flour	2 tbs. flour	1 tbs. flour
1 cup milk	1 cup milk	1 cup milk
Salt and pepper to taste	Salt and pepper	Salt and pepper

Thick sauce is for binding vegetables together as in soufflés or loaves or patties. Medium sauce is used for creaming vegetables and for making gravies and scalloped dishes. Thin sauce is a good base for other, more complex sauces. It is also used to "cream" soups.

Method of preparation: Melt butter or fat over a fire. If you are using a double boiler, add flour and salt to fat and stir until it starts to bubble. Add liquid slowly, stirring constantly until sauce thickens. If you are using a saucepan, remove pan from burner after fat has melted. Add flour and seasoning and stir smooth. Return to burner and add liquid gradually, stirring all the while. Remove from heat when mixture thickens. Yields 1 cup of sauce.

CLASSIC BROWN SAUCE

2   tbs. butter or fat
2½ tbs. flour
1   cup meat, vegetable or fish stock
    Salt and pepper

Method of preparation: Melt fat in skillet or heavy-bottomed saucepan. Mix in flour and cook, stirring, until mixture starts to brown. Add stock slowly, stirring continually until sauce bubbles and thickens. Add seasonings. Cook on low flame for a few additional moments. 1 cup of sauce.

LEMON BUTTER SAUCE

4   ozs. butter
    Juice and rind of 1 lemon
1   tbs. parsley, chopped
    Salt and pepper, dash paprika

Melt butter. Add lemon juice and other ingredients. Blend well. Serve over vegetables. ½ cup of sauce.

CLASSIC HOLLANDAISE SAUCE

½ *cup butter*
4 *egg yolks*
2 *tbs. lemon juice*

½ *tsp. salt*
Dash Tabasco or cayenne
⅓ *cup boiling water*

Cream butter in the top of a double boiler. Add egg yolks one at a time and beat in well. Slowly blend in lemon juice and seasonings. Place pan over heating water. Add boiling water slowly, beating constantly with a wire whisk or egg beater. Continue to beat mixture over hot but *not boiling* water until sauce thickens to the consistency of soft custard. Remove from heat and serve at once. Sauce separates upon standing, or if cooked too long or over too high a temperature. To redeem separated sauce, add a tbs. of boiling water and a few drops of lemon juice, a drop at a time, beating constantly as you add.

ITALIAN STYLE TOMATO SAUCE

1 *onion, diced*
1 *clove garlic, minced*
3 *tbs. olive oil*
1 *lb. can tomatoes (Italian style, if desired), diced*

2 *tbs. parsley, chopped*
1 *bay leaf (opt.)*
½ *tsp. basil, chopped*
Salt and pepper

Sauté onion and garlic in olive oil. When onions are transparent, add tomatoes, herbs and other seasonings. Simmer over low heat for about a half hour. Discard bay leaf. Pour over vegetables and serve.

DEVILLED VEGETABLE SAUCE

3 *tbs. melted butter*
½ *tsp. dry mustard*
1 *tsp. Worcestershire sauce*
Juice of ½ lemon
Salt and pepper to taste

Melt butter. Add remaining ingredients and mix well. Pour over hot vegetables and toss through. Serve.

HERB BUTTER SAUCE

2 *ozs. butter*
2 *tbs. onion, chopped*
2 *tbs. celery, chopped*
¼ *tsp. your favorite herb*

Melt butter. Sauté onion and celery till soft. Add herb and simmer for an additional few moments. Pour over vegetable, toss and serve.

BÉCHAMEL SAUCE

3 *tbs. butter or fat*
2 *tbs. flour*
1 *cup stock (chicken, preferably)*
½ *cup cream*
½ *tsp. salt*
   Dash paprika
1 *tsp. lemon juice*

Melt the butter in the top of a double boiler. Blend in the flour, and stir until smooth. Add stock slowly, stirring until bubbles form. Stir in seasonings and then cream, gradually. Bring almost to boiling point. Reduce heat and simmer for five minutes or until thickened. Remove from heat. Add lemon juice. Serve.

TOMATO WINE SAUCE

3 *tbs. butter or fat*
3 *tbs. flour*
1 *cup canned tomato sauce*
1 *bay leaf*
1 *tbs. onion, minced*
¾ *cup bouillon*
¼ *cup dry red wine*
3 *peppercorns*
   Salt to taste
   Pinch of your favorite herb

Melt butter. Sauté onion until butter turns golden. Add flour and stir, cooking, until it begins to brown. Stir in tomato sauce, bouillon, spices and seasonings and cook to boiling point, stirring constantly. Add wine, and bring just to a boil over moderately high heat. Remove from heat, discard bay leaf and serve.

MUSHROOM SAUCE

3 *ozs. butter*
1 *small onion, chopped*
½ *lb. mushrooms, sliced or chopped*
1 *small clove garlic, crushed (opt.)*
¼ *tsp. marjoram*
  Salt and pepper to taste
1 *cup white or brown sauce (pages 46–47)*

Melt butter in skillet. Sauté mushrooms, onion and garlic in butter until mushrooms turn dark. Remove from pan. Drain. Add to white or brown sauce along with marjoram, adjust seasonings of sauce, and heat in double boiler until flavors blend. (A few minutes.)

SOUR CREAM SAUCE

1 *cup dairy sour cream*
2 *egg yolks*
  Juice of ½ lemon
1 *tsp. chopped parsley*
  Salt and pepper, paprika to taste

Beat together egg yolks and sour cream in top part of a double boiler. Use wire whisk or egg beater. Heat over just-below-boiling water and cook, stirring, until mixture thickens like custard. Remove from heat. Add remaining ingredients, mix well. Pour over vegetable and serve.

ONION SAUCE

½ *cup onions, chopped or thin sliced*
1 *tbs. butter or fat*
1 *tbs. flour*
1 *cup milk or stock*
  Salt and pepper to taste
  Pinch of thyme or sage, if desired

Sauté onion in butter or fat until transparent. Blend in the flour. Slowly add milk or stock, stirring constantly. Continue stirring and cooking over low heat until sauce thickens. Season, simmer for a few more minutes. Remove from heat and serve.

CHEESE SAUCE

1 *cup grated cheese*
1 *cup thin or medium white sauce, hot*

Add cheese to white sauce in top part of double boiler. Stir and cook until cheese melts into sauce.

EGG SAUCE

2 *hard-boiled eggs, chopped or grated*
½ *tsp. dry mustard (or curry powder)*
1 *cup white sauce (thin), hot*

Add eggs and mustard to white sauce. Simmer together for a few moments. Season and serve.

SWEET AND SOUR SAUCE

2 *tbs. butter or oil*
2 *tbs. flour*
1 *cup vegetable or meat stock*
2 *tbs. brown sugar*
3–4 *tbs. lemon juice (to taste)*
½ *tsp. salt*
  Pepper

Melt butter or heat oil. Blend in flour. Slowly add stock, stirring, and salt and pepper. Bring to a slow boil and simmer 5 minutes. Add sugar and lemon juice and cook a moment or two longer. Pour hot over vegetables and serve.

🍂 SOME UNUSUAL HOT SAUCES FOR VEGETABLES

BACON OR BEEF FRY SAUCE FOR GREENS

1 tbs. salad oil
5 strips bacon or beef fry, minced
2 tbs. flour
5 tbs. white wine or cider vinegar

1 tsp. sugar
½ cup bouillon
2 egg yolks
Salt and pepper to taste
Good dash paprika

Fry out the bacon or beef fry. When meat is brown and crisp, add flour to pan and cook, stirring, over moderate heat until mixture begins to bubble. Slowly add vinegar, sugar and broth, stirring constantly. Bring to a slow boil. Reduce heat and beat in egg yolks and seasonings. Do not allow mixture to boil again once egg yolks are added. Serve hot over cooked or raw greens.

CARAWAY SAUCE

1 tbs. caraway seeds
2 tbs. water
4 tbs. butter
1 tbs. grated onion

½ clove garlic, crushed (opt.)
Salt and pepper to taste
Dash paprika
1 tsp. lemon juice

Cook caraway seeds in water until water is absorbed. Melt butter in skillet. Sauté seeds and onion in butter for just a few moments, until seeds brown slightly. Remove from heat. Season and add garlic (if desired) and lemon juice. Pour over hot vegetables.

SPANISH SAUCE

¼ cup olive oil
1 clove garlic, crushed
¼ cup onions, chopped
2 tbs. green or red pepper, chopped

1 tbs. parsley, chopped
Salt and pepper to taste
Good dash paprika
Juice of ½ lemon

Sauté garlic, pepper and onion in oil. When pepper wilts and onion becomes transparent, remove from heat. Add seasonings and lemon juice. Pour over hot vegetables. Serve.

RAISIN SAUCE

1 *cup sultana raisins*
2 *tbs. butter or margarine*
2 *tbs. flour*
¾ *cup liquid from sultanas*
2 *tbs. dry red wine*

2 *tbs. sugar*
1 *tbs. lemon juice*
   Grated rind of 1 lemon
½ *tsp. salt*

Add 1 cup of boiling water to sultanas and plump in a saucepan over low heat for a few moments, until raisins swell. Remove from heat, drain, and reserve raisin liquid. Melt butter in a skillet. Blend in flour. When flour starts to color, add raisin liquid, wine, sugar, salt and grated rind. Stir constantly until sauce thickens. Add raisins and simmer an additional few moments. Remove from heat, add lemon juice, pour over hot vegetables and serve. Particularly good with carrots, sweet potatoes, winter squash, beets, turnips, rutabagas and onions.

CREOLE SAUCE

¼ *cup fat or oil*
1 *green pepper, diced*
2 *onions, sliced thin*
2 or 3 *stalks celery with tops,*
   diced
1 *clove garlic, minced*
1 *2 lb. can tomatoes, strained*
   or chopped

1 *tsp. chili powder*
1 *tsp. sugar*
2 *whole cloves*
3 *peppercorns*
1 *tbs. parsley, chopped*
2 *tbs. cornstarch mixed with*
   2 tbs. water
   Salt to taste

Heat oil or fat. Sauté onion, pepper, celery and garlic over moderate heat until onion turns transparent. (Make sure you do not brown vegetables.) Add tomatoes, chili powder, sugar, cloves, salt, peppercorns and parsley. Simmer over low heat for about ½ hour, stirring from time to time. Remove cloves, peppercorns. Adjust seasoning. Add cornstarch mixed with water and stir in well. Simmer for an additional 5 or 10 minutes. Serve.

BELGIAN GRAPE SAUCE

1 *tbs. butter or margarine*
1 *tbs. flour*
⅔ *cup chicken broth*

½ *cup seedless grapes, halved*
Dash salt, white pepper
1 *tsp. lemon juice*

Melt butter or margarine. Mix in flour and cook, stirring, until color turns golden. Slowly add chicken broth and stir until mixture thickens. Add grapes and seasonings and simmer together an additional few moments. Pour over vegetables and serve.

PEANUT SAUCE SUPREME

½ *cup processed cheese spread*
¼ *cup milk*
1 *tbs. grated onion*
1 *tbs. grated celery*
1 *tbs. mayonnaise*
¼ *cup chunk-style peanut butter*
1 *hard-boiled egg, grated (opt.)*
  Salt to taste
  Dash Tabasco

Melt cheese and milk in top part of double boiler. When creamy, mix in mayonnaise and peanut butter. Stir and cook until thoroughly blended. Remove from heat. Add celery, onion and seasonings. Mix in grated egg. Pour over hot vegetables and serve.

HOT APPLE CREAM SAUCE

½ *cup unsweetened apple*
  sauce
  Rind of 1 lemon, grated
2 *tbs. butter*
2 *tbs. flour*
1 *cup light cream or milk substitute such as Mocha Mix*

1 *small onion, grated*
2 *tbs. ground almonds (opt.)*
  Salt to taste
2 *egg yolks*
  Dash nutmeg

Melt butter in top of double boiler. Sauté onion and ground almonds in butter until onions are transparent. Add flour and blend in well. Place over hot water. Slowly add cream or substitute. Stir constantly over hot, not boiling, water until mixture thickens. Slowly add apple sauce mixed with lemon rind. Continue to stir until blended. Beat in egg yolks with whisk or egg beater. Heat until sauce thickens like custard. Do not allow to boil. Remove from heat, season, and pour over vegetables. Excellent for peas, celery, carrots, beets, winter squash, sweet potatoes, regular potatoes, turnips, rutabagas.

QUICK BUTTERMILK HOLLANDAISE

1 *cup buttermilk*	$\frac{1}{4}$ *tsp. mustard powder*
2 *tbs. butter*	$\frac{1}{2}$ *tsp. salt*
2 *tbs. flour*	*Pepper*
1 *egg, beaten*	*Dash paprika*

Melt butter in top part of double boiler. Add flour and mix well. Allow to cook for a minute or two. Slowly add buttermilk, stirring constantly. Add seasonings and mix in well. When sauce thickens, beat in raw egg with wire whisk or egg beater. Continue beating until sauce is hollandaise consistency. Remove from heat at once. Pour over hot vegetables and serve.

For information on marinating vegetables see salad chapter, pages 61–66.

Condensed canned soups that may be used undiluted as sauces:
1. Tomato soup
2. Onion soup
3. Cream of mushroom soup
4. Cream of celery
5. Cheese soup
6. Cream seafood soups
7. Cream of tomato
8. Cream of chicken

Heat soups, pour over hot vegetables and serve.

COLD SAUCES FOR HOT OR COLD VEGETABLES

GREEN SAUCE

3 *tbs. water cress or spinach, chopped*
1 *tbs. parsley, chopped*
1 *tbs. green onion, chopped*
Pinch dry mustard

$\frac{1}{4}$ *cup wine vinegar*
$\frac{1}{2}$ *cup olive oil*
Salt and pepper to taste
1 *clove garlic, crushed*

Pour ingredients into blender (or mash through sieve) and purée. Chill in refrigerator and serve over hot or cold vegetables. You can marinate vegetables you wish to serve as salad elements or cold hors d'oeuvres in this sauce. To do so, chill raw or par-cooked vegetables in sauce overnight. Remove from sauce and serve.

COLD DILL SAUCE

1 *cup dairy sour cream*
2 *tbs. lemon juice*
$\frac{1}{4}$ *cup fresh dill, chopped*

Salt and pepper to taste
1 *tsp. sugar*
2 *tbs. grated onion*

Mix ingredients together. Serve over hot or cold vegetables or use as marinade over raw or blanched vegetables.

CUCUMBER POPPY SAUCE

1 *cup plain yoghurt*
1 *cucumber, peeled, seeded and grated*
1 *tbs. ground poppy seeds*
   Dash garlic powder (opt.)
1 *tbs. onion, chopped (opt.)*
   Salt and pepper to taste

Combine ingredients. Chill at least 1 hour. Use as a marinade or over hot or cold vegetables.

* Poppy seeds can be ground quickly in a blender.

COLD CHEESE SAUCE

4 ozs. soft cheese spread
(Velveeta, wine Cheddar,
Cheddar spread, Blue
cheese spread, etc.)
1 tsp. lemon juice

2 tbs. mayonnaise
2 tbs. salad oil
1 tsp. paprika
  Salt and pepper to taste
¼ tsp. salad herbs

Mash cheese with oil until blended. Add lemon juice, mayonnaise, herbs and seasonings. Whip until light and fluffy. Serve over cold cooked vegetables.

HUNGARIAN MUSTARD SAUCE

½   cup mayonnaise
1½ tbs. sharp mustard
1   cup dairy sour cream
2   tbs. white horse-radish in vinegar
¼   tsp. sugar
    Dash salt

Combine all ingredients. Chill for an hour or more. Serve over cold or hot vegetables or use as a marinade.

ARABIC SESAME SEED DRESSING

½ cup Techina (prepared
  sesame seed dressing)*
  Juice of ½ to 1 whole lemon
  to taste
1 clove garlic, crushed

2 tbs. water
2 tbs. olive oil
1 tbs. parsley, chopped
  Salt to taste
  Good dash paprika

Mix lemon juice (start with juice of ½ lemon and add more later if you desire,) and water and blend into Techina. Add remainder of ingredients and blend in a blender or beat until sauce whitens somewhat. Pour over hot or cold vegetables or use as a marinade. Particularly good with peas and beans of all kinds.

* Techina is obtainable at Oriental (Mid-Eastern and Indian) specialty stores.

AVOCADO SAUCE

1 *avocado pear, mashed*
½ *cup mayonnaise*
½ *cup dairy sour cream or whipped sweet cream*
1 *tbs. prepared white horse-radish*
  Salt and pepper to taste

Blend ingredients thoroughly. Chill. Pour over hot or cold vegetables.

4

The Adventure of Salad Making

Every good cook has his forte. It may be a mystique for creating extraordinary sauces, a knack for combining unexpected ingredients in just the right way or a talent for subtle and rare flavorings. These specialties require time, experience and patient hard work. There is another fame a cook may lay claim to whose prerequisites are courage and imagination alone: that is, the art of salad making.

If your ingredients are fresh, your dressing well-mixed and applied at the proper time, chances are you can be a great salad chef. Often, in this country, the man of the house prides himself on his charge of the salad bowl. Try to lure the same head of the household to stir-cooking over a hot stove and wild horses won't do the job. Why? Because salads are fun, needing little time for preparation and a minimum of experience. There's something

59

festive about a well-tossed salad that makes it a memorable dinner-table event. A molded salad, shimmering jewel-like on a plate, can make your diners protest that it's too pretty to eat. (Have no fear. They'll lick their platters clean.) A cooked vegetable salad beaded with drops of aromatic marinade will start the gastro-intestinal juices running on first sight. If these results appeal to you follow me into the adventure of salad making.

The raw vegetable salad is the most generally popular in the United States. Purists like to make single ingredient salads such as lettuces, tomatoes, mushrooms, radishes, etc. Combination salads are likely to be gayer looking and more flavorful. Whatever your preference, here is a list of raw materials you may use.

Cabbage, carrots, cauliflower, celery, corn, cucumbers, greens, such as: iceberg, leaf, romaine, Boston and Bibb lettuces, curly endive, Belgian endive, water cress, chicory, escarole, dandelion greens, fennel, parsley, spinach, beet tops, mushrooms, onions, green peas, red and green peppers, tomatoes, radishes.

Raw vegetable salads may contain additional ingredients such as: nuts, cold, cooked fish, meat or poultry, cheese, hard-boiled eggs, olives, canned pimiento, toasted bread croutons, fruit, left-over cooked rice or pasta, any cooked vegetable that is neither too soft nor watery. These are just a few suggestions. I'm sure you will think of many more.

PREPARING RAW SALADS

1. Select your ingredients and line them up before you.
2. Wash all greens carefully to remove grit and dirt. Drain them dry in a colander or in a kitchen towel. If you use a towel, pat them dry gently. Greens bruise and wilt easily.
3. Wash, trim and pare those vegetables that require it. If you wish to crisp your celery, radishes, peppers, carrots, etc., before use, put them in ice water for a few minutes.
4. Make sure all your ingredients are dry before combining them in a salad bowl. Soggy salad fixings will make for wilted salads and diluted dressings.

5. To make your lettuce leaves into bite-size pieces, tear them into desired size. Never use a knife on them.

6. If you are using any hard vegetables, such as carrots, in your salad, make sure you cut them into pieces thin enough to be chewed conveniently. Salad morsels that take extra chewing effort are enough to ruin your guests' pleasure.

7. Vegetables (other than lettuce) may be diced, sliced, julienned, minced or grated for salads. The important thing is that they be the right size for fork and mouth.

8. A good combination salad has neither a superabundance of soft nor hard ingredients but a balance between the two.

9. Combine your bite-size salad ingredients in a bowl and refrigerate till ready to use. Do not prepare your salad fixings more than a few hours before use. The idea is to keep them looking and tasting fresh.

10. Do not add dressing to your raw salad till it reaches the table.

11. Look for a variety of color, texture and flavor in your raw vegetable salads. Just as your salad should not have too many hard nor too many soft ingredients, it is best that you use a majority of mild-flavored ingredients. Strong-flavored ingredients such as onion, anchovy, olives, etc., are good as accents. Don't forget that salad dressing will provide the over-all flavor.

Potato salad is probably the best known cooked vegetable salad. There are multitudes of others. Beet salad, Niçoise salad, cold asparagus salad, salad of artichoke hearts, green bean salad are a few more standards. Here, too, purists use single ingredients for their cooked vegetable salads. Combination salads of cooked ingredients are equally delightful to me. The choice is yours. Whether your cooked products originated in a can, frozen package, or yesterday's dinner casserole, if they still retain flavor, color and a somewhat solid state, my advice is: marinate for salad. Unlike raw vegetable salads, cooked vegetables will taste better if they are dressed and refrigerated hours before serving. Some cooks marinate their cooked salads overnight. I prefer to do it in the morning of the day they are to be used. I find that most cooked vegetables get too soft under overnight conditions. But be your own judge. A hint of raw onion, a few tablespoons of chopped green pepper, some radish slices and fresh-cut celery will transform yesterday's side dish into an original salad creation. The family will never know. The taste will improve immeasurably. (One of the reasons for marinating a cooked vegetable salad in dressing is to put back flavor where prior cooking may have taken it out.) Use the applicable rules for making cooked vegetable salads noted above for raw. An important difference is where you are using a variety of cooked vegetables, try to cut them in approximately the same shape or size. They'll look prettier if carrots, green beans, potatoes, onions, peas, corn and beets are all dice-size.

Cooked vegetables you may use: artichokes, asparagus, beans, beets, broccoli, carrots, cauliflower, celery, corn, eggplant, kohlrabi, leeks, lentils, mushrooms, okra, onions, turnips, parsnips, rutabagas, peas, peppers, potatoes, squash.

MY FAVORITE SALAD DRESSINGS AND MARINADES

FRENCH DRESSING AND MARINADE WITH VARIATIONS

BASIC RECIPE:

$\frac{1}{4}$ cup wine vinegar (white or red)

$\frac{1}{4}$ tsp. mustard powder

Dash paprika

$\frac{1}{4}$ tsp. sugar (if desired)

1 tsp. chopped parsley

$\frac{2}{3}$ cup salad oil

Salt to taste

Shake together in a covered jar and refrigerate till needed.

Variations:

1. Add 1 tbs. chopped or grated onion.
2. Add 1 crushed garlic clove.
3. Add $\frac{1}{4}$ tsp. celery seed.
4. Cook 2 tbs. caraway seeds in 2 tbs. water until water evaporates (few minutes) and add seeds to marinade or dressing.

5. Add ¼ tsp. crushed herbs: thyme, marjoram, basil, tarragon, chervil, oregano, or whatever you prefer. Try a combination of herbs such as: thyme, marjoram and basil, or tarragon and chervil, etc.

6. Add 1 fresh, diced tomato to your dressing, particularly good if you plan to use it as a cooked vegetable marinade.

7. 1 tbs. prepared chili sauce, catsup or pickle relish.

8. 1 tsp. Worcestershire sauce.

9. 1 tbs. capers.

10. 2 tbs. chopped olives.

11. 2 tbs. chopped gherkins or sour pickles.

12. 1 tbs. mustard relish (omit mustard powder from recipe).

13. Use all lemon juice or a combination of lemon and vinegar.

14. Add 1 tbs. chopped anchovies.

15. Add 2 tbs. chopped pimientoes.

16. Add 2 mashed, hard-boiled egg yolks.

17. Add 1 beaten raw egg.

18. Substitute white or red dry wine for vinegar and lemon.

LIME DRESSING FOR FRUIT AND LETTUCE SALADS

2 tbs. lime juice

2 tbs. honey

¾ cup mayonnaise

Dash pepper, salt to taste

¼ tsp. celery seed

¼ cup chopped pecans (opt.)

Mash well together. Chill till used. For an interesting variation, substitute 6 ozs. softened cream cheese for mayonnaise.

CREOLE DRESSING

½ cup evaporated milk

2 tbs. white wine or cider vinegar

2 tbs. catsup

1 clove garlic, crushed

¼ tsp. thyme, crushed

¼ tsp. basil, crushed

Dash Tabasco

Salt to taste

½ cup salad oil

Shake in a covered jar till well blended. Refrigerate till needed.

SESAME SEED DRESSING

$\frac{1}{3}$ *cup red or white wine vinegar*
3 *tbs. cold water*
 Salt and pepper to taste
3 *tbs. salad oil*
$\frac{1}{2}$ *clove garlic, crushed*
1 *tbs. onion, grated or chopped*
$\frac{1}{4}$ *tsp. mustard powder*
$\frac{1}{4}$ *cup sesame seeds*

Place seeds in a skillet over a high flame. Shake pan vigorously as seeds start to brown. (It should take just a few minutes.) Pour seeds while still hot from the pan into combined ingredients above. Seeds should sizzle as they hit the liquid dressing. Refrigerate at least 1 hour before serving. Good over mixed greens, cooked broccoli, green beans, boiled new potatoes, green peas.

CURRY DRESSING AND MARINADE

1 *cup dairy sour cream or yoghurt*
1 *tbs. white vinegar*
1 *tbs. mayonnaise*
2 *egg yolks, hard boiled*
1 *tbs. (if you don't like strong flavors, use 1 tsp.) curry powder*
1 *clove garlic, crushed*
 Salt, pepper, paprika, to taste

Mash egg yolks with vinegar and mayonnaise. Mix in curry powder, garlic and other seasonings. Whip into sour cream. Refrigerate till needed. Particularly good over seafood, meat, poultry, cheese, pasta, rice or cooked vegetable salads.

SWEET AND SOUR CREAM DRESSING

1 *tsp. salt*
2 *tbs. white or cider vinegar*
$\frac{1}{4}$ *cup water*
$\frac{1}{4}$ *tsp. prepared mustard*
$\frac{2}{3}$ *cup dairy sour cream*

Heat together all ingredients except sour cream. Bring to a boil and simmer for 3 to 5 minutes. Remove from heat and add sour cream. Pour while still warm over potato salad, cole slaw, beet salad, cucumber salad or any other raw or cooked vegetable combination you choose.

BLUE CHEESE DRESSING

¼ lb. Blue cheese, Gorgonzola
   or Roquefort
2 tbs. red wine vinegar
2 tbs. olive oil

Dash Tabasco (opt.)
½ cup mayonnaise
Dash salt, if desired

Mash cheese to a paste with vinegar. Blend oil and Tabasco. Whip mayonnaise into mixture thoroughly. Season to taste. Serve on bite-sized greens, tomato wedges or cooked vegetable combinations.

HONEYED YOGHURT DRESSING

1 cup plain yoghurt
1 tbs. dry Sherry
½ tsp. celery seed
¼ tsp. prepared mustard (opt.)
   Dash salt
2 tbs. mild-flavored honey

Combine ingredients and mix together thoroughly. Refrigerate 1 hour before use. Excellent over greens or fruit salads.

AUSTRIAN CARAWAY MARINADE

¼ cup celery tops, coarse chopped
½ tsp. caraway seeds
1 tsp. white horse-radish (fresh, if possible, grated)
½ tsp. sugar
½ cup white vinegar

Boil vinegar, caraway seeds and celery tops together and allow to simmer for 5 minutes. Remove from heat, remove celery, if desired, and combine with other ingredients. Pour while still hot over cooked vegetables and marinate in the refrigerator until needed. Good for peas, beets, carrots, potatoes, summer squash, etc. Oil may be added at the table.

LEMON-BUTTER DRESSING

Juice of one lemon
⅓ cup melted butter
Juice of ½ clove garlic (or few drops liquid garlic)
Juice of ¼ medium onion (or few drops liquid onion)
Salt and pepper to taste

Melt butter and cool. Combine with other ingredients. (Garlic and onion may be crushed in garlic press for juice.) Do not refrigerate dressing as butter will harden below room temperature. It is advisable to use this dressing shortly after making it. Be sure your greens are at room temperature before pouring this dressing over them. Excellent on Bibb or Boston lettuce, spinach greens, or any vegetable combination where a delicate dressing is desired.

FAVORITE SALADS IN MY HOUSE

GREEN SALAD WITH TOASTED ALMONDS

1 *head Boston lettuce, torn*
1 *head Iceberg lettuce, torn*
1 *small bunch water cress, trimmed and torn (opt.)*
½ cup blanched, sliced almonds
2 *tbs. cooking oil (corn or peanut)*

Clean greens thoroughly. Drain and pat dry. Combine in salad bowl and chill till just before needed. Pour oil into wide-bottomed skillet. Heat and add blanched almonds. Toast over medium heat, shaking pan constantly to avoid scorching. When fairly evenly browned, turn out almond slices onto absorbent paper to drain off oil. Make sure you remove most or all of the excess oil. Just before serving, sprinkle toasted almonds over greens. Dress with the following:

$\frac{1}{4}$ cup lemon juice
$\frac{1}{4}$ tsp. mustard powder
   Salt to taste, black pepper
$\frac{1}{2}$ to $\frac{2}{3}$ cup salad oil (other than olive)

You can add dressing ingredients to salad bowl directly at the table. It is not necessary to combine them in advance. Make sure, however, that ingredients are well tossed and blended. Add enough oil to give salad a mild flavor; let your palate be the judge. (You may taste a leaf out of the bowl for testing purposes without losing a bit of *savoir faire.*)

CRACKED WHEAT (BORGHUL) SALAD

1 cup cooked borghul
2 cups Iceberg lettuce, torn
$\frac{1}{3}$ cup scallions, diced (opt.)
2 navel oranges, peeled, sectioned and skinned

Combine in salad bowl. Dress before use with same mixture as for Green Salad with Almonds. (See above.)

RICE SALAD

2 cups (leftover) cooked rice
1 green pepper, chopped fine
2 canned pimientoes, drained and minced
$\frac{1}{4}$ cup cooked (or canned) mushrooms, diced (if available)
1 tbs. parsley, chopped
2 tbs. scallions, chopped

Combine ingredients. Trim with sliced, pitted olives, hard-boiled egg wedges, pepper rings, anchovies, etc. Dress at the table with the following:

$\frac{1}{4}$ *cup wine vinegar and lemon juice combined*
$\frac{2}{3}$ *cup olive oil*
  Dash Worcestershire sauce
  Salt and pepper
$\frac{1}{4}$ *tsp. crushed basil*
  Dash sugar

and serve over lettuce leaves. This is a basic rice salad recipe. You may add to it cubed, cooked meats, seafood, eggs or cheese to make a meal-size salad.

MACARONI SALAD

2 *cups small cooked macaroni shells*
$\frac{1}{4}$ *cup celery, chopped*
$\frac{1}{4}$ *cup sour or dill pickles, chopped*
1 *green pepper, diced*
2 *tbs. stuffed olives, chopped*
2 *tomatoes, diced*
$\frac{1}{4}$ *cup radishes, thin sliced*
2 *tbs. parsley, chopped*

Combine and chill. Prepare dressing in advance, as follows:

2 *tbs. wine vinegar*
1 *small clove garlic, crushed*
1 *tsp. curry powder*
  Dash sugar
  Dash cayenne pepper (opt.)
  Salt and pepper to taste
1 *cup mayonnaise*

Dress salad shortly before serving. (At least $\frac{1}{4}$ hour to allow ingredients to absorb flavors.) You may serve salad on lettuce, if you wish. Cheese cubes (Gruyère is good, or any other mild-flavored variety), cooked poultry, fish or meat may be added to this salad.

SCANDINAVIAN BEET SALAD

1   cup cooked beets, julienne-sliced
1½ cups cooked potatoes, diced
⅓ cup celery, diced
1   Spanish or Bermuda onion, medium size, thin-sliced in rings
1   head Iceberg lettuce, torn in bits
2   hard-boiled egg whites, shredded

Combine ingredients. Dress before use with the following:

2 hard-boiled egg yolks
1 raw egg yolk
1 tbs. white vinegar
1 tsp. sharp, prepared mustard
  Salt and pepper to taste
1 tsp. sugar
1 cup unsweetened whipped cream (or dairy sour cream)

Mash hard yolks with vinegar and mustard. Beat in raw yolk.
Add all ingredients except whipped cream. Fold in cream gently,
last. Combine with salad at the table.

SALADE PROVENÇAL

½ cup cooked carrots, diced
½ cup cooked potatoes, cubed
½ cup cooked whole green peas and diced green beans
  (combined)
¼ cup raw celery, diced
¼ cup raw green pepper, diced

Combine in bowl and marinate overnight in the following dressing:

2 tbs. wine vinegar
  Dash mustard powder
  Salt and pepper to taste
½ clove garlic, crushed
1 tbs. parsley, chopped
½ cup olive oil
  Sprinkling of your favorite salad herbs, crushed (opt.)

CHINESE RADISH SALAD, SWEET AND SOUR

2 cups small, crisp radishes, trimmed	1½ tbs. plain vinegar
1 tsp. soya sauce	1 tbs. sugar
1 tsp. salt	1 tbs. corn or peanut oil

Take a heavy knife and with the flat side, crush each radish with one blow, leaving them whole, however. Sprinkle them with salt and allow to stand for 5 or so minutes. Combine other ingredients as you would a sauce. Marinate radishes in mixture for ½ hour before serving. This salting and marinating process may be used with sliced turnips, seeded cucumber wedges, flowering parts of mustard greens, broccoli, but eliminate crushing process with these.

EGGPLANT SALAD

1 eggplant, baked in skin
1 firm ripe tomato, peeled* and cubed
1 cup sharp Cheddar cheese, grated
½ onion, grated
   Dash cayenne
   Salt and pepper to taste
2 hard-boiled eggs, chopped

Peel and cube cooked eggplant. Combine in serving bowl with other ingredients and blend well. Dress with the following:

2 tbs. white wine vinegar
¼ tsp. tarragon leaves, crushed
5–6 tbs. olive oil

Dress and chill salad one hour or more before serving.

---

* To peel tomatoes: plunge into boiling water, remove at once and hold under cold running water. Skin will peel easily, leaving tomatoes whole.

RED SALAD

2 *raw red peppers, sliced*
  julienne and seeded
2 *cloves garlic, halved*
¼ *cup salad oil*

Juice of 1 lemon
2 *tomatoes, cubed*
½ *cup radishes, sliced thin*

Cook peppers and garlic in oil until peppers soften and wilt. Pour hot mixture into salad bowl. Remove garlic halves. Add tomatoes, radishes, lemon juice and seasoning. Toss until well coated. Refrigerate for one or more hours. Serve on lettuce or alone.

ITALIAN PEPPER SLAW

1 *head cabbage, shredded*
1 *green pepper, grated*
1 *medium-sized jar pimien-*
  toes, julienne sliced
1 *tsp. celery seed*
  Dash Tabasco
3 *tbs. fine bread crumbs*
1 *small can tomato paste*

6 *tbs. water*
  Salt to taste
  Dash sugar
¼ *cup cider or white vinegar*
  Juice of ½ lemon
⅓ *cup olive oil*
1 *clove garlic, crushed*

Place shredded cabbage, pimientoes, grated pepper and celery seed in salad bowl. Make dressing separately, as follows:

Soak bread crumbs in water. When water is totally absorbed, add tomato paste, spices and seasonings (garlic, salt, Tabasco, sugar, etc.). Add vinegar, lemon juice and oil and mix well together. Pour over slaw. Toss vigorously. Refrigerate overnight.

MENNONITE SALAD

3 *carrots, grated*
1 *cup celery, chopped*
½ *cup peanuts, chopped*
2 *tart apples, grated*

Combine. Serve on lettuce topped with honeyed yoghurt dressing, sweet-sour sour cream dressing, mayonnaise or sour cream.

THE BEAN BOWL

1 *pkg. frozen cut wax beans, thawed over heat*
1 *pkg. frozen cut green beans, thawed over heat*
1 *medium size can kidney beans, drained*
1 *medium size can chick-peas, drained*
1 *large sweet onion, sliced thin in rings*
⅓ *cup celery, diced*
¼ *cup fresh parsley, chopped*

Combine the above. Dress as follows:

½ *cup wine or cider vinegar*
½ *cup salad oil*
½ *cup sugar*
1 *small clove garlic, crushed (opt.)*
  Salt and pepper to taste

Serve chilled. Marinate four or more hours in dressing. If you haven't four hours till dinner and you need to make a quick job of marinating: heat dressing ingredients together in a saucepan until they start to boil. Pour boiling hot over vegetables. Cool and chill quickly in the freezer. Results will be almost as good as lengthy marinating.

FRENCH SPINACH SALAD

1 *bag pre-cleaned spinach (or 1 lb. loose)*
¼ *lb. Gruyère cheese, cubed*
¼ *cup celery, diced*
1 *pear, peeled, trimmed and diced*

Combine and dress as follows:

2 *tbs. evaporated milk*
  Juice of 1 lemon
  Salt and pepper
  Dash sugar

GRAPEFRUIT-AVOCADO SALAD

1 *head Boston lettuce, torn*
2 *avocado pears, pitted, skinned and sliced into wedges*
1 *medium grapefruit, peeled, sectioned and seeded*
2 *tbs. toasted coconut (opt.)*

Combine and dress with:

¼ *cup lemon juice*   2 *tbs. mild honey*
¼ *cup dry Sherry*   ¼ *tsp. celery seed*

LITERARY SALAD

(Inspired by a recipe of Alexander Dumas)

1 *bunch water cress, trimmed*   1 *can tuna fish, drained and*
  and washed   *flaked*
⅓ *cup celery, sliced*   8 *large stuffed olives, sliced*
½ *cup cooked beets, sliced*   2 *tbs. onion, diced*
1 *cup cooked potatoes, cubed*   *Handful of Iceberg lettuce,*
1 *tomato, diced*   *torn in bits*

Combine ingredients in a large bowl. Make the following dressing:

3 *cooked egg yolks*
⅔ *cup good olive oil*
¼ *tsp. mustard (French, if possible)*
1 *tbs. soya sauce*
2 *gherkins, diced*
1 *tsp. Worcestershire sauce*
1 *hard-boiled egg white, shredded*
  Juice of 1 lemon
¼ *tsp. crushed tarragon leaves*
  Dash salt, if desired

Mash egg yolks in oil. When a thin paste is made, add mustard, soya sauce, gherkins, lemon juice, Worcestershire, egg white and tarragon. Blend together with a fork. Taste, add salt if desired. Salad may be dressed and chilled ½ hour before serving.

ATHENS SALAD

1 *head Iceberg lettuce, torn in bits*
2 *tomatoes, diced*
1 *cup raw spinach leaves, torn in bits*
1 *cucumber, cubed*
1 *green pepper, sliced in rings*
2 *tbs. onion, chopped*
½ *cup cooked beets, diced*
½ *lb. Feta cheese, cubed*
½ *cup Greek olives*

Combine ingredients in a large salad bowl. (The size of the salad makes it suitable for parties or large dinners.) Chill until used. Dress before bringing to the table with the following:

⅔ *cup olive oil*   *Salt and pepper to taste*
¼ *cup wine vinegar*   *Good dash paprika*
1 *clove garlic, crushed*

CHINESE HOT VEGETABLE SALAD

1 *head cabbage (Chinese style, preferably) in bite-size pieces*
1 *can bean sprouts, drained*
2 *cans water chestnuts, sliced*
2 *cans bamboo shoots, sliced*
½ *lb. fresh snow peas or 1 pkg. frozen peas*
2 *cloves garlic, crushed*
2½ *tbs. soya sauce*
2 *tbs. light salad oil*

Rinse all vegetables under running water. Place them in a strainer or colander and shake off most excess water. (Make sure that some beads of moisture remain.) Select a large heavy-bottomed pot such as one used for soup. Place oil on bottom of pan. Coat vegetables with garlic, soya sauce and oil by mixing in pot. Place pot over medium high heat and steam for a few moments, until cabbage softens slightly. Turn out on platter and serve hot. Serves 4–6.

ASPARAGUS SALAD

1 *bunch asparagus*   *Grated rind of 1 lemon*
   Juice of 1 lemon   2 *drops garlic juice (opt.)*
2 *tbs. soya sauce*   ½ *cup olive oil*
½ *cup stuffed olives, sliced*

Cook asparagus till tender in boiling, salted water. Drain and cool. Place in a refrigerator dish and dress with other ingredients. If salad is too tart for your taste, add a dash of sugar. Refrigerate a few hours before serving. Serves 4–6.

AVOCADO SALAD

1 *ripe avocado pear*   *Pulp and juice of 1 tomato*
1 *small onion, grated*   *Salt and pepper, to taste*
1 *canned pimiento, diced*   2 *tbs. olive or salad oil*
   Juice of ½ lemon   ½ *cup crushed corn flakes*
   Dash Worcestershire sauce   ½ *cup mayonnaise (opt.)*
2 *hard-boiled eggs yolks,*
   mashed

Remove pit from avocado and spoon out flesh into mixing bowl. Mash together with above ingredients. This salad will keep under refrigeration for one or two days, if kept covered. Before serving, trim with chopped parsley or sprinkle with paprika. Serve on lettuce or as a dip.

MID-EAST SALAD PLATTER

3 *ripe tomatoes, sliced thin*
2 *cucumbers, unpeeled, sliced thin*
½ *lb. fresh mushrooms, cleaned, sliced thin*
   Juice of 1 lemon
⅓ *cup good olive oil*
   Dollup of yoghurt
8–10 *Greek olives*

On a platter, make a row or ring of tomato slices, another of cucumbers and a third of mushrooms. Squeeze a lemon over the vegetables and pour olive oil evenly over that. Sprinkle with salt and pepper. Garnish platter with olives, leaving room in center for yoghurt. Trim with fresh chopped parsley. Serve.

DUTCH GLUNARENSLA

1 *cup boiled beets, cubed*
2 *cups boiled potatoes, cubed*
2 *tart apples, peeled, seeded and cubed*
1 *medium onion, diced*
1 *large sour pickle, cubed*
½ *cup walnuts, coarse chopped (opt.)*
1 *cup herring fillets,* in bite-size pieces*
  Mayonnaise

Combine all ingredients in a refrigerator bowl. Moisten thoroughly with mayonnaise. Use as much or as little as you prefer. Chill overnight before using.

RUSSIAN SALAD

Similar to Glunarensla, the flavor difference is marked enough to convince me to include it here.

2 *cups boiled beets, sliced*   1 *dill pickle, cubed*
½ *cup scallions, diced*   3 *hard-boiled eggs, diced*
2 *cups cooked potatoes, diced*   ⅓ *cup radishes, sliced*
⅓ *cup celery, diced*   8 *anchovy fillets*
1 *cup sauerkraut, rinsed and*   2 *tbs. chopped parsley*
  drained

Combine in a refrigerator bowl. Prepare a mild French dressing:

¼ *cup white wine vinegar or*   *Good dash paprika*
  lemon juice   *Salt and pepper to taste*
¼ *tsp. mustard powder*   ¾ *cup light salad oil*

Dress salad and chill overnight. This salad may be trimmed with fresh, chopped dill, if desired.

---

* You may substitute sardine fillets or any leftover meat or poultry for herring.

CHEESE SALAD

1 *cup grated Cheddar or Gruyère cheese*
1 *tomato, diced*
1 *medium dill pickle, diced*
8 *radishes, sliced thin*
1 *red pepper or canned pimiento, diced*
2 *hard-boiled eggs, diced*
1 *head Boston or Iceberg lettuce, torn in bits*

Toss in salad bowl. Dress with vinegar and oil, salt and pepper and serve.

VEGETABLE ASPIC

1 *envelope unflavored gelatin*
1¾ *cups vegetable juice cocktail*
2 *tbs. lemon juice*

Few drops onion juice
Dash Worcestershire sauce
Pinch salt
½ *tsp. sugar*

Sprinkle gelatin on ½ cup of juice. When softened (5 or so minutes), place in saucepan over low heat, add lemon juice, onion juice and Worcestershire sauce. Heat until gelatin is thoroughly dissolved. Remove from heat. Add remaining ingredients. Turn into a 2 cup, lightly greased mold and chill until firm. Turn out on serving platter. Garnish with tomato wedges, scallions, olives, cucumbers or whatever salad ingredients you prefer. Serve immediately.

JELLIED SALAD

1 *pkg. lemon-flavored gelatin*
1 *cup boiling water*
1 *tbs. vinegar*
1 *cup carrots, fine chopped*

1 *cup celery, diced*
1 *tbs. onion, grated*
Dash salt

Dissolve gelatin in boiling water. Cool and refrigerate. When mixture starts to thicken, add vinegar, carrots, celery and onion. Pour into individual, lightly greased molds which have been slightly chilled. Refrigerate until firm.

5

A Soup for All Seasons

Soup is a venerable food. It has an ancient history which dates back to the dawn of civilization. In Biblical times, it was the hallmark of a gracious host to present his guests with a rich and nourishing broth after a long and tedious journey. Soups had magical, life-giving properties in old times. They were given to the sick or convalescent to speed his recovery. Priests and shamans concocted bubbling bouillons of weird ingredients whose consumption gave to the drinker extraordinary and sometimes supernatural powers. There were soups to make you healthy, soups to make you strong, virile, amorous, victorious, or wealthy. There were soups to make you powerful and soups to make you wise.

In cultures around the world to this day, the composition and blend of the soup you eat is the mark of your social status. In China, for example, until the Revolution at any rate, the peasant dined on simple broths of rice or noodles and vegetables. The nobleman consumed delicate distillations of such rare ingredients as bird's nests and shark's fins. The multiplicity of ingredients, the subtlety of flavoring, the time and method of preparation involved are indicators of wealth and position in life.

Fortunately for us the natural bounty of our country allows us all to share the palatal pleasures of diverse soup preparations. Unlike the Chinese peasant, we can all afford the best culinary ingredients. Meat, poultry, seafood, grain or vegetable products are abundant here. Those food lovers who dine on hearty, peasant-style stock-pots do so because they prefer it. Delicate seasonings and flavor agents are as close to hand as the nearby supermarket.

For us, soups can be the overture to a meal or the main melodic line. As a first course, their function is to arouse and tempt the tastebuds into a state of full awakening. It is a mistake to flavor meal starters so strongly that the palate is knocked out of tasting for the remainder of a meal. A disciplined, seasoning hand is what is needed here. Not so for meal-in-one or main course soups. In these cases, your flavor conscience is your guide and preference is king.

As you may begin to suspect, there is a wide range of soup styles from which to choose. They may be served hot, chilled or jellied. Hot or chilled soups can be thick or thin, strained and clear such as consomme and bouillon, creamed and puréed or stocked with cuts of meats, vegetables and/or grains. The meal-in-one soups consist of richly flavored, long simmered broths from which the vegetables and meats or seafood are removed to be served as separate portions. Some soups must be simmered for twenty-four to forty-eight hours to attain their flavor peak. Others are overdone after a half-hour of cooking. Soups known as stock (to be discussed) are the basis for other kinds of preparation. Thin cuts of meat, seafood, poultry may be quickly poached to perfection in broth. Vegetables cooked in stock achieve a unique seasoning blend. Eggs can be poached in a slow simmering pan of bouillon and served alone or with the liquid. The possibilities are unlimited. As a base for sauces, the liquid in which to cook vegetables, a part or totality of a meal, soup is indispensable.

American housewives and amateur chefs have the choice of

dehydrated soup mixtures commercially prepared, frozen or un-
frozen cans of soup, instant soup bases (bouillon cubes and
powder) for soup starters or starting from scratch in creating
their soups. There is something to be said for each. I have tried
and enjoyed each in my own kitchen. The dehydrated soup mixes
when added to some fresh ingredients and re-seasoned are quickly
prepared and tasty. Canned ready-soups are great emergency
meal adjuncts and can be dressed up simply and prettily with
few additions. Some of them are excellent sauce material (see
page 55). Bouillon cubes and powders save on time tremen-
dously. Where stock or broth is called for as a single ingredient
of a recipe you can cut the preparations by half (at least) with
the aid of these commercial products. Of course, it is marvelous
to have a refrigerated or frozen container of your own created
stock always at hand. Few cooks I know do so. While the flavor
of homemade broth far surpasses that of its processed, mass-
marketed brother, time, labor and expense of preparation hardly
warrant the result. In my own home I find that my homemade
stocks just don't go far enough. A day's simmering produces only
enough liquid for a few days of use. As to starting from scratch,
I have done that often in the making of a soup. When I find my
vegetable bin overflowing with wilted vegetables or slightly
over-ripe or over-mature ones, soup is the order of the day. These
vegetables which can be used successfully in no other dishes are
perfect for soups when combined with stock. Their strong and/or
pungent flavors mellow out over the cooking hours. Their tough,
fibrous or over-soft tissues are of no concern to us here.

If you are concerned with the good nutrition of your household, soup can be your ally. You may know that certain vitamins
are water-soluble. This means that the vitamin content of these
dissolve in the cooking liquid. If you throw away the cooking
water and consume the vegetables only, you are literally throwing
away the vitamins. If the idea of quaffing doses of pallid vegetable water does not appeal to you, keep a "stock-pot." The French
are noted for it. They save the liquid by-products of their cooked
foods all together in a refrigerated container. Remnants of vegetable juices, bits of broth or cooking water, along with such
vegetable bits as were discussed above, are saved for such time

as a soup is being made. They are incorporated into the soup. The result is enriched flavor and nutrition. Once you're in the saving habit, a stock-pot is easy. I encourage you to try it.

The recipes I include here are some of my friends' and family's favorites. They range in length of preparation, complexity and manner of cooking. Some are for the connoisseur. Others are simply put together and un-fancy. A few are combinations using commercially prepared soup products. Others require all fresh ingredients. I hope they are comprehensive enough to provide something for everyone.

🍂 DEFINITIONS

The following are a few definitions pertaining to soups that may clarify your thoughts. Between some, only shades of difference exist. Others are quite individually named.

STOCK — The liquid resultant from long-simmering meats or poultry or fish, with or without flavorful vegetables and herbs.

BROTH — An aromatic, richly flavored thin soup produced in the same manner as the above. The difference between the two is that broth connotes a finished soup, seasoned, skimmed and strained of all materials not to be served in the soup bowl.

CONSOMMÉ — A clear, thin concentrated broth, seasoned for serving.

BOUILLON — Like consomme, it is clear, seasoned and brothy. Generally, it is lighter and less concentrated in flavor.

To CLARIFY — To remove any meat scum and fat from the soup liquid. This may be done by spooning off this material from the top of the broth or by straining the soup through cheesecloth, refrigerating it until it jells slightly, and then removing the hardened fat on top of the soup. (Of course, only soups made with bones will jell under refrigeration.) Another method is to beat egg whites until stiff and to add them with or without egg shells to the soup pot. All foreign matter will be absorbed by egg whites and shells and can be easily removed.

CREAM SOUPS — These can be broadly categorized as puréed vegetables or seafood added to a thin white sauce made with either stock, milk, cream or a combination.

CHOWDER — Usually, a soup with a milk or cream base in which vegetables and/or seafood have been quick-cooked. A chowder should never cook longer than twenty to thirty minutes and should be served with the ingredients presenting a just-done taste and texture.

BISQUE — A thick rich soup with a cream base. Seafood bisques are the most common variety.

THE STOCK-POT

BROWN STOCK — Brown stock has a meat base, either veal bones and meat, beef bones and meat, or ham or lamb or a combination of meat, bones and/or poultry. To this can be added celery, mushroom stalks, carrots, onion and/or leek, parsnips and/or turnips, parsley, dill, peppercorns, bay leaf, your favorite herbs and/or spices. (Any or all of the foregoing may be used.) Sautéed, browned onions may be added to this kind of stock, as well. Cut up sausage may be added or bacon, beef fry or corned beef. Any spicy meat adds flavor.

YELLOW OR WHITE STOCK — Usually, such a stock has a poultry base; chicken or duck. Delicate and strong-flavored vegetables can be used here, depending on how much of a purist you are. Some like the liquid of a stewing chicken alone. Others prefer garlic, onion/leek combinations, celery, parsnip, dillweed, parsley, lettuce greens and various herbs. You should experiment to find your favorites.

VEGETABLE STOCK — Celery and tops, onions, leeks, carrots, cucumber skins, tomatoes with liquid centers removed, mushroom stalks, turnips or parsnips, lettuce leaves, bay leaf, parsley, dillweed, thyme or marjoram or other favorite herbs, peppercorns, cloves.

MY FAVORITE BROWN STOCK

1 *clove garlic, diced*
2 *carrots, halved*
3 *celery stalks and tops, cut in large pieces*
1 *white turnip, cubed*
2 *onions, quartered*
  Stems of ½ lb. mushrooms

1 *veal knuckle with meat, split*
1 *beef bone with meat, split*
  Sprigs of parsley and dill
  Some peppercorns
  Bay leaf

Bring ingredients together with 2 quarts of water to a boil. Reduce heat. Simmer for at least 4 hours. The longer the stock cooks the better. Skim top surface of any scum that surfaces during the first hour of cooking. Strain stock through cheesecloth or fine strainer and refrigerate till needed. Any fat that coagulates on top of chilled soup may be removed.

MY FAVORITE YELLOW STOCK

1 *whole stewing chicken, in pieces*
2 *leeks, split*
2 *cloves garlic, split*
3 *stalks celery and tops, cut in pieces*
  Sprigs of parsley

1 *parsnip*
  Some peppercorns
2 *slices fresh ginger or a pinch of powdered, dry ginger (opt.)*
  A few leaves of Swiss chard
2 *qts. water*

Prepare as for brown stock.

MY FAVORITE VEGETABLE STOCK

2 *onions, sliced*
2 *tbs. light oil*
3 *carrots*
1 *white turnip*
2 *stalks celery with tops*
2 *leeks*
  Handful of mushroom stems

2 *tomatoes, seed centers removed*
  Skin of 1 green pepper
  Skin of 1 or more cucumbers
  Handful of fresh dillweed
  Bay leaf
  Pinch of thyme

Sauté the onions in the oil until golden brown. Add the rest of the ingredients to the pot, cover them with water and bring to a boil. Reduce heat and simmer for 2 or 3 hours. Strain and refrigerate till needed.

HOT SOUPS

HEARTY TOMATO SOUP

1½ *lbs. very ripe tomatoes, diced*
2 or 3 *favorite soup meat bones with meat (ham, veal, beef, etc.)*
¼   *cup raw rice*
    Salt
1   *large onion, chopped*
2–3 *tbs. light oil*
1   *tbs. or more sugar*
1½ to 2 *qts. water*

Cook tomatoes and meat bones together in a soup pot with water. Bring to a boil, lower heat and simmer for 1½ hours. (You may skim surface of soup if you wish.) Strain out tomato skins and remove soup bones. If you prefer it, you may dice soup meat and return to pot. Add rice and some salt and simmer, covered, for ½ hour. Stir soup occasionally while rice is cooking. Meanwhile, sauté the onion in the oil until golden brown. At end of cooking period, add browned onion and sugar (to taste) to soup. Re-season. Serve at once or reheat at later time. Soup improves on second day.

RUSSIAN MEAT BORSCHT

2 *bunches small to medium beets, peeled and grated*
2 *large meaty beef knuckles*
1 *carrot, peeled and halved*
1 *onion, quartered*
2 *qts. water*

Salt to taste, pepper
2 or 1½ *lemons, juice only*
¼ *cup sugar (or more to taste)*
2 *cloves fresh garlic, pressed*
Hot potatoes

Bring grated beets, bones, carrot, onion, water and a good pinch of salt to a boil. Lower heat to simmering and add the juice of 1 lemon. Simmer for about 1½ hours. If desired, at this time you can remove the bones. Some people like to remove the bone scum on the soup's surface, others don't bother. Meat, in any case, should be left in the pot. Add sugar, ½ to 1 whole more lemons (juice only), freshly squeezed garlic, pepper and more salt to taste. Cook about 15 minutes more. Serve over hot, peeled potatoes and quartered hard-boiled eggs.

LENTIL-BARLEY SOUP

2 cups lentils
½ cup pearl barley
2 onions
3 stalks celery
2 carrots
2 cloves garlic
8 small dried brown mush-
rooms (European or Chinese, opt.)
1 bay leaf
3 tbs. light olive oil or corn oil
2 qts. water
Salt and pepper
Pinch curry powder (opt.)

Soak lentils, barley and mushrooms together overnight. Dice onions, carrots and celery. Sauté in oil until onions are golden and other vegetables are soft. Add lentils, barley and mushrooms and curry powder and quickly toss through browned vegetables over medium high heat. (2 or 3 minutes only.) Add hot water, garlic, bay leaf and salt and pepper. Bring to a boil, reduce heat and simmer for approximately 2 hours. This soup, like most, improves with age.

QUICK KIDNEY-NAVY BEAN SOUP

1 qt. beef stock
1 cup mixed kidney and navy beans
Chopped parsley
¼ tsp. chopped basil
Salt and pepper to taste
Butter or margarine

Soak beans overnight to soften. Simmer beans in stock for about 1 hour. Pour into blender and purée. Return to pot and reheat with chopped basil. Serve with pat of butter or margarine and sprinkled with chopped parsley.

Variations: 1 tbs. of brandy can be added to soup when it is reheated.

Try adding 1 small sautéed, chopped onion to purée. Heat together.

Sprinkle the green parts of scallions, chopped, over soup and serve.

A healthy dash of garlic salt will spice up the flavor during the initial cooking.

MUSHROOM BISQUE WITH BRANDY AND CHIVES

1 *lb. fresh mushrooms, sliced*	$\frac{1}{4}$ *cup flour*
1 *quartered small onion*	2 *cups milk or half & half*
$\frac{1}{2}$ *tsp. salt*	$\frac{1}{3}$ *cup chopped chives*
Enough water to cover	2 *tbs. brandy*
3 *tbs. butter*	

Simmer mushrooms and onion in salted water for about $\frac{1}{2}$ hour or until they are tender. Purée liquid and vegetables in a blender or by forcing through a sieve. Melt butter in the top part of a double boiler. Gradually add the flour. Mix until smooth. Slowly add the cream or milk, mixing constantly. Stir mixture until thick and smooth. Add the purée, chives and brandy. Re-season with salt. Heat before serving but do not boil.

VEGETABLE CHOWDER

1 *large onion, chopped*	3 *cups boiling water*
2 *tbs. butter*	1 *tbs. celery flakes*
1 *lb. new potatoes*	1 *pkg. frozen corn or* 1$\frac{1}{2}$ *cups*
2 *carrots*	*fresh kernels*
1 *lb. fresh peas*	3 *cups scalded milk*
1 *bay leaf*	$\frac{1}{2}$ *tsp. thyme*
Salt and pepper	1 *tbs. chopped parsley*

Sauté onion in butter until golden. Add the sliced peeled potatoes, carrots and the water. Add celery leaves and bay leaf. Bring to a boil, reduce heat and simmer, covered, for approximately 15 minutes or until potatoes and carrots are tender. Remove bay leaf. Add milk, corn, peas and simmer an additional 10 minutes. In final cooking moments, add thyme, parsley and seasoning. You can serve this chowder topped with a pat of butter. For a variation, try adding chopped water cress (1 bunch, no stems) during last moments of cooking.

QUICKIE FRENCH ONION SOUP

1 *pkg. dehydrated onion soup mix and water as package directs*
½ *cup water (additional)*
½ *cup dry white wine*
3 *pearl onions, sliced*
½ *cup beef bouillon or pot roast gravy*
1 *clove garlic, crushed*
3 *tbs. olive oil or butter*
4 to 6 *rounds of day-old French bread (1 per serving)*
1 *tbs. of grated Parmesan per serving*

Combine onion soup mix and water, wine, onions, broth and extra water. Bring to a simmer and continue cooking over low heat for 5 to 10 minutes. Sauté stale French bread rounds in fat or oil into which garlic has been squeezed. Fry bread till golden. Place 1 slice of fried bread at the bottom of each soup bowl, pour soup over it and sprinkle with cheese. Serve.

CREAM OF YAM SOUP

1 *lb. yams, peeled and*
  quartered
1 *medium onion, quartered*
1 *cinnamon stick*
3 *cups water*
3 *tbs. butter*

3 *tbs. flour*
3 *cups milk or half & half*
1 *tsp. salt (or more to taste)*
  Pepper
  Dash nutmeg
2 *tbs. Sherry*

Cook yams, onion, and cinnamon stick in water till vegetables are soft, about 20 minutes. Force through a strainer or purée in a blender, first removing cinnamon stick. In the top part of a double boiler, melt butter. Mix in flour slowly. When well blended, pour in milk or cream, stirring constantly. Continue stirring until sauce thickens. Add salt, pepper and Sherry to mixture. Pour in purée, reheat but do not boil. Sprinkle with nutmeg and serve.

Variation: To make Cream of Carrot soup, substitute an equal quantity of carrots for yams and proceed as directed in previous recipe.

OLD-FASHIONED POTATO SOUP

4 *medium potatoes, peeled*	*Water*
and cubed	*Salt and pepper*
2 *medium onions, chopped*	2 *stalks celery, diced*
3 *tbs. oil or butter*	

Cook potatoes in enough salted water to cover them, in a covered saucepan, until tender. (20–30 minutes.) Sauté onions and celery in oil or butter until golden brown. Add cooked potatoes and potato cooking water. Season with salt and pepper to taste. Simmer for 5 or 10 minutes and serve.

POTATO CHOWDER

1 *medium onion, chopped*	1 *tbs. butter*
2 *tbs. butter*	1 *tbs. flour*
2 *cups potatoes, peeled and*	2 *cups scalded milk*
cubed	1 *bay leaf*
1 *carrot, peeled and diced*	*Chopped parsley*
2 *stalks celery, diced*	¼ *tsp. chopped marjoram*
3 *cups boiling, salted water*	

Sauté onion in butter until golden brown. Add raw potatoes, carrot, celery, bay leaf, and salted, hot water and simmer in covered saucepan until potatoes are tender. (About 15 minutes.) Blend melted 1 tbs. of butter with flour. Combine with scalded milk and mix until smooth. Add to potato mixture, stirring constantly until soup thickens. Remove bay leaf. Sprinkle with marjoram and parsley. Re-season and heat before serving but do not allow to boil. Serve with hard-boiled egg quarters.

HEARTY MINESTRONE

2 qts. beef bouillon
2 tomatoes, diced
$\frac{2}{3}$ cup medium barley, soaked a few hours
$\frac{1}{2}$ cup large dry lima beans, soaked a few hours
$\frac{1}{2}$ cup small macaroni (shells or tubes)
1 red or green pepper, diced
2 medium onions, diced
1 pkg. frozen green beans (or $1\frac{1}{2}$ cups fresh beans, diced)
$\frac{1}{2}$ pkg. frozen peas (or $\frac{2}{3}$ cup fresh peas)
2 carrots, diced
$\frac{1}{2}$ cup celery and tops, diced
1 small bunch escarole, leaves only, chopped
$\frac{1}{2}$ cup green squash, diced (opt.)
2 white turnips, diced (opt.)
$\frac{1}{2}$ lb. lean beef, diced
  Bay leaf
2 garlic cloves, diced
$\frac{1}{4}$ cup fresh dill, chopped
5 peppercorns
4 slices bacon or beef fry
2 tbs. flour
  Salt to taste

Place all ingredients except bacon or beef fry and flour and salt in a soup pot. Simmer over low heat for at least 3 hours. Fry out bacon or beef fry. Put strips in the soup. Cook fat from strips with flour until lightly browned paste is formed. Stir slowly into soup. Continue to stir until well incorporated. Simmer additional 20 minutes. This soup can be served the same day, refrigerated up to five days and reheated for the table or frozen indefinitely for future use. It is a healthful, filling meal-in-one.

SPRING SOUP

1 *bunch carrots, peeled and sliced*
1 *small bunch hearts of celery, diced*
1 *small cabbage, shredded fine*
¼ *cup chopped parsley (fresh) or 2 tbs. dry parsley flakes*
2 *onions, diced*
1 *red or green pepper, diced*
3 *tomatoes, peeled and diced*
½ *cup green beans, cut in 1 in. pieces*
1 *parsnip, diced*
½ *cup green peas*
  Corn kernels from two fresh ears of corn
  Peppercorns, salt to taste
2 *quarts water*

Place all ingredients except salt in soup pot. Bring to a boil, lower heat, simmer for 35 to 45 minutes. When all vegetables are tender, soup is done. Season with salt. You may add cut thin noodles and rice (½ to ⅔ cup together) to soup during last twenty-five minutes of cooking. In this case, cover soup and simmer until rice and noodles are tender.

YANKEE BAKED BEAN SOUP

1 *large can baked beans (any style)*
1 *pint beef stock*
1 *cup water*
1 *medium onion, diced*
2 *stalks celery, diced*
1 *cup tomato juice*
  Salt and pepper to taste
2 *tbs. flour*
2 *tbs. butter or margarine*

Simmer beans, stock, water, onion, celery, tomato and garlic together in a soup pot for about 45 minutes. Pour mixture into a blender and purée. Return to pot. Add juice and reheat to simmering. Melt butter in a saucepan. Blend in flour till a paste is made. Slowly, stir in paste to soup. Mix in well. Re-season. Allow to cook, simmering, for 20 or more minutes.

HOME-STYLE MINESTRONE

$\frac{1}{3}$ cup olive oil or butter

3 cups mixed, diced fresh vegetables such as the following:
  onions, cabbage, carrots, string beans, mushrooms, celery,
  potatoes, summer squash, green pepper, spinach or Swiss chard

2 pints hot vegetable or chicken stock

$\frac{1}{3}$ cup small macaroni

$\frac{1}{4}$ cup green peas

2 peeled, diced tomatoes

$\frac{1}{2}$ cup total canned chick-peas, broad beans and/or kidney beans,
  rinsed and drained

1 bay leaf

2 tbs. chopped Italian parsley
  Salt and pepper
  Grated Parmesan cheese

Heat oil in heavy-bottomed soup pot. Add first three cups of vegetables. Stir and cook them in the hot oil till the vegetables begin to wilt visibly. Add stock, bay leaf, macaroni, salt and pepper and parsley and bring to a boil. Reduce heat and simmer until vegetables are tender. Remove bay leaf. Add tomatoes, green peas and beans. Season once again. Add 4 or 5 tbs. grated cheese (fresh grated, if possible). Simmer 5 to 10 minutes longer. Serve with additional grated cheese.

SCANDINAVIAN ROOT SOUP

3 ozs. sweet butter

2 carrots

1 large potato

1 parsnip

1 white turnip

1 onion

3 stalks tender celery

$\frac{1}{2}$ cup pearl barley (soaked
  overnight to soften)

$\frac{1}{4}$ tsp. thyme

1 tbs. chopped fresh dillweed
  (or 1 tsp. chopped dry dill)

1 tbs. chopped fresh parsley

4 cups vegetable bouillon

2 cups scalded milk, hot
  Salt and pepper

Melt butter in the bottom of heavy-duty soup pot. Peel and dice all the vegetables. Brown them lightly in butter over a moderate fire. Add stock and seasonings: dill, parsley, thyme, salt and pepper, and simmer together until vegetables are tender. (About 30 minutes.) Add barley, again bring to a boil, reduce heat and simmer for 15 to 20 minutes more, covering the pot. Add hot milk, some additional butter, if desired (2 ozs.), season again, and serve.

DUTCH PEA SOUP

$2\frac{1}{2}$ *quarts water*
1   *lb. split peas (soaked overnight)*
1   *ham bone (veal may be substituted)*
$\frac{1}{2}$ *lb. sausages or other savory meat, cubed*
$\frac{1}{2}$ *celery knob or 3 stalks outer celery plus 1 tsp. celery seed*
2   *leeks, split in half*
$\frac{1}{4}$ *cup tops of celery*
1   *tsp. thyme*
$\frac{1}{4}$ *tsp. basil*
$\frac{1}{4}$ *tsp. marjoram*
    Salt to taste
    Dash cayenne or Tabasco
    Toasted croutons

Boil peas in soaking water (plus fresh water to total $2\frac{1}{2}$ quarts) along with bone for about 2 hours. Add diced vegetables and sausage or meat. Cook until vegetables are tender. Remove bone. Add salt, pepper and herbs. Simmer for a few moments. Serve with fried bread croutons.

EAST INDIAN QUICK SOUPS

To vegetable soups, cream soups, pea soups and tomato soups in cans, add:

$\frac{1}{4}$ *cup lemon juice*
$\frac{1}{4}$ to $\frac{1}{2}$ *tsp. turmeric powder*

POLISH CABBAGE SOUP

1   2 lb. cabbage, shredded
1   large onion, chopped
3   tart apples, chopped and
     peeled
½ to ⅔ lb. lamb with lamb
     bones (you may substitute
     2 or 3 lamb chops)

2   tomatoes, diced
1½ lemons, juice only
2   tbs. flour
2   tbs. fat or oil
     Sugar to taste — ⅓ to ½
     cup
1   tsp. salt

Salt cabbage and allow to stand for 5 to 10 minutes. Squeeze out as much liquid as possible from cabbage leaves. Place cabbage, onion, chopped apples and lamb and tomatoes in soup pot and add about 2 qts. of water. Bring to a boil, reduce heat and simmer twenty-four to forty-eight hours. (That is, cook it all day the first day and return to stove and cook it most of a second day, as well.) Liquid should reduce by half. Do not allow to burn at bottom. When ready, brown 2 tbs. of flour in fat. Remove soup bones (which should be clean of meat as this should fall to pieces in the soup during cooking). Add browned flour to soup and stir till soup thickens. Add the juice of 1½ lemons, sugar and salt (these must be varied to taste) and cook over low heat for twenty minutes more. Serve.

MENNONITE VEGETABLE SOUP

1½ lbs. soup bone and meat
1   2 lb. cabbage, chopped
      fine
2   cups celery, chopped
1   cup onions, chopped fine
2   pkgs. frozen mixed
      vegetables

1   #2 can tomatoes
2   qts. water
     Salt and pepper
1   or more tbs. sugar, to taste

Cook soup bone and meat, cabbage, tomatoes, salt and water for 2 or 3 hours. Remove any scum that forms on top of soup. 15 to 20 minutes before serving, add celery, onions and frozen vegetables. Re-season and serve.

CRÈME LUISE

1 *cup sweet onions, sliced*
  (Spanish onions, if possible)
1 *cup white turnips, diced*
¼ *cup light oil and butter,*
  combined
¼ *tsp. curry powder*
¼ *tsp. French mustard*
¼ *tsp. celery seed*
2 *diced tomatoes, very ripe*

3 *cups hot vegetable or*
  chicken bouillon
1 *cup boiling water*
1 *cup broad egg noodles*
2 *ozs. condensed milk or milk*
  substitute such as Mocha
  Mix
2 *tbs. cornstarch and 2 tbs.*
  water, mixed
  Salt to taste

Sauté onions, turnips, curry powder, celery seed, mustard and some salt in oil-butter combination until vegetables soften and turn yellow. Cook over moderate heat, stirring occasionally, for about five minutes or until vegetables are soft. Add tomatoes and cook additional 10 minutes or until tomatoes become mushy. Add bouillon, boiling water and noodles. Cover and cook soup gently until noodles soften. Stir in milk or milk substitute and blend well. Mix cornstarch with water. Add some hot soup to the cornstarch mixture and mix together. Stir in the cornstarch liquid to the soup, slowly and blending all the while. Continue stirring until soup thickens. (5 to 10 minutes.) Season with salt. Do not allow to boil again. Serve soon after soup is ready—soup will separate on standing.

VIETNAMESE FESTIVAL SOUP

1 *can cream of asparagus soup*
1 *cup chicken bouillon*
1 *small can shredded crabmeat*
1 *tsp. soy sauce*
½ *garlic clove, crushed*
¼ *tsp. powdered ginger*
1 *can white asparagus (diced) and juice*

Heat together all ingredients in the top of a double-boiler. Season to taste. Serve with crisp Chinese noodles, if desired.

MAX'S MAN-IN-THE-KITCHEN SOUP

1 *can diluted cream of celery soup*
1 *can diluted pea soup*
1 *tsp. chopped dillweed*
1 *tbs. dehydrated celery flakes*
1 *tsp. chopped parsley*
1 *tbs. dehydrated vegetables*
2 *tbs. dry Sherry*

Combine all ingredients, except Sherry. Bring to a boil, reduce heat and simmer for 10 to 15 minutes or until done. Add Sherry. Simmer an additional 3 or 4 minutes. Serve.

CHINESE HOT AND SOUR SOUP

$1\frac{1}{2}$ *qts. chicken stock or bouillon*
1 to 2 *tbs. lemon juice, to taste*
   A few drops Chinese sesame oil (opt.)
   Pinch powdered ginger
   Ground pepper, salt
1 *chicken breast, deboned and shredded*
$\frac{1}{3}$ *cup dry mushrooms (soaked 20 minutes)*
$\frac{1}{4}$ *cup bamboo shoots*
2 *eggs, well beaten*
2 *cakes bean curd, cubed (opt.)*
2 *tbs. cornstarch mixed with 2 tbs. water*
2 *tbs. scallion greens, chopped*

Combine all ingredients through bamboo shoots and simmer for 5 minutes. Add bean curd, simmer 2 more minutes. When soup is just below boiling point (but not boiling), slowly spoon in the beaten egg. As each spoonful forms threads in the soup, add more. Next, mix cornstarch with water and some hot broth from the soup. Pour into the soup, stirring constantly. Keep stirring gently until soup thickens slightly, about 6 minutes. Add chopped scallion greens and serve.

TEN-MINUTE DIFFERENT-INGREDIENT SOUP

1 *pkg. dehydrated chicken-rice soup mix and water as pkg. directs*
2 *additional cups water*
½ *cup coarse chopped spinach leaves*
⅓ *cup bamboo shoots*
¼ *cup fine sliced water chestnuts*
⅓ *cup dry black mushrooms (soaked for 20 minutes)*
⅓ *package cellophane noodles (if available) or fine egg noodles*
2 *cakes Chinese style bean curd, cubed (opt.)*
1 *breast of chicken, deboned and shredded*
¼ *lb. snow peas or ¼ cup green peas, raw*
¼ *tsp. powdered ginger*

Combine all ingredients and simmer together for eight minutes, except peas. Add snow-peas or green peas. Simmer for 2 more minutes. Season with salt to taste, if needed. Serve.

🍃 COLD SOUPS

COLD MEATLESS BORSCHT

2 *bunches raw beets (medium size), peeled and grated*
3 *celery stalks and tops, cut in pieces*
1 *large onion, quartered*
1 *carrot, peeled and halved*
  Juice of 1 lemon
2 *qts. water*
1 *tbs. coarse salt*
2 *egg yolks*
3 or 4 *tbs. dairy sour cream*
  Sugar to taste
  Some more salt (to taste)

Bring soup pot to a boil with water, beets, celery, onion, carrot, lemon juice, salt. Reduce heat and simmer for about ½ hour. Strain soup. While still quite warm, add well-beaten mixture of egg yolks, sour cream, sugar and salt. Slowly add to soup mixture, stirring constantly until totally combined. Chill in refrigerator until needed. Serve with added sour cream.

CHILLED WATER CRESS SOUP

2 *cups thin white sauce made with half & half (see pages 46–47)*
2 *bunches water cress*
2 *leeks, split (1 onion may be substituted)*
2 *cups water*

Cook 1½ bunches of water cress in the water with leeks. Simmer for 10–15 minutes. Strain broth and add to creamy white sauce. Season with salt to taste. Chill. Serve garnished with fresh chopped water cress.

SOURGRASS OR SORREL SOUP (SCHAV)

½ *lb. sorrel or sourgrass, stems removed*
1½ *qts. lightly salted water*
2 *beaten egg yolks*
½ *cup dairy sour cream*
  Good pinch of salt (to taste)

Cook leaves in salted water for about 20–25 minutes. Remove all but a few leaves. While still warm, beat eggs with salt and sour cream to a smooth, creamy mixture. Pour warm soup into mixture, slowly, stirring constantly. Refrigerate overnight. Serve topped with chopped scallions.

JELLIED BORSCHT

1 *#2 can sliced beets*
1 *cup bouillon (chicken or vegetable)*
1½ *tsps. red wine vinegar*

¼ *cup cold water*
1 *tbs. unflavored gelatin*
  Salt to taste

Drain beets, reserving liquid. Soften gelatin in cold water. Heat beet liquid and bouillon in a saucepan. Add softened gelatin and simmer until gelatin dissolves. Remove from heat. Add vinegar and adjust seasoning. Pour liquid into a blender along with sliced beets. Blend until beets are puréed. Pour mixture into individual serving cups. Chill until jelled. Serve topped with dairy sour cream or plain yoghurt. Serves 6–8.

JELLIED MADRILÈNE

2 *cups tomato or vegetable juice*
2 *cups bouillon (beef or vegetable)*
2 *envelopes (tbs.) unflavored gelatin*
½ *cup cold water*
½ *tsp. Worcestershire sauce*
1 *tbs. lemon juice*
  Dash Tabasco (opt.)
  Salt and pepper, if desired

Heat juice, bouillon and lemon juice until boiling. Soften gelatin in cold water. Pour gelatin into hot broth and stir until dissolved. Remove from heat. Add other seasonings and mix well. Pour into wet mold and chill until set. Beat jelly slightly and spoon into cold serving dishes. Trim with fresh chopped dill or parsley, chopped scallion greens or pimiento-stuffed olive slices. Serves 6–8.

6

Casseroles for Carefree Living

The advantages of casserole cookery have made it ubiquitously popular from the shoals of Maine to the Barbary Coast. It is the one type of cooking which may be called truly national in practice. So much so that in many homes across the nation it is a rare dinner that does not include one casserole course. Women like casserole cookery because it is economical in time of preparation and cost. Men like it because casseroled foods are robust rather than "fancy," fun to eat because of the multitude of ingredients and, usually, because there's plenty to go around. Children find an element of exploration in casseroled dinners; they can search and discover the ingredients they favor. Truly, the art and science of casserole cooking is an American contribution to world cuisine.

There are a great many things to be said for casseroling vegetables. First, the natural juices, flavors and nutritional elements are kept within the pot rather than lost in the cooking process. Second, as I have been told by many wives and mothers, it is a painless way to get the family to eat vegetables. In uncounted homes where (I hate to admit) the name of vegetables is anathema, children and husbands will wolf down a vegetable casserole where they would not touch greens or yellows in any other form. The reason for this is unknown to me. I only report the fact as I have heard it again and again. Another legitimate reason for the success of casseroles is that they neither have to be stirred, basted nor watched. You put the dish in the oven, set your timer and forget it. The oven does all the work. Remove, and serve in the self-same pot. No extra serving bowls to wash.

I have great fun inventing casseroles for meals-in-one. My husband claims I have never made or served him a casserole dish more than once. It may be so, I honestly don't recall. What I put together in my casserole depends on what is left over in my refrigerator and what is plentiful in my pantry. So it should be with all casserole ingredients. The best are made with what is readily available. If you have to go out and shop for casserole fixings half the fun is gone. For that reason, the casserole dishes included here are presented with the thought that the recipe elements are likely to be in your kitchen at this or any time. The advantages of the casserole are gone if they force you to shop for special ingredients of limited usefulness.

Don't be afraid to vary to your taste my casserole recipes. They are presented as basic preparations. You might wish to vary the seasoning or exchange one food element for another. It is perfectly all right to do so. In that way, you make the recipe yours. Almost any recipe included here can be expanded to a full dinner meal. The addition of meat, fowl, fish, or sometimes, cheese or eggs will do the trick. Salads are a pleasant accompaniment to casserole dinners. Fresh or cooked fruits make a delightful ending to a casserole supper for family or guests. Bread and a beverage will complete your meal.

VEGETABLES À LA CRÈME

2 *frozen pkgs. artichoke hearts or asparagus, green beans,*
  broccoli, Brussels sprouts, cauliflower, carrots, mushrooms,
  peas, potatoes or squash
½ *cup bouillon (beef, chicken or vegetable)*
1 *tbs. margarine or butter*
  Salt and pepper, paprika
1 *cup dairy sour cream*
1 *pkg. frozen French fried onion rings or ½ can of same*
3 *tbs. grated yellow cheese*

Cook vegetables first in bouillon with butter or margarine until
half-done or not quite tender. Drain. Place at bottom of a greased
casserole. Cover with thawed onion rings, pour over top sour
cream, sprinkle with salt and pepper and paprika. Spoon grated
cheese on top. Place in preheated oven at 350° for about 20
minutes.

SCALLOPED VEGETABLE CASSEROLE

3 *cups canned tomatoes*
1½ *cups of one or more of the following: limas, eggplant cubes,*
  summer squash cubes, celery crescents, green pepper rings,
  whole kernel corn, green peas, diced green beans or 2 cups
  onion sliced thin.
2 *tbs. butter*
1 *tsp. sugar*
  Salt and pepper to taste
1 *tbs. grated onion (substitute grated celery if onions are used in*
  recipe)
  Bread crumbs
3 *tbs. buttered bread crumbs*

Sauté your vegetables till softened but not brown. Combine
with tomatoes, sugar, salt and pepper, grated onion or
celery. Blend in just enough fine bread crumbs to thicken mixture
slightly. (This will depend on what vegetable combination you
choose.) Pour into a lightly greased casserole, top with buttered

crumbs and bake at 350° for about 35–40 minutes. Serve bubbly hot.

Variation: Instead of thickening with bread crumbs, add ½ can of French fried onion rings to recipe and omit the grated onion.

VEGETABLES POLONAISE

4 *cups zucchini, cubed*
2 *cups onions, coarsely chopped*
2 *cups celery, sliced in crescents*
1 *cup buttered bread crumbs*
2 *tbs. butter*
1 *cup yellow cheese cubes, American or Cheddar, (opt.)*
  Seasoned salt

In a greased casserole, place 1 layer of zucchini, 1 layer of onions, 1 layer of celery, 1 layer of cheese cubes and a layer of buttered crumbs. Sprinkle with seasoned salt. Repeat layers till all ingredients have been used. End with a topping of buttered crumbs and dots of butter. Bake in a moderately slow oven (325°) for 45 minutes to 1 hour.

CALIFORNIA VEGETABLE RING

1 *lb. (approx. 2 cups) vegeta-*
  *bles, fresh, chopped fine**
4 *tbs. butter*
2 *tbs. chopped onions*
¼ *to ½ tsp. chili powder*
  (to taste)

½ *garlic clove, pressed (opt.)*
  Salt and pepper
4 *tbs. flour*
1 *cup milk*
4 *eggs, separated*

Clean and chop vegetables fine. Melt butter in large skillet. Sauté onions till golden. Add vegetables and chili powder. Stir-cook for about 5 minutes or until vegetables soften. Add salt and pepper to taste and flour. Blend well. Slowly, stirring constantly, add

---

* Fresh vegetables you can use in this recipe: carrots, celery, mushrooms, broccoli, green beans, spinach, red or green peppers, rutabagas, potatoes, turnips, squash.

milk. Continue to stir over low fire until mixture thickens to sauce consistency. Beat egg yolks. Add some of hot sauce mixture to yolks and blend. Turn off heat under skillet and slowly, stirring, add egg yolks. Beat egg whites until stiff peaks are formed. Fold into warm (not too hot) sauce. Turn into greased ring mold and bake at 350° until firm. (Approx. 30 minutes.)

BAKED VEGETABLE GUMBO

3 *tbs. butter*
1 *small to medium eggplant*
2 *cups onions, sliced*
1 *red or green pepper,*
  coarsely chopped
1 *#2 can tomatoes*
1 *garlic clove, crushed*

Salt to taste
Dash Tabasco sauce
Dash powdered cloves
$\frac{1}{4}$ *tsp. oregano*
$\frac{1}{2}$ *cup fried bread croutons*
Additional butter for
  dotting top

Sauté eggplant cubes and onion slices in butter till softened but not mushy. Pour mixture into greased casserole dish. Add pepper, tomatoes, salt to taste, Tabasco, garlic and oregano. Top with well-buttered crumbs and dots of butter. Bake for about 1 hour (or until brown at edges of pan) in moderate (350°) oven.

BAKED EGGPLANT FIESTA

1 *medium eggplant*
2 *medium onions*
1 *green pepper*
1 *clove garlic, crushed*
1 *tbs. vinegar (wine vinegar,*
  if possible)
1 *diced tomato*
1$\frac{1}{2}$ *tbs. grated Italian cheese*
1 *tbs. minced parsley*

2 *cups toasted, flavored*
  bread croutons
1 *small can unflavored*
  tomato paste
1 *cup milk*
3 *eggs*
Salt and pepper
Dash of cayenne pepper

Bake eggplant, onions and pepper whole in skins for 1 hour in a moderately hot oven (375°). Cool, remove skin of vegetables and chop (together) edible parts. When finely chopped, transfer to a mixing bowl and add garlic, vinegar, tomato, cheese, parsley and salt and pepper. Oil a glass casserole with butter or olive oil. Pour mixture into casserole. Sauté bread croutons in additional butter or oil (3 tbs.) until lightly browned. Make a second layer of the croutons in the casserole. Smooth the tomato paste over the croutons. Beat the eggs with milk until frothy. Pour over paste. Season with additional salt and pepper and cayenne. Bake in a moderate oven (350°) for 50 minutes to 1 hour. When egg-milk custard is set and browned, casserole is done. This dish is an excellent Lenten or dairy meal-in-one.

AU GRATIN POTATOES AND TOMATOES

2 *lbs. tiny new potatoes, halved*
4 *tomatoes, thin sliced*
½ *cup favorite grating cheese*
1 *tsp. sugar*
  Salt and pepper
½ *cup scallions, chopped*

Half cook potatoes in salted water. Remove from pan and drain. Place on bottom of greased casserole. Lay out tomato slices on top of potatoes. Sprinkle with salt and pepper and sugar. Scatter chopped scallions over tomato slices. Top with grated cheese. Bake about 25 minutes in moderate oven (350°) or until cheese top is brown and bubbly.

BROCCOLI DIVINE

2 *pkgs. frozen broccoli, thawed*
2 *cans condensed cream of mushroom soup*
1 *small can water chestnuts, rinsed, drained and thin sliced*
1 *#2 can bean sprouts, rinsed and drained*
½ *cup grated cheese, (opt.)*
1 *can onion rings*
  Salt

Grease a large casserole (2½ qt. capacity). Place at the bottom a layer of broccoli stalks. Pour ½ can concentrated mushroom soup over these and sprinkle with 1 tbs. of grated cheese and a little salt. Place a layer of French fried onion rings over this and another layer of water chestnuts and bean sprouts above that. Pour remaining ½ can soup on this and again sprinkle with cheese and salt. Repeat these layers until all your ingredients have been incorporated. Top with fried onions and grated cheese. Bake at 350° for 40–45 minutes.

Variations: Substitute frozen cauliflower, whole green beans, asparagus, Brussels sprouts, or potatoes for broccoli.

SPANISH POTATO CASSEROLE

2 *cups leftover mashed potatoes*
1 *clove garlic, crushed (opt.)*
2 *eggs*
½ *cup chicken broth or bouillon*
1 *red pepper (or canned pimiento), minced*
1 *onion, minced and browned in 2 tbs. oil*
¼ *cup chopped green olives*
¼ *tsp. mint leaves, crushed*
1 *small can seasoned tomato sauce*

Combine mashed potatoes, garlic, pepper, onion, olives. Beat eggs and broth until frothy. Add to potato mixture and blend until well mixed. Pour into round, greased casserole. Top with tomato sauce and mint leaves. Bake in moderate oven (350°) for 20 to 25 minutes.

SQUASH-POTATO PIE

1 *medium butternut squash*
2 *large potatoes*
1 *large carrot*
2 *ozs. melted butter*
½ *cup milk*
1 *egg*

1 *tbs. brown sugar*
¼ *tsp. salt*
½ *tsp. French mustard*
1 *medium can sliced peaches,*
  drained

Cook squash, potatoes and carrot either by boiling in little water or steaming over water. Peel vegetables. Remove seeds from squash. Mash together potatoes, squash and carrot, butter and milk beaten with egg. Season mixture with salt, sugar and mustard. Pour into greased round casserole. Lay out slices of peaches to make a single pinwheel pattern. Sprinkle with additional brown sugar (2 tbs.) and dot with more butter (2 tbs.). Bake in moderate oven for about 35 minutes or until top is browned and set.

ARTICHOKE POTATOES ITALIENNE

1 *pkg. frozen artichoke hearts, half-cooked as directed on pkg.*
3 *medium potatoes, peeled and cubed*
  Garlic powder, salt, pepper
3 *tbs. olive oil*
3 *eggs*
½ *cup bread crumbs*
1 *cup grated Parmesan cheese (fresh grated is best)*

Half-cook potatoes in salted water. Remove, drain and place in oblong baking pan which has been oiled with 1 tbs. olive oil. Mix drained artichoke hearts with potatoes. Sprinkle with salt, pepper and garlic powder. Pour the 2 remaining tbs. of olive oil over potatoes and artichokes. Mix together the following: 3 eggs, fine bread crumbs, grated cheese. Pour over the artichoke-potato combination. Bake in moderate oven (350°) for about 40 minutes.

CARROT SCALLOP

2 *cups carrots, pared and thin sliced*
1 *medium onion, chopped*
1 *tbs. flour*
3 *tbs. butter*
1 *can condensed cream of celery soup*
¼ *can milk*
  Salt, pepper and paprika

Sauté carrots and onion in butter until onion turns yellow and carrots soften partially. Pour into a baking dish. Sprinkle with salt and pepper and flour. Mix the celery soup and milk until smooth. Pour over carrots. Sprinkle with paprika. Bake in moderate oven (350°) for about 40 minutes.

VEGETABLE RICE

½ cup fresh mushrooms, chopped
1 small onion, chopped fine
1 carrot, peeled and chopped fine
1 red or green pepper, chopped fine
3 tbs. oil or fat
1 tsp. celery flakes
1 tsp. minced parsley
1 cup raw rice
1 can beef consomme, concentrated
1¼ cans water
  Salt and pepper
  Good dash soya sauce

Sauté mushrooms, carrots, onion and pepper in fat or oil until all vegetables have softened and onions are lightly browned. In a covered saucepan, combine rice, sautéed vegetables, water, celery flakes and parsley and soya sauce. Bring pot to a rapid boil, stir through once, lower heat and simmer for about 12 minutes, covered. Remove cover. If water is still visible in pan, continue to heat over lowest heat, uncovered, up to 5 minutes more so water will evaporate. Do not stir pot. Serve as a base for sauced meats, poultry or fish.

STUFFIN' VEGETABLES

2 cups cooked sliced vegetables: carrots, green beans, celery,
  mushrooms, asparagus, peppers or potatoes
1 8 oz. pkg. seasoned stuffing (as for poultry)
½ cup bouillon (vegetable or chicken)
1 cup half & half
  Dash Tabasco
½ tsp. onion salt
2 tbs. butter
2 eggs, beaten

Moisten stuffing with bouillon. Make a layer of $\frac{1}{3}$ of stuffing in the bottom of a greased, square baking dish (8 inch). Spread $\frac{1}{2}$ of vegetables over stuffing. Mix together half & half, eggs, Tabasco and onion salt. Pour $\frac{1}{3}$ of mixture over vegetables. Place another third of stuffing over this, the rest of the vegetables above the stuffing and pour over this more sauce, leaving some in reserve. Top with the rest of stuffing and sauce. Dot with butter. Bake in hot oven (425°) for 20 or 25 minutes. Casserole is done when top is browned and stuffing is firm to the touch.

CABBAGE AU GRATIN

1 *medium cabbage, cut in wedges*
2 *cups seasoned medium white sauce (see page 46)*
1 *cup grated American and Cheddar cheese plus 2 tbs.*
2 *tbs. chopped canned pimiento*

Place cabbage wedges in a pot with water to cover. Bring slowly to a boil. Remove pot from heat, cover, and allow cabbage to cool in water. Drain cabbage and place on the bottom of a greased baking dish. Combine white sauce and grated cheese (minus 2 tbs.) in the top part of a double boiler. Add chopped pimiento and stir until cheese is entirely melted and blended. Pour sauce over cabbage wedges and sprinkle with reserved grated cheese. Bake in a moderate oven (350°) for about 25 minutes or until cabbage is tender.

Variations: Substitute thawed frozen broccoli or cauliflower or Brussels sprouts for cabbage. Do not blanch, however. For 1 pkg. frozen vegetables, use 1 cup cheese sauce.

MUSHROOM MACARONI

2 *cups cooked macaroni*
1 *lb. fresh mushrooms*
1 *medium onion, chopped*
3 *ozs. butter*
2 *eggs, beaten*

3 *ozs. condensed milk*
Salt and pepper
3 *tbs. favorite grated cheese*
or $\frac{1}{4}$ cup buttered bread crumbs

Clean mushrooms and remove stems. Chop together onion and mushroom caps. Place chopped vegetables, butter and 2 tbs. water in a blender. Purée mixture. Pour into a frying pan and simmer, stirring occasionally, until liquid diminishes and color darkens somewhat. (About 5 minutes.) Combine with all other ingredients except cheese or crumbs. Pour into a buttered casserole. Top with cheese or buttered crumbs. Bake at 350° for 20–25 minutes or until top is golden. Serve hot and sliced like a cake.

Variations: You may substitute 1 bunch of raw carrots for mushrooms. This dish may be served with a sauce at the table. (See Chapter 3 for suggestions.)

GOLDEN GLOW CASSEROLE

2 *ozs. butter*
5 *medium white turnips*
3 *large carrots*
1 *medium onion*
   Salt and pepper
4 *tbs. condensed milk*
2 *eggs*
2 *cups cooked white meated fish, chopped*
1 *tsp. Worcestershire sauce*
   Juice of 1 lemon
   Salt and pepper, paprika
1 *tbs. butter, melted*
3 *tbs. cracker crumbs*

Steam or cook pared turnips, carrots and onion in small amount of water till tender. Place in blender (or mash together) with seasoning, butter, condensed milk and eggs. If fish is used, in a separate container, mix together fish, Worcestershire, lemon juice, salt and pepper, and melted butter. Butter a casserole dish. Pack fish mixture on bottom of dish. Pour vegetable mixture over fish. Sprinkle with paprika. Bake in moderate oven (350°) for about 40 minutes or until golden on top. This recipe works equally well with or without fish mixture.

CREAMED CORN AND CELERY

2 *cups fresh from the cob or canned and drained corn kernels*
1 *cup celery, diced*
½ *cup buttered bread crumbs*
2 *tbs. butter*
  Seasoned salt, pepper
1 *cup rich milk or half & half*
1 *red pepper or canned pimiento, diced*

Combine corn, celery, pimiento and seasonings. Blend in buttered crumbs. Grease a casserole with 1 tbs. butter. Pour in vegetable-crumb mixture. Pour over the rich milk. Dot with 1 tbs. butter and sprinkle with paprika. Bake in moderate oven (350°) for about 20 minutes or until casserole is browned on top.

✂ 7

Leftovers Redressed

It must be the fate of most newly married housewives to end the week with a refrigerator full of day-to-week-old leftovers. It was mine. I rued the moment when my husband, in all innocence, would open the refrigerator door in search of an odd-hour snack and find the remnants of the four-layer casserole we ate for dinner three days before. "Say, isn't that the eggplant and meat dish we had a few days ago??" he would inquire. "I could have that again anytime, don't let it go to waste," he would remark, meaning to flatter me, I'm sure. Everything in my gourmet novitiate soul rebelled against it. The thought of reheating not quite two portions of a formerly delectable creation now past its prime in flavor and freshness appalled me. Any way you re-sauced it, it would remain a faded memory of past glory. Despite my prideful rejection of leftovers, conscience would not allow me to toss out the remains of a meal. As a result, shelf upon shelf of well-wrapped cooked tidbits would accumulate in both my freezer and refrigerator until such time as lack of space forced me to do in one fell swoop what I could not do day by day.

In time, the absurdity and lack of thrift of this housekeeping method of mine became painfully clear to me. Like all young brides, I wanted my husband to feel that I was a wise budgeter and a thrift-minded shopper as well as a sensible and orderly homemaker. I wanted him to have the same confidence in my ability to do a job that I felt about his professional capabilities. The day he delicately suggested that I prepare smaller portions for our meals so we wouldn't have so many leftovers, I realized the jig was up.

Somehow, what I cooked was always too much for two. Particularly when I was improvising dishes, a small-intentioned recipe had a way of growing out of hand. The best I was able to manage was generous servings for three.

I inquired of friends noted for their budgeting wisdom how they managed the problem of leftovers. One young housewife whom I particularly admired for her cuisine and thriftiness replied, "why, I just add other things to them or dress them up a little and reserve them. I never waste anything." I was on the trail of an answer. "How do they taste when you reserve them?" I asked her. "Frankly," she told me, "I don't eat them but my husband cleans his plate." This comment and others elicited in my grass roots poll convinced me that the problem of leftovers was not uniquely mine as I had assumed but universal in scope.

As my research has convinced me, there are ways to redress leftovers that make them tasty, even delicious servings. Whether you are fixing re-prepared food (réchauffés, as the French put it) or newly made dishes, there is never an excuse for mealtime monotony. The following are a list of cooking methods you may use in recreating dishes. Basic recipes using previously cooked ingredients are included.

1. SAUCES. Cooked vegetables not previously sauced may be blended with a white sauce, cheese sauce, hollandaise sauce, etc., and served over buttered or curried rice or pasta, wild rice, buckwheat groats, cracked wheat (Burghul), toast points, or in pop-

overs, patty shells, pie pastry or on quick breads. (See Chapter 3 for sauce variety.)

2. OMELETS. Previously sauced and cooked vegetables can be used, sometimes, as original and unusual omelet fillings. Saucy vegetable combinations that are left over can be put at the bottom of individual casseroles and eggs can be poached on top in the oven.

3. GRILLED SANDWICHES. Some leftover foods can be spread over toast or muffins, and with the addition of sliced meats, tomato and/or cheese, grilled open-faced under the broiler.

4. PURÉES. Vegetables cooked with or without simple sauces can be puréed for cream soup bases. (See Chapter 5.)

5. OTHER FILLINGS. Small amounts of leftover foods can be used as filling in refrigerator dinner roll dough. The food to be used as filling is spooned into center of a dough triangle which is then wrapped securely around the filling and baked according to package directions. Allow slightly more time for baking rolls that are filled than for plain ones.

6. CASSEROLES. See Chapter 6 for recipes that call for cooked vegetable ingredients.

7. SOUFFLÉS. (See basic recipes at the end of this chapter.)

8. VEGETABLE LOAVES. (See recipes at end of chapter.)

9. VEGETABLE FRITTERS AND CROQUETTES. (See recipes at end of chapter.)

10. VEGETABLE PUDDINGS. (See recipes at end of chapter.)

11. VEGETABLE PATTIES. (See recipes at end of chapter.)

12. VEGETABLE PIES. (See recipes at end of chapter.)

BASIC VEGETABLE SOUFFLÉ RECIPE

1 *cup chopped, drained leftover vegetables*
½ *cup thick white sauce*
3 *eggs, separated*
  Salt and pepper to taste
  Your favorite herb, spice or seasoning for vegetable (see seasonings chapter).

Combine white sauce and well-beaten egg yolks. Fold in chopped vegetables and blend well. Season as desired. Beat egg whites till stiff and in peaks. Gently fold into vegetable mixture. Pour into greased casserole and set dish in pan of hot water in preheated oven. Bake at 325° for about 1 hour. Serves 4.

BASIC VEGETABLE LOAF RECIPE

2 *cups leftover vegetables, mashed, chopped or puréed*
2 *beaten eggs*
1 *cup fine white bread crumbs*
3 *tbs. cream or broth*
2 *tbs. melted butter*
  Salt and pepper
  Seasonings, such as: chopped onion or chives, Worcestershire sauce, lemon juice, herbs, spices or condiments as desired.

Mix all ingredients together. Blend well. Pour into well-greased loaf, ring or casserole type pan. Sprinkle top with buttered crumbs, paprika or grated cheese. Bake at 350° in preheated oven until set and lightly browned on top and around edges of pan. Serves 6–8.

BASIC VEGETABLE FRITTER RECIPE

2 *cups drained, chopped or mashed vegetables*
½ *cup milk or broth*
1 *egg*
1½ *cups flour*
2 *tsp. baking powder*
1½ *tbs. melted fat or oil*

Beat egg. Mix liquid and vegetables into it. Slowly incorporate flour, blending well. Add fat or oil and baking powder. (Blend minimally after addition of baking powder.) If batter is too thick to spoon onto skillet, add a small amount more of liquid. (If too loose, add additional flour.) Spoon into deep, hot fat in skillet. Fry till golden brown. Remove from oil, drain and serve. Serves 6–8.

BASIC VEGETABLE CUTLET RECIPE

1½ *cups cooked vegetables (one kind or combination), chopped (such as: peas, green beans, carrots, cauliflower, potatoes, cabbage, etc.)*
½ *cup mushrooms (fresh or canned) or raw onions, chopped*
3 *tbs. butter or oil*
3 *slices stale white bread soaked in milk and squeezed out*
3 *eggs*
Salt and pepper
2 *tbs. chopped parsley*
⅓ *cup flour*
⅓ *cup fried bread crumbs*

Fry mushrooms, onions or combination of two in butter or oil until golden brown. Add to pan seasonings, parsley and squeezed out bread along with other vegetables. Mash together in skillet and cook, stirring constantly, over medium heat until mixture darkens somewhat. Remove from heat and cool. Beat 2 eggs. Add cooled vegetable mixture to them. With your hands, form into small cutlet patties. Dip cutlets first in flour, then into a beaten egg and last, into fried bread crumbs. (Pat cutlets to make crumbs stick.) Fry in deep, hot fat until brown. Serves 6–8.

BASIC VEGETABLE PUDDING

2 *cups leftover vegetables, puréed*
3 *well-beaten eggs*
2 *cups milk or milk plus Sherry or other flavoring liquids to equal 2 cups (example: 1¾ cups milk and ¼ cup Sherry, fruit or vegetable juice)*
2 *tbs. melted fat or oil*
Salt and pepper
Other seasonings, if desired

Blend purée into beaten eggs. Add milk, other liquid and seasoning. Mix in fat or oil. Beat together until smooth and frothy. Pour into well greased casserole. Place in pan of hot water in preheated oven. Bake at 350° for about 1 hour or until set. (Test center for degree of doneness.)

BASIC VEGETABLE PATTIES

1½ *cups cooked vegetables, chopped and well drained*
2 *eggs, separated*
1 *heaping tbs. sour cream*
1 *tsp. melted fat or oil*
1 *tbs. flour*
  Salt, pepper, additional seasonings, if desired

Combine vegetables, beaten egg yolks, cream, fat, flour and seasonings. Mix well. Beat egg whites until stiff and standing in peaks. Carefully fold into vegetable mixture. Drop spoonfuls of mixture onto a greased, heated griddle. Brown on both sides. Serve hot or cold.

BASIC VEGETABLE PIE #1

6 *slices stale white bread, crusts removed*
3 *eggs, beaten*
¼ *cup milk*
2 *cups leftover chopped vegetables*
  Salt, pepper, seasonings

Beat eggs and milk together and season. Soak white bread in egg mixture until soft. Fit bread snugly into bottom of greased pie plate. Pour vegetables over bread and spread evenly. Cover vegetables with egg-soaked bread and pour any remaining egg mixture over top. Dot with butter or top with grated cheese. Bake in 350° oven for about ½ hour or until top is evenly browned. Serve hot or cold.

VEGETABLE PIE #2

1 *baked pie shell, cooled*
2 *cups cooked vegetables, puréed*
1 *cup medium white sauce*
2 *egg yolks, well beaten*
  Salt, pepper, seasoning (refer to chart, pages 36–42)

Blend white sauce, egg yolks and purée together. Season to taste. Pour into pie shell. Top may be decorated with rosettes of whipped potatoes forced through a pastry decorator and brushed with egg yolk or with a meringue or sprinkled paprika. Bake in 325° oven until set, about 45 minutes.

8

The Vegetable Lover's Diet

The questions that might occur to any thoughtful reader noting the title of this chapter should be: doesn't the public have enough "gimmicky" diets in its domain already, and, don't most diet regimens prescribe vegetables? The answer to both queries is affirmative. However, nutritionists tell me that overweight is the single most serious nutritional problem in our country. The glut of diet fads paraded before an eager, willing public in the United States has had little effect not because they are inefficient methods of losing weight as much as because the public has not "bought" them. It is my belief that a prime reason for the lack of diet adherents is that these suggested weight-losing programs are so far removed from a normal eating plan habitually followed through most of life that dieters lose interest after a short period of time and revert to old habits.

A normal diet, for most of us, is comprised of protein foods, fatty foods and carbohydrates. Proteins, the so-called body-building foods, are the first to be turned into energy by the body. There is some indication that fats aid in the breakdown and transformation of these energy-giving foods. Carbohydrates are more complicated in chemical structure and slower to be used by our systems. For this reason, most diet plans are strict in curtailing the consumption of foods high in carbohydrates.

Most vegetables, those low and high calorically, contain a preponderance of carbohydrate calories. The usual diet list cuts down the vegetable allowance dramatically, limiting the choice to leafy greens, raw salad ingredients and carefully counted measures of some cooked vegetables permitted on occasion if served plain.

A normal dinner in this country comprises a first course of fruit, hot appetizer or soup. A salad, dressed in tangy fashion may precede or more usually accompany a main course of meat, fish, poultry, eggs and/or cheese, a starch such as potatoes or noodles or rice, a cooked vegetable such as carrots, peas, green beans, etc., followed by a dessert of fruit, pudding, pastry or ice cream. Let us investigate what happens to this dinner pattern under ordinary weight-control programs.

Fruits, high in sugary carbohydrates, are generally restricted to desserts, once or twice daily. Combination dishes and the sauces or gravies they usually require cannot be allowed. I have seen very few diets that encourage the consumption of soup. Diet dinners commonly begin with salad (unoiled), go on to main course meat, fish or other protein and end with a diet-right (low calorie) beverage. A snack of crackers or fruit may be tolerated during long, hungry evenings.

It is my contention that breakfasts and lunches, usually consumed on the run between busy daily activities, are not a barrier to diet hopefuls. It is at dinner when you are relaxing tired limbs and mind after the strenuous efforts of work, in the leisurely confines of home, that a meager dinner seems poor reward for the day's accomplishments. A diet dinner such as I outline above can be served and eaten in little more than ten minutes. The small amount of time given to the activity alone can make a dieter feel hungry; that he has not eaten enough. The ideal solution is a full 4-course meal that is bountiful, various and dietetic. It can't be done, I'm sure you're thinking. I disagree.

Vegetables, in their abundant varieties and unlimited recipe possibilities, are my solution. There are enough low or moderate caloric vegetables to allow a diet-conscious cook to prepare three a day and not repeat the recipes or combinations in a year or more. With the aid of such vegetables you can enjoy multi-coursed meals, feel sated, your palate and appetite appeased, and lose weight too. For skeptics, I include here my own personal testimonial of how I lost weight on the vegetable lover's diet. Rules to guide your weight loss plan and recipes follow at the end of this chapter.

Three months after I began work on this book, my husband and I decided to lose weight. Our clothes no longer fit. We felt flabby and unattractive. At the end of each working day we found ourselves exhausted, too tired considering our labors. We faced the fact that overweight was affecting our health and well-being.

Dieting was not new to us. Through most of our adult lives, my husband and I have been on and off diets. From time to time, we achieved moderate weight losses with great effort. When we stopped counting calories, the pounds returned. One or the other of us tried out each new reducing regimen as it hit the market. On one of these diet programs, my husband actually ended up gaining nine pounds the first week. He was tempted to believe, after this discouraging result, that it was his body chemistry never to be thin.

Our greatest problem in the past was our attitudes. We didn't enjoy suffering to be slender. Every prohibition our diets imposed on us was a cause for depression. The foods we were allowed were so far removed from the ones we enjoyed that each dieting moment was a torment. A dieter is like a child. If you keep saying no to him, the forbidden things become irresistible.

This time, we vowed to find a way to slim down and stay that way. We knew that the years were kinder to thin people than to heavy ones. We had a child to consider. Aware that most overweight parents have overweight children, and having experienced the unhappy fates of fat children ourselves, we resolved never to let it happen to our own.

I was the homemaker. It was up to me (and my kitchen) to make it work. I knew that success would hinge on three conditions: good nutrition, high spirits, and a continuous feeling of satiety. It was no easy task at the time we had chosen. I had just started work on a cookbook. The prospect of hundreds of recipes to create and test lay before me. We were engaged in a great deal of entertaining. I couldn't expect my dinner guests to eat diet fare. Our six-month-old daughter kept me close to home; temptation had to be met and vanquished daily. Of course, no time is the right time for starting a diet. I had given my husband my word that I would devise a program that was interesting and varied enough to make us stick it through. I intended to keep it.

I studied the problem. Books on nutrition began to fill our home. Weight-reducing plans were read and compared, fad diets as well as standard medically approved ones. I poured over calorie charts and carbohydrate lists. I pondered material on vitamin and mineral dietary requirements. I sought the advice of friends who had dieted successfully and interviewed physicians of our acquaintance on the subject. One medical advisor bluntly proclaimed that I was fooling myself. He couldn't see how I could hope to write a book on food and lose weight at the same time. Besides, he offered good-humoredly, he'd never known a good cook who was slender.

Nine months after the start of our diet we achieved our weight reduction goals. My husband reduced a total of forty-eight pounds, I lost forty. We have maintained our new figures and intend to continue to do so. Our friends and family are amazed. They say we look years younger. We certainly feel years younger from the point of view of energy. Our eating habits have changed forever. We are incapable of eating the high carbohydrate foods we used to love. Now, they actually, physically, sicken us. Our work habits are better. We accomplish more in our waking hours and we enjoy our new, glamorous appearance immensely. After a recent physical check-up, our family physician announced that our health is optimum.

Through all the months of losing weight, never once did either of us feel deprived, dismayed, depressed, weak-kneed, or unsatisfied, food-wise. The general run-down feeling that dogs most dieters, making them susceptible to every contagion in the air, never affected us. We became neither tense, overtired, nervous, edgy nor humorless. Our states of mind were generally pleasant and we never felt we were missing out on others' fun. That haggard, gaunt look that marks a dieter and sets him apart from the rest of humanity didn't afflict us. People who meet us now are amazed to learn of our great weight loss. Invariably, they comment, "I can't believe you ever looked any different from now."

To what do I attribute our success? I believe it is the product of the foods we ate plus our attitudes. The diversity and balance of our foods provided the fuel to keep us going. The regimen we followed is here for you to try. It worked for us. That it will work for you I cannot promise. Each metabolic system is individual, requiring different qualities and quantities of raw material to function at peak. However, if the diet program appeals to you there is a good chance of your success on it. Unfortunately, it is not as easy to dictate attitudes as it is dietetic recipes. That is entirely up to you. I can only advise you to forget the negative aspects of dieting, that is, all the foods prohibited to you. Keep in mind the positive factors, the range of foods that are allowed you and the many ways you can enjoy them.

At first, you'll probably feel what seems like hunger pangs between and/or after meals. Hold fast. These feelings will disappear by the end of the first week. It's not really hunger but overgrown appetite. The appetite of an overweight person is like a pent-up jungle beast. It constantly rattles the bars seeking to break loose in order to forage (for food) to its heart's content. If you keep the beast penned for even a few days he calms down and grows tame. You have to work at it. There's no other way. Remember, you have the advantage over this inner beast. You're stronger, more determined and more intelligent than he is.

On the eve of our diet, my husband and I conferred across the kitchen table. On the paper before me I had drawn a three column heading: FOODS BEST LIKED, FOODS MODERATELY ENJOYED, FOODS NOT TO BE GIVEN UP. Together, we filled in the columns. The first two headings are self-explanatory. The third refers to foods we didn't wish to give up under any dieting circumstances. Here are our lists. Yours will be different. If ice cream (or some other high carbohydrate food) is on your NOT TO BE GIVEN UP list, that doesn't mean you are free to indulge in unlimited quantities of it daily. A spoonful or two won't hurt twice a week, or a half a scoop on a special occasion. Moderation and sanity should be your guide.

FOODS BEST LIKED

Sweet carbonated drinks
Tea
Coffee with whole milk
Wine (dry)
Pasta dishes
Chinese food
Batter and deep fried foods
Well-seasoned foods
Butter and bread
Cheese of all kinds
Ice cream
Desserts (not too gooey
  or sweet)

Some cakes
Nuts and nut products
Eggs, any way
Salads
Home-made salad dressings
Meats
Fruits (fresh)
Vegetable dishes
Soups
Dried fruits
Dairy sour cream
Yoghurt

FOODS MODERATELY ENJOYED

Milk
Cold cereals
Some cooked cereals
Rolls, crackers, pancakes
Rice and wheat casseroles
Cookies
Chocolate products
Pies

Gelatine desserts
Sherbets and Ices
Sandwiches
Mayonnaise and commercial
  dressing
Fish and poultry
Saucy foods
Some candy
Some preserves

FOODS NOT TO BE GIVEN UP

Coffee with whole milk
Tea
Occasional glass of wine
Occasional slice of bread
Cheeses
Egg dishes
Salads and salad dressing
Vegetable dishes

Fresh fruits
Some nuts
Occasional soup
Occasional fried food
Spicy foods
Chinese food
Meat, fish, and poultry
Some kind of dessert

Are you surprised, looking at your list, as we were scanning ours? The foods we found easiest to omit were the sweets and rich dishes. Our NOT TO BE GIVEN UP list was comprised of wholesome, body-building foods. These were to be the basic elements of our diet with a few additions from columns one and two. The more varied and complete your selection of diet foods, the less you will be reminded of what you're missing.

Most foods can be adapted to weight reduction programs. Obvious starches, such as potatoes, noodles, rice, and breads, have to be severely limited. Richly creamed or fatty foods have to be cut down. Sugary foods, sweets, jams and jellies, many desserts, must be curtailed. As for the rest, you're allowed quality but not quantity. When a diet indicates "a portion" of meat, fish or poultry, three to six ounces are intended (depending on how severe you intend to be). You can eat more chicken and lean fish than you can most meats because their calorie counts are lower. (Check a popular calorie counter.) Many vegetables are low enough in calories to allow you to eat your fill of them at meals. A salad is a good beginning to any diet dinner. You can eat as much as you like and feel full, despite the smaller portions of other foods. (The dressing is the thing to watch. It is loaded with calories. Instead of drowning your salad with sauce, coat it lightly. It'll taste just as good.)

I suggest constructing a diet meal like any other. At breakfast, start with fruit. A list will follow of kinds and portion sizes of fruits you can safely allow yourself. Next, protein is in order. An egg, poached, coddled or boiled is suggested, or $\frac{1}{3}$ cup of cottage cheese or a one inch square of yellow cheese. If you enjoy meat at breakfast, three ounces of your favorite lean meat will fill the bill. If, after the first few dieting days, this regimen leaves you unsatisfied, instead of adding bread-stuffs to your morning meal, increase your portion of protein. Coffee or tea can conclude your meal.

Lunch is usually eaten on the run in this country. Therefore, it makes sense to keep it simple. If a sandwich is what you insist on, eat only one slice of the bread (preferably rye or wheat for good nutrition's sake), and go easy on the mayonnaise. One spoonful of dressing will make you feel satisfied. Remove the surplus. Avoid creamy restaurant fish, meat or egg salad concoctions. They're usually full of high caloric stuff. Order sandwich fillings that are plain, baked, boiled or broiled. Ask for lettuce and tomato on it, if you like. Restaurant cole slaw is relatively low in calories and filling. Salad tossed with protein food is a good lunch for dieters in a hurry. If you find yourself unsatisfied, order a side dish of cooked vegetables in addition. A sugar-free beverage and a fresh fruit dessert will complete your lunch. If you are eating lunch in your home, your choice is less limited. A portion of a protein food, greens or cooked vegetables, beverage and fruit or diet gelatine dessert is the basis. Keep starches low. Eat moderate portions. If you've just fed the children and they've left over part of their meal, if you can't save it, toss it out. It's better in the garbage pail than in your stomach.

Between meal snacks are a dieter's nemesis. When you feel like nibbling, try an artificially sweetened carbonated beverage. Sometimes the sweetness will satisfy your craving. Diet jello is a good between meal filler. Of course, you can nibble on raw vegetables such as celery, cucumbers, lettuce, green peppers, radishes and scallions (if you dare) to the limit.

At dinner, the accent is on the gala. Start with an appetizer. Raw or cooked vegetable salads, cooked vegetables prepared in an unusual manner, thin soups, vegetable juices and calorie-reduced stuffed vegetable canapes are good ideas. (Recipes follow.) With your main course protein food (fish, meat, poultry, cheese or egg dishes), serve two vegetable side dishes. These may be hot or cold, marinated, dressed or sauced in a dietetic fashion. (See recipes at the end of this chapter.) If you and your family are in the habit of eating a dinner-time starch such as: potatoes, rice, noodles, corn or beans, try these substitutions: whipped turnips or mashed kohlrabi, Hungarian squash, sautéed mushrooms, sweet and sour celery, eggplant scallop, lemony carrots, creamed green beans (with yoghurt and dill). The calorie count will be substantially reduced and the appetite sated. Fruit, cheese or dietetic puddings and gelatine molds will finish your meal. Chances are, you won't feel the need for bread in such a meal. Don't eat it if you don't really want it. With starches cut back and sweets eliminated except for artificially sweetened dishes and beverages, you will lose weight.

A FEW IMPORTANT GUIDES

1. Limit your liquid intake during meals to one glass. Up to one hour before or one hour after you may drink as much as you desire of low calorie beverages.

2. Cut down on salt. It makes your body retain fluids. If you like well-seasoned foods, rely on herbs and spices to satisfy your taste buds.

3. Keep bread down to 1 or less slices per day. If you eat any (not much, I hope) rice, beans, potatoes, corn or noodles, omit that day's bread.

4. If you feel you just have to consume a forbidden food, try 1 or 2 spoonfuls and see if it doesn't stanch the desire for more. It's better to taste and savor than never to have tasted at all.

5. If you are caught in a situation where you are served rich, creamy or gravy-laden foods and it is beyond your control to change them for diet fare, brush aside the rich sauces as best you can and eat moderately. Leave over what is obviously fattening. Eat for quality not quantity.

6. When you feel unsatisfied, instead of gobbling down high carbohydrate fruit, cakes or rich dishes, if raw vegetables leave you cold, try a few spoons of cheese or a small slice of meat or poultry.

7. Weigh yourself as often as you like but don't expect to show a real weight loss except once or twice a week. Weigh in at the same time of day. Your weight shifts upward and down in the course of a day as a result of the liquids and solids you consume.

8. Impress this maxim on your mind: I must eat to be sated not to be bloated.

9. Try to discipline yourself to go without between meal snacks.

10. Treat yourself to one slightly more elaborate meal each

week. This is for morale purposes. It will assuage your deprived feeling. The meal may be in a restaurant or at home. I don't suggest that you revert back to eating high-carbohydrate foods. Simply, allow yourself to taste foods ordinarily not allowed you. On these occasions, skip dessert, breads and obvious calorie-loaded sauces.

11. Pay attention to every morsel you put into your mouth. Pounds are gained because we eat absent-mindedly, unaware of the amounts and kinds of food we are consuming.

12. You owe it to yourself (and to whomever is dieting with you) not to serve any dish in the same form twice in a dieting week. If you are bored with your diet, chances are you will not stick to it.

13. On diet day number one, set a weight goal for yourself. Allowing for minor deviations, keep to your diet until your goal is reached.

14. At the start of your diet, get a check up from your family physician. This is to insure that your health is up to restricted food intake and to convince yourself that there is no organic reason why you cannot lose weight. Discuss your diet with your physician. Let him advise you. Ask your doctor for vitamin and iron supplements to take while dieting. Restricting your calories may be cutting down your body's needed vitamin and mineral requirements.

15. Think positively. Tell yourself you can and will lose weight and you will succeed. If you don't think you can do it, there's a good chance you won't.

16. Make it a rule to keep obvious fattening foods out of the house while dieting. If the children insist on their cookies, candy and ice cream snacks, keep these in a place you are not likely to see and be tempted by them during the better part of the day. Ice cream can hide in a portion of the freezer out of eye range. Cookies and candy can sit unnoticed in a cabinet you don't often get into. If your husband is not dieting with you, ask for his cooperation. He'll probably jump at the chance to help as it's in his interest that his wife be svelte. It'll be much easier for you if he consumes his favorite pie, cake, or other rich goody out of your sight.

Raw Fruits You Can Eat on Your Diet

TYPE	QUANTITY PER PORTION	TYPE	QUANTITY PER PORTION
Apple	$\frac{1}{2}$ medium	Olives	5 or 6
Apricots	1 or 2 small	Orange	$\frac{1}{2}$ medium
Blackberries	$\frac{1}{2}$ cup	Peach	$\frac{1}{2}$ large
Blueberries	$\frac{1}{4}$ cup	Pear	$\frac{1}{2}$ large
Cantalope or muskmelon	$\frac{1}{2}$ small	Pineapple	1 thin slice
		Plum	1 medium
Cherries	10 to 12 medium	Dried raisins	1 tbs.
		Cooked rhubarb	1 cup (no sugar)
Grapefruit	$\frac{1}{2}$ small		
Green seedless grapes	20 to 30 medium	Strawberries	10 large
		Tangerine	1 medium
Honeydew	$\frac{1}{4}$ of a small	Watermelon	$\frac{1}{2}$ cup cubes or balls
Mango	$\frac{1}{4}$ of a small		
Nectarine	1 medium		

Vegetables You Can Eat on Your Diet

VEGETABLES LIMITED TO 1 CUP

Asparagus
Bean sprouts
Cabbage
Cauliflower
Celery
Chicory, endive
Water cress
Cucumber

Cucumber (any kind) pickles
Escarole
All other greens
All lettuces
Parsley
Green or red peppers

Radishes
Sauerkraut
Soybean cake (Chinese style)
Spinach
Summer squash or zucchini

VEGETABLES LIMITED TO ½ CUP

Artichokes
Bamboo shoots
Snap beans
Broccoli
Brussels sprouts
Swiss chard
Eggplant

Kohlrabi
Leeks
Mushrooms
Okra
Onions
Canned pimiento

Rutabagas
Tomatoes
Tomato juice
Turnips
Vegetable juice (V-8)
Water chestnuts

Vegetables You Can Eat on Your Diet (Continued)

VEGETABLES LIMITED TO ¼ CUP

Beets	Green peas
Carrots	Pumpkin
Parsnips	Winter squash

🍃 VEGETABLE RECIPES FOR DIETERS

CUCUMBER-CHEESE BALLS

8 ozs. low calorie commercial cheese spread
¼ cup grated cucumber, seeds removed, skin unpeeled
2 tbs. grated onion
  Dash Worcestershire sauce
  Salt and pepper to taste
  Dash Tabasco

Put ingredients into mixing bowl. Blend well with wooden spoon. If necessary to thin mixture, add 1 or 2 tbs. of milk. Form into balls and sprinkle with parsley. Chill a few hours before serving. This mixture can be used to stuff celery or lettuce leaves. Trim with dice of green pepper and canned pimiento. Serves 4.

CAULIFLOWER À LA GRECQUE

1 raw cauliflower
  Boiling water to cover

MARINADE:

2 cups water
1 cup dry white wine
  Juice of 2 lemons
2 tbs. plain white vinegar
1 bay leaf
3 peppercorns
⅛ tsp. thyme (opt.)
1 heaping tsp. fennel seed

Separate cauliflower into flowerettes. Trim off leaves and tough stalk material. Wash thoroughly. Place in casserole dish, pour in enough boiling water to cover vegetable and cover casserole dish. Allow cauliflower to steep in hot water for five minutes. In a saucepan, heat marinade ingredients and bring to a slow boil. Allow to simmer for a few moments. Drain cauliflowerettes and add to simmering mixture. Simmer over low heat until cauliflower is tender but still crisp. Remove from heat and cool in marinade. Drain, discard marinade. Refrigerate until needed. This recipe is excellent with broccoli, snap beans, celery, Brussels sprouts, mushrooms, squash and carrots. It can be used as an appetizer, salad or main course side dish.

TOMATO ASPIC

1 envelope unflavored gelatin	$\frac{1}{2}$ tsp. Worcestershire sauce Dash Tabasco
1$\frac{1}{2}$ cups tomato juice Salt to taste	2 tbs. lemon juice
$\frac{1}{2}$ tsp. sugar substitute (equivalent to $\frac{1}{2}$ tsp. sugar)	$\frac{1}{4}$ cup chopped stuffed olives $\frac{1}{4}$ cup chopped celery

Sprinkle gelatin on $\frac{1}{2}$ cup of tomato juice to soften. Allow to set five minutes. Fold into saucepan, add remainder of tomato juice and lemon juice. Heat on low heat until gelatin dissolves, stirring constantly. Add remainder of ingredients. Blend together. Pour into individual greased molds. Chill until firm. Serves 4–5.

DIET COCKTAIL

1 qt. V-8 or tomato juice	1 lemon, sliced very thin
2 tbs. onion juice	Salt to taste
1 bay leaf	1 sprig fresh parsley
$\frac{1}{2}$ tsp. chili powder	

Heat all ingredients together in a pot. Bring to a slow boil and simmer for approximately three minutes. Strain, cool and re-season to taste. Refrigerate until used. Serves 6–8.

EGGPLANT APPETIZER SALAD

1 *medium eggplant*
2 *green peppers*
2 *onions*
Juice of 1 lemon
1 *tbs. wine vinegar*

Salt and pepper to taste
¼ *tsp. prepared light mustard*
2 *generous tbs. plain yoghurt*
Dash cayenne (opt.)

Bake eggplant, green peppers and onions in skins for 1 hour in 375° oven. Remove and cool slightly. Peel vegetables and chop together. Add other ingredients. Mix well. Chill before serving. Can be used for a dip or as a salad.

BEET SALAD MOLD

1 *envelope diet raspberry gelatin (to serve four)*
1 *cup boiling water*
½ *cup cooked beets, grated*
½ *cup coarse chopped nuts*
1 *tbs. wine vinegar*
½ *tsp. salt*

Dissolve gelatin in boiling water. Chill until mixture starts to thicken. Remove from refrigerator, mix in other ingredients. Pour into greased molds.

MARINATED CUCUMBER SALAD

2 *cucumbers, sliced very thin, unpeeled*
1 *sweet onion, sliced thin*
Salt and pepper
Equivalent substitute for 1 tsp. sugar
⅓ *cup white vinegar*
1 *tsp. chopped dill (fresh, if possible)*

Sprinkle cucumbers lightly with salt. Drain in strainer or colander for ½ hour. Press out liquid and blot on absorbent paper. Add onions and seasoning. Chill for a few hours in marinade.

VEGETABLE CHEESE SALAD

1 *lb. pot cheese*
¼ *cup radishes, diced*
1 *cucumber, diced unpeeled*

¼ *cup scallions, chopped*
½ *cup plain yoghurt*
Salt and pepper

Thin pot cheese with yoghurt. Mix in vegetables and seasoning. Serve on lettuce beds or stuffed in hollowed tomatoes or celery branches. Serve chilled. Serves 6–8.

PARTY SALAD MOLD

1 *envelope diet orange*
gelatin (to serve four)
1 *cup diet ginger ale*
1 *cucumber, peeled, seeded*
and grated
1 *carrot, pared and grated*
½ *green pepper, grated*

1 *tsp. onion juice*
¼ *tsp. salt*
½ *tsp. prepared light mustard*
3 *tbs. plain yoghurt*
Red and yellow food coloring to give orange color

Heat ginger ale to just below boiling point. Pour over gelatin and stir until dissolved. Mix in all other ingredients. Stir well. Pour into greased party mold. Chill until firm. Turn out on platter of mixed greens.

DRESSING FOR MOLD:
¼ *cup lemon juice*
¼ *cup dry Sherry*
Sugar substitute to sweeten to taste
¼ *tsp. celery seed*

SPINACH SALAD DRESSING

¼ *cup lemon juice*
1 *tbs. sesame seeds, toasted*
Salt and pepper
⅛ *tsp. dry mustard (opt.)*

Place sesame seeds in skillet over medium heat. No oil is required, they contain their own. In a few moments, they will start to brown and pop. Shake pan so they brown evenly. Pour them while hot into lemon juice mixture. Mix well. Pour over spinach or other greens.

CHUTNEY DRESSING FOR FRUIT SALADS

1 *cup plain yoghurt*
½ *tsp. prepared light mustard*
  Salt to taste
  Grated rind of 1 lemon

1 *tbs. orange juice*
  A few drops sugar
  substitute (½ tsp. sugar)
2 *tbs. mango chutney*

DIET SALAD DRESSING, FRENCH STYLE

⅓ *cup wine vinegar*
2 *tbs. water*
2 *tbs. salad oil (opt.)*
1 *tbs. sweet pickle or India relish*

1 *tbs. grated onion*
⅛ *tsp. mustard powder*
  Salt, pepper and paprika

Shake well together. Pour over salad (greens and raw vegetables) at table.

COLD YOGHURT SAUCE FOR HOT VEGETABLES

1 *cup plain yoghurt*
  Dash Tabasco
1 *garlic clove, crushed*
2 *tbs. salad oil*

2 *tbs. dry red wine*
  Pinch crushed tarragon
  leaves
  Salt and pepper, paprika

ANOTHER YOGHURT DRESSING

1 *cup yoghurt*
¼ *cup pimiento, diced*
½ *green pepper, chopped*
1 *small onion, grated*

2 *tbs. chili sauce*
¼ *tsp. prepared light mustard*
  Juice of ½ lemon
  Salt and pepper

Mix well. Serve on hot or cold vegetables. Or use this dressing as a marinade for part-cooked vegetables.

LOW CALORIE CHEESE SAUCE

½ *cup buttermilk*
½ *cup part-skim milk cheese,*
*grated**

Dash paprika
⅛ *tsp. mustard powder*
Salt and pepper

Heat buttermilk in top of double boiler. Add cheese and stir until melted. Stir in seasonings. Pour hot over your favorite vegetable.

SOYA SAUCE DRESSING

¼ *cup soya sauce*
Juice of ½ lemon
1 *tsp. sugar or equivalent*

1 *clove garlic, crushed*
¼ *tsp. powdered ginger*
1 *tbs. dry Sherry*

Heat ingredients together over moderate flame. When just beginning to boil, reduce heat and simmer for a few minutes. Pour hot over vegetables and bring to the table or marinate in the refrigerator for a few hours.

BAKED TOMATOES WITH CHEESE

4 *tomatoes, stem top removed*
1 *cup mozzarella cheese, cubed*
1 *tbs. salad oil*
½ *tsp. sweet basil*
Seasoned salt, paprika, pepper

Scoop out pulp of tomatoes. Mash with salad oil, basil, and seasonings to taste. Mix well with cubes of cheese. Refill tomato shells with mixture. Sprinkle with paprika. Stand upright in lightly greased baking pan and bake at 350° for 20–25 minutes. Brown 1 or 2 minutes under broiler before serving. Serves 4.

---

* Part-skim milk cheeses are available at cheese specialty stores. They include: Baronet, French Swiss, Danish Muenster, certain Cheddar cheese spreads and many more.

STUFFED ZUCCHINI

6 *young, evenly shaped zucchini*
2 *hard-boiled eggs, chopped or grated*
2 *tbs. onion, minced*
1 *tbs. oil or fat*
1 *tbs. chopped parsley*
  Cracker crumbs
  Salt and pepper, paprika

Clean zucchini and slice off stem end. Blanch in boiling water
and allow to cool in water. Remove from water, drain. Reserve
blanching liquid. Split zucchini down the middle, lengthwise.
Scoop out center portion. Chop centers and fry with onion in oil
or fat. When brown, remove from fire and mix with chopped
eggs. Add parsley and seasoning and stuff mixture into zucchini
shells. Sprinkle tops with cracker crumbs and paprika. Moisten
each zucchini half with 1 tsp. blanching water. Bake at 350° for
approximately ½ hour. Serves 6.

CURRIED STEWED CELERY

½ *bunch of celery, trimmed and cut into serving pieces*
1 *onion, sliced*
  Salt
1–2 *tbs. oil or fat*
¼ *tsp. curry powder*
1 *tomato, diced*
1 *tbs. blanched slivered almonds (opt.)*
1 *tbs. sultana raisins (opt.)*

Place celery in pan with enough boiling water to cover. Bring to
boil once more and cook rapidly for 10 minutes. Drain, rinse
celery, drain again. Sauté onion in fat or oil until transparent.
Add tomato, curry powder, celery, salt to taste. If desired, you
may add raisins or almonds. Cover and simmer for 15 minutes.
Serves 6–8.

BAKED MUSHROOMS

1 *lb. fresh mushrooms*
½ *cup vegetable or chicken*
  stock
1 *tbs. chopped parsley*
½ *tsp. marjoram*

1 *garlic clove, crushed*
2 *tbs. minced onion*
1 *tbs. Italian grated cheese*
2 *tbs. dry Sherry*
  Salt and pepper

Clean and slice mushrooms. Place in lightly oiled casserole. Pour over them stock plus seasonings except for cheese. Toss gently until mushrooms are evenly moistened. Sprinkle with grated cheese. Cover tightly. Bake at 350° for 25–30 minutes.

FRENCH FRIED CUCUMBERS

4 *young cucumbers*
1 *egg, well beaten*
½ *cup cracker crumbs*

Salt and pepper
Deep fat for frying

Pare cucumbers. Quarter them, remove seeds and cut shells into 2–3 inch sticks. Sprinkle with salt and pepper and allow to drain for 10 minutes. Dip sticks in beaten egg and roll in cracker crumbs. Immerse in very hot fat and cook until crust is golden. Remove from oil and drain well on absorbent paper.

GREENS IN CURRY CREAM

1 *lb. mustard greens*
1 *tbs. oil*
½ *cup buttermilk*
2 *egg yolks*

1 *tbs. parsley*
½ *tsp. curry powder*
  Salt to taste

Trim and wash greens. Cut into convenient lengths. Oil the bottom of a heavy-duty skillet and place undrained greens in it. (There should be beads of moisture on the leaves to insure against scorching.) Steam over moderate heat, covered. Be sure to toss leaves occasionally so they cook evenly. Cook until tender, about fifteen minutes. In the top of a double boiler, heat buttermilk, egg yolks, parsley, curry powder and salt. Stir continuously until sauce thickens. Pour over cooked greens and serve.

SWEET AND SOUR CELERY

2 *cups celery, diced*
⅓ *cup plain or white wine vinegar*
   Sucaryl equivalent to ¼ cup sugar
   Salt and pepper
½ *tsp. allspice*
½ *cup yoghurt*
1 *egg*

Cook celery in boiling salted water, covered, until tender. Drain. Heat together in skillet the vinegar, sugar substitute and salt and pepper. When liquid begins to boil, add celery and reduce heat. Pour yoghurt mixture into skillet, stirring constantly. Heat until pan liquids bubble for a few moments. Serve. Substitute carrots, onions or turnips for celery, if desired.

STEWED MUSHROOMS

1 *lb. mushrooms, whole or*
   sliced
1 *tbs. butter or oil*
1 *onion, chopped*

1 *tbs. Sherry (opt.)*
¼ *cup bouillon (chicken or*
   vegetable)
   Salt and pepper

Heat oil in a skillet. Sauté onion until transparent. Add mushrooms and toss over heat in pan for a few minutes. Add wine, bouillon and seasonings. Cover and simmer for about ten minutes or until tender. Serve.

HUNGARIAN SQUASH

4 *thin yellow squash*
1 *medium onion, sliced thin*
1 *tbs. oil*
1 *tbs. paprika*
2 *tbs. tomato paste*

1 *cup plain yoghurt*
1 *tsp. dill weed, chopped*
½ *tsp. salt*
   Sucaryl equivalent to 1 tsp.
   sugar

Peel, halve and remove seeds from squash. Grate coarsely. Sauté onion in oil until transparent. Add squash, tomato paste and just enough hot water to keep mixture from scorching. Simmer, covered, for about 10 minutes. Add sugar substitute, dill, salt, paprika and yoghurt. Reheat to just below boiling. Serve.

MASHED KOHLRABI

4 or 5 *kohlrabi, peeled and quartered*
 Salt and pepper
 Dash nutmeg
½ *cup dietetic cheese sauce (see recipe, page 134)*

Boil kohlrabi in salted water until tender, about ½ hour. Drain. Remove to mixing bowl and mash with seasonings. Add hot cheese sauce, mix well and serve. Serves 6–8.

WHIPPED TURNIPS

6 *medium white turnips, pared and quartered*
½ *tsp. salt, pepper to taste*
½ *cup skim milk and 1 tbs. powdered skim milk, hot*
1 *tbs. parsley, chopped*
 Sprinkling of cinnamon

Cook turnips in boiling salted water, covered, for 20 to 30 minutes, until tender. Drain. Remove to mixing bowl and mash. Gradually add hot milk and beat in vigorously. Season. Serve topped with cinnamon. Serves 6–8.

TOMATO-EGGPLANT SCALLOP

1 *small to medium eggplant*	1 *small onion, grated*
1 *lb. can tomatoes*	1 *tbs. parsley, chopped*
Salt and pepper	4 *white crackers, crushed*
Sucaryl equivalent to 1 tsp.	1 *tbs. grated cheese*
sugar	

Peel and cube eggplant. Add tomatoes which have been diced. Add onion, seasonings and cracker crumbs. Pour into lightly greased baking dish. Sprinkle with grated cheese. Bake in 375° oven until brown on top and bubbly. (1 hour.) Serves 8–10.

LEMONY CARROTS

1 tbs. oil or butter
6 young carrots
Juice of 1 lemon
Grated rind of 1 lemon
½ tsp. salt

1 wineglass Sherry or orange juice
Sucaryl equivalent to ½ cup sugar

Peel or scrape carrots. Slice fairly thick. Place in skillet with just enough cold water to cover. Bring to a boil, reduce heat, cover and simmer until not quite done. Add oil, salt, lemon juice, rind, wine or orange juice and simmer for 15–20 minutes more. Add sugar substitute and serve. Serves 6–8.

CREAMED GREEN BEANS, DILL STYLE

1 lb. green beans
1 onion, chopped
1 egg yolk
½ cup yoghurt

Pepper and salt
½ tsp. dillweed, chopped
½ tsp. celery seed

Cook the beans, onion and celery seed in a small amount of water, covered, until firm but done. Beat egg yolk into yoghurt and mix in salt and pepper and dillweed. Slowly pour yoghurt mixture over green beans, stirring constantly. Heat on very low fire until just before boiling. Serve.

BAKED STUFFED CUCUMBERS

4 large cucumbers
1 small onion, chopped
1 tbs. oil or fat
1 cup stewed tomatoes, chopped

1 tbs. parsley, chopped
2 tbs. pimiento olives, chopped
Salt and pepper
4 soda crackers, crushed

Pare and trim cucumbers. Halve them, scoop out seeds and set them aside. Simmer cucumbers in salted water for about 10 minutes or until half-done. Drain. Sauté onion in oil, add tomatoes, olives, cucumber centers, cracker crumbs and seasonings. Simmer mixture to reduce liquid. Fill cucumber shells with stuffing mixture. If desired, sprinkle tops with grated cheese. Place in buttered baking tin and broil under flame for about 2 minutes or until browned. Serve. Serves 4–8.

SQUASH PUDDING

1 *butternut or large acorn squash*
⅓ *cup unsweetened orange juice*
  Rinds of 1 lemon and 1 orange
½ *tsp. salt*
  Sucaryl equivalent to ½ cup sugar
1 *whole egg, beaten*
2 *egg whites, beaten stiff*
¼ *tsp. cinnamon*
¼ *tsp. clove*

Bake squash in skin in 375° oven until quite soft. (About 1 hour.) Cool partially. Remove skin and mash. Gradually add all ingredients, saving beaten egg whites for last. Mix in thoroughly. Fold in egg whites, pour into lightly greased baking dish and bake until browned on top, about 1 hour on moderate heat. Serves 6–8.

RHUBARB WHIP

1 *bunch rhubarb, trimmed and cubed*
½ *cup water*
1 *cinnamon stick*
  Sucaryl equivalent to 1 cup sugar
2 *tbs. unflavored gelatin*
¼ *tsp. salt*
¼ *cup cold water*
2 *egg whites, beaten till stiff with a pinch of salt*

Cook rhubarb in ½ cup water containing cinnamon stick, covered, until soft. Soak gelatin in ¼ cup cold water. Allow to stand 5 minutes. When soft, stir into hot rhubarb mixture and stir over low heat until gelatin dissolves. Remove cinnamon stick, add sucaryl and salt. Pour into refrigerator dish and cool until half jelled. Remove from refrigerator and whip with egg beater or whisk until frothy. Carefully fold in stiff egg whites. Pour into serving dishes and chill. Serves 5–6.

☙ ADAPTING RECIPES TO REDUCING DIETS

Most vegetable recipes can be altered to contain fewer carbohydrates and calories. The flavor of these altered dishes may change somewhat from the originals. The point to remember is that it is only a change, not a loss of flavor. There is nothing to substitute for the rich buttery taste of classic cream dishes. A yoghurt or buttermilk sauce provides its own delicious savor. Expect of your diet cuisine not the flavors you've grown accustomed to through a lifetime but ones equally as good. Try out your diet-adapted dinners on friends. You will probably find, as I did, that your guests never suspect they're eating low-calorie fare.

These are the principles of recipe changes for weight watchers:

1. When milk is called for in a recipe, substitute an equal amount of liquid skim milk. If the skim milk is too thin for your recipe, add 1 or 2 tbs. of powdered skim milk to the liquid. It will take on the consistency of regular milk.

2. When a recipe calls for many eggs (and many calories, as a result), try substituting egg whites for every two out of three eggs specified.

3. When sweet or sour cream is listed, replace it with an equal quantity of buttermilk or plain yoghurt.

4. If butter, fats or oils are among listed ingredients, cut them down to lowest possible amount. ($\frac{1}{4}$ cup oil or fat can be replaced by 1 tbs. of oil plus $\frac{1}{4}$ cup minus 1 tbs. of beef, chicken or vegetable bouillon.)

5. Where flour is required, eliminate it. The absence will change the consistency but not the flavor of your vegetable dishes. If you feel, for esthetics' sake, you must thicken your dish with something, used crushed soda crackers. They have fewer calories than other flour products used in cooking. Crushed soda crackers in moderate amounts can be substituted for bread crumbs, as well. Use just enough to bind the ingredients together. 4 crushed crackers can, passably, do the work of $\frac{1}{2}$ cup of crumbs or more.

6. Again, for breading your vegetables, use cracker crumbs or crushed corn flakes.

7. If your recipe specifies a yellow cheese such as Cheddar or Gruyère, etc., use a part-skim milk cheese instead. A wide variety of these are available at cheese specialty stores. They are quite as tasty as products with higher fat contents.

8. Where sugar, honey, syrups, jams, molasses, etc. are called for, use a sugar substitute such as sucaryl. If the artificial aftertaste bothers you in foods sweetened with these products, add some vanilla extract to your recipe. It will mask the aftertaste.

9. Reduce the portion quantity suggested in non-dietetic recipes by $\frac{1}{3}$ to $\frac{1}{2}$.

10. Remember that well-drained deep-fried foods retain less fat than sautéed or shallow-fried foods. It is better to eliminate most fats from your diet but if you feel you must indulge from time to time, deep-fried foods will be kinder to you calorically.

Example of Recipe Adapted for Dieters:

STRING BEANS IN EGG SAUCE (Original)

1 *pkg. frozen green beans, cooked according to directions but half-done*
2 *tbs. butter*
2 *tbs. flour*
$\frac{1}{2}$ *cup milk*
Dash celery seed
Salt and pepper
3 *hard-boiled eggs, sliced*

Brown flour in melted butter. Slowly add milk and all liquid from green beans. Stir over heat until thickened. Add celery seed, salt and pepper and blend. Pour over hot beans. Garnish with sliced egg and serve.

STRING BEANS IN EGG SAUCE (Diet Version)

1 *pkg. frozen green beans, cooked till half-done*
$\frac{1}{2}$ *cup buttermilk*
2 *egg yolks*
Dash celery seed
Salt and pepper
1 *hard-boiled egg, coarsely grated*

Heat bean juice, buttermilk beaten with egg yolks in top of a double boiler until thick. Add celery seed, seasonings and blend. Add green beans and cook 5–10 minutes, until beans are tender. Garnish with grated hard-boiled egg. Serve.

Part Three

9

Individual
Vegetable Recipes

❧ GLOBE ARTICHOKES AND ARTICHOKE HEARTS

To CLEAN ARTICHOKES: Dip repeatedly in a bowl of cold water, tips down.

To TRIM: Cut off the stems. Pull off the tough or discolored outer leaves. With a scissors or knife, cut off the top third of vegetable to include any spiny leaf tips.

To AVOID DISCOLORATION AFTER TRIMMING: Dip in or rub on lemon juice on all parts that have been cut.

To BOIL: Set on stem ends in pot of lightly salted water to cover. Cover pot, bring to a boil, reduce heat and simmer for 20–50 minutes, until tender. (Boiling time depends on age and size of vegetable.) Artichokes are done when leaves come off stem easily.

To STEAM: Set the artichokes, stem ends down, on a steamer rack over 2 inches of boiling water. Bring water to a boil, reduce heat, cover pan and steam till tender.

ARTICHOKE HEARTS PROVENÇAL

1 pkg. frozen artichoke hearts
1 small onion, chopped
1 ripe tomato, diced
2 tbs. olive oil
¼ cup water
1 tbs. lemon juice (fresh)
½ tsp. sugar
Pepper and salt
½ cup cooked new potatoes, diced
1 tbs. chopped parsley (fresh, if possible)

Mix oil and water in a skillet. Bring to a boil. Add onion and tomato. Allow to cook for a few moments or until tomato disintegrates in liquid. Add sugar, lemon juice, salt, pepper and frozen artichoke hearts. Cover and simmer for about 20 minutes. Add cooked potatoes. Simmer an additional few moments, gently tossing potatoes until well coated with sauce. Serve hot as a side dish or cold as an hors d'oeuvre. Sprinkle with fresh chopped parsley before serving. Serves 3–4.

CREAMED ARTICHOKE HEARTS

1   pkg. frozen artichoke hearts
1½ tbs. butter
¼   cup light cream
1   tbs. chopped parsley
½   tsp. French-style mustard
1   egg yolk
    Salt and pepper

Cook hearts in salted water as directed on the package. Melt butter in skillet. Drain hearts and toss in butter over moderate heat. Slowly add cream mixed with mustard. Simmer but do not allow to boil. Add parsley and salt and pepper. Beat yolk. Add to it some of hot liquid from skillet. Pour slowly into skillet, stirring constantly. When sauce thickens, serve.

Variation: 2 tbs. dry white wine may be substituted for mustard.

DRESSING FOR PLAIN BOILED ARTICHOKES

To prepare boiled artichokes, follow boiling instructions given on page 145.

2 *cooked egg yolks, mashed*
2 *tbs. white wine or tarragon vinegar*
  Green parts of 2 scallions, chopped
1 *small clove garlic, crushed*
  Sprinkling onion powder

Juice of ½ *lemon*
¼ *tsp. sugar*
¼ *tsp. dry mustard (opt.)*
  Salt and pepper
1 *cup olive oil*
2 *tbs. fresh chopped parsley*

Combine ingredients and blend well. This dressing may be heated to simmering and served with hot artichokes or may be chilled for service with cold, cooked artichokes.

STUFFED BAKED ARTICHOKES

10 to 12 *artichokes, half-cooked*
1 *lb. ground veal*
2 *tbs. chopped parsley*
¼ *cup chopped scallions*
1 *egg*
2 *tbs. fine white bread crumbs*

1 *clove garlic, crushed (opt.)*
1 *lemon*
¼ *cup olive oil*
½ *cup water, hot*
  Salt and pepper

Remove center choke from vegetables. Prepare filling of chopped meat, parsley, scallions, salt, pepper, egg and bread crumbs. Stuff centers of artichokes with meat mixture and tie buds with string or thread so they will hold their shape. Stand upright on stem ends in a baking pan. Cut ½ lemon into thin slices. Place 1 slice on top of each artichoke. Combine oil, juice of ½ lemon, hot water and crushed garlic. Pour over artichokes. Bake in a moderate oven until filling is set, about 35 minutes. Baste with liquid from pan from time to time.

ARTICHOKES WITH CHICKEN, GREEK STYLE

6 *small or medium artichokes*
1 *chicken breast*
$\frac{1}{4}$ *cup light olive oil*
2 *cups hot water*
  Juice of 1 lemon
2 *tbs. chopped dill*
2 *tbs. chopped parsley*
  Salt and pepper

Trim stem end of artichoke. Remove largest outer leaves and cut off top third of each vegetable. Cut each vegetable in half, lengthwise. Pour oil on bottom of large skillet. Add chicken breast, lemon juice, hot water, dill, parsley and seasonings. Place artichoke halves in pan, baste with liquid. Cover pan and simmer for about 50 minutes. Serve halves with slivers of chicken and pan-sauce spooned over.

Plain boiled artichokes may be served as an appetizer or side dish with the following hot sauces (served on the side). The leaves are pulled away and dipped in the sauce at the table:

1. Hollandaise sauce. (See page 48.)

2. Melted butter with salt and pepper and, if desired, delicately flavored with onion and/or garlic juice.

3. 1 cup medium white sauce (see pages 46–47) made with chicken stock or bouillon (rather than with milk) to which you add the following in final cooking moments: herbs, spices and condiments. (See page 29.)

4. Mayonnaise (sparked with lemon juice, dry mustard, tarragon, scallions, dillweed, garlic, onion or any of the foregoing.)

5. Your favorite French or Italian style salad dressing.

6. Cold sour cream or yoghurt salad dressings.

❧ ASPARAGUS

There are three varieties available in our markets. White or early asparagus is tender, mild flavored and quick cooking. Violet asparagus (named for the color of its stalk base) is thick, strong flavored and likely to be fibrous in texture. Green or young, thin asparagus have the greatest edible part and the most delicate flavor when fresh. There is another kind known as wild asparagus that is highly prized in parts of Europe. The flavor and delicate texture of these is said to be best of all.

To CLEAN: Rinse under cold running water.

To TRIM: Cut or snap off lower tough portion of stalk. (Tough portion can generally be recognized by color difference from rest of vegetable; it will either be white or violet rather than green.) Keep the stalk ends for flavoring stews and soups.

To BOIL: Tie the trimmed asparagus into convenient bunches. Stand on cut ends upright in large soup pan or special asparagus cooker. Pour into pan about 2 inches of water. Cover (either with pot cover or inverted top of double boiler) and steam asparagus till tender. (10–15 minutes.)

In France, asparagus are sometimes served boiled, drained and presented on folded cloth napkins to be eaten with fingers as an hors d'oeuvre.

ASPARAGUS WITH EGGS, ITALIENNE

1 *lb. tender green asparagus, trimmed and cut to fit pan*
1 *small onion, chopped*
2 *tbs. olive oil*
1 *small can Italian-style plum tomatoes*
1 *cup hot water*
  Salt and pepper
4 *eggs*

Sauté onion in oil in large skillet until softened. Add tomatoes, water and seasoning. Simmer for about 5 minutes or until tomatoes cook down somewhat. Place asparagus in pan. They should be covered or almost covered by pan liquids. If they are not, add small amount of additional water. Cover skillet. Simmer over low heat for about 20 minutes or until asparagus are tender. Uncover pan, push asparagus gently to the side. Carefully, crack eggs open and drop into pan broth to poach. Serve asparagus topped with eggs over which sauce from skillet has been poured. Serves 4.

AU GRATIN ASPARAGUS

2   *pkgs. frozen asparagus, thawed partially (enough to separate stalks)*
1   *cup grated Cheddar or American cheese*
6   *slices white toast, trimmed of crust and lightly buttered on both sides*
1½ *cups hot milk*
2   *eggs, beaten*
    Salt, pepper, paprika
¼   *cup dry white wine (opt.)*

Cut buttered, trimmed toast into 1 inch strips. Place strips in a greased loaf-shape baking dish, to make a layer. Cut asparagus in half and make a single layer of halves over toast. Sprinkle ⅓ of cheese over asparagus. Repeat layers until bread, asparagus and cheese are used up. Beat eggs with wine (if desired) and slowly blend in hot milk, making sure that eggs do not cook in hot liquid. Season with salt and pepper. Pour mixture over layers. Sprinkle top with paprika. Place baking dish in pan of hot water in oven and bake at 325° for about 1 hour. Serves 8.

ASPARAGUS TIPS, FRENCH STYLE

1 *lb. asparagus*
2 *tbs. olive oil*
1 *cup light bouillon (chicken or vegetable)*
1 *tbs. chopped parsley*
¼ *tsp. crushed chervil (opt.)*
  Salt and pepper
  Good dash ground nutmeg

Cut 2 inch pieces from top of raw stalks to include tips. Reserve the other portion of stalks for future use in soups, casseroles or other dishes. Sauté tips in oil in skillet until slightly softened. Add parsley, chervil, salt and pepper and nutmeg. Pour in bouillon. Cover pan and simmer for 15–20 minutes until tips are tender. Drain and serve as a side dish.

ASPARAGUS WITH LEEKS

1   *lb. asparagus, trimmed of tough portion of stalks*
1½ *cups light chicken bouillon*
2   *leeks, cleaned, trimmed and sliced thin*
2   *tbs. melted fat or oil*
2   *tbs. flour*
¼   *cup cream or milk substitute*
    Salt and pepper

Place asparagus and leeks in pan with bouillon and cook till tender (15–20 minutes). Combine fat and flour to make a paste. Slowly pour into pan and stir, gently, until liquid thickens. Season to taste. Add cream or milk substitute. Simmer for a few more minutes but do not allow to boil. This dish may be served as is or on a bed of noodles, rice or potatoes.

ASPARAGUS OMELET

2   *tbs. oil or butter*
3   *eggs, well beaten*
    Salt and pepper
¼   *cup liquid from cooked asparagus*
1   *cup cooked asparagus tips, drained*
    Dash Tabasco

Melt butter or oil in skillet or omelet pan. Beat eggs, seasoning and asparagus liquid until frothy. Pour into hot omelet pan. Quickly pull cooked portions of egg away from sides and bottom with a fork, 3 or 4 times. Reduce heat to lowest. Spoon tips onto eggs. Cover skillet and cook till done. Serve with fresh chopped parsley and/or dairy sour cream.

FRENCH FRIED ASPARAGUS

1 *lb. asparagus, trimmed*
½ *cup pancake flour*
2 *eggs, well beaten*
  Salt and pepper

Place trimmed asparagus in lightly salted, cold water. Bring to a slow boil and allow to simmer for 5 minutes. Remove from water and plunge into cold water. Drain. Tie asparagus stalks into bundles of 5. Roll asparagus bundles in flour and dip in egg. Plunge asparagus bundles into deep, hot fat and allow to brown. Remove from oil, drain well and serve as an appetizer or side dish.

SYRIAN ASPARAGUS

1 *pkg. frozen asparagus*
1 *onion, sliced thin*
3 *tbs. olive oil*
  Salt and pepper
½ *cup hot water*
  Fresh chopped parsley
  Lemon wedges

Sauté onion in oil in a skillet until onion is soft. Add hot water, salt and pepper to pan. Place frozen asparagus in liquid and, over high heat, separate stalks with a fork quickly. Lower heat to simmering, cover pan and cook for 10 minutes. Remove asparagus from liquid, sprinkle with fresh chopped parsley and serve with lemon wedges.

ASPARAGUS À LA RATATOUILLE

1 *lb. fresh asparagus,*
  trimmed and cooked
2 *tbs. olive oil*
1 *onion, sliced*
1 *green pepper, cut in strips*
1 *clove garlic, crushed (opt.)*
1 *bay leaf*
1 *medium zucchini, diced*
  Salt and pepper
1 *medium can tomatoes*
½ *cup fresh green peas*

Sauté onion in oil in a large skillet until soft. Add tomatoes, green pepper, garlic, salt and pepper, bay leaf. Simmer, uncovered, for

10 minutes. Add drained, half-cooked asparagus, squash and peas. Cover pot securely. Simmer for about ½ hour. Sprinkle with fresh chopped parsley before serving. This dish may be served on toast points, over rice or pasta.

✄ *BAMBOO SHOOTS*

WHERE TO BUY: Purchase fresh, young, edible plants from Chinese green grocers. Canned bamboo shoots are available in Oriental food stores and in some supermarkets and groceries.

HOW TO USE FRESH SHOOTS: Slice on the bias (diagonal) into pieces ½–1 inch long. Boil in water to cover 10–15 minutes, or until tender. Drain and incorporate in recipes.

Bamboo shoots can be prepared Chinese style (see page 22) or incorporated into most stir-fry vegetable and/or meat recipes.

HOW TO USE CANNED SHOOTS: Drain liquid from can. Remove any salty residue from vegetables by rinsing with vigorously boiling water. Cut into convenient slices (it's best to cut slices thin) and incorporate into recipes.

To store leftover shoots, place in a refrigerator container, covered. Shoots will keep about 5 days.

✄ *SNAP BEANS*

Green, yellow or mottled beans are a universally popular vegetable. Some of the best-looking and tasting beans I've ever encountered are sold by the quart in the Farmers' Markets of the Pennsylvania Dutch. Other areas of the world vie for the title of best in growing snap greens. According to Alexander Dumas, "until my last visit to Asia I would have said that beans from Soissons were the best in the world. But I feel obliged to recognize that beans from Trebizond are better."

To TRIM BEANS: Snip off top and bottom ends.

To PREPARE FOR COOKING: Cut in 1 inch pieces, in half, on the diagonal (French-style), slice them down the length or leave them whole.

To BOIL: Drop beans into boiling water. Return to the boil, lower heat and simmer until tender. (15–30 minutes.) Season after cooking.

To STEAM: Place on steamer rack over boiling water, cover, cook till tender.

VEGETARIAN LIVER PÂTÉ

2½ cups cooked green beans
    or 2 pkgs. frozen, cooked
    beans
3 medium onions, sliced fine
3 tbs. oil
3 hard-boiled eggs, grated

½ cup walnuts
½ tsp. celery seed
    Salt and pepper
2 tbs. mayonnaise
    Juice of ½ to 1 whole
    lemon (to taste)

Sauté onion in oil. Allow to brown but not burn. Remove from pan and pour into mixing bowl along with pan oil. Add grated egg to bowl and mash together. In a blender, purée beans, nuts, mayonnaise, salt and pepper and celery seed. Pour into egg-onion mixture and blend. Re-season and dress with lemon juice. This can be served on lettuce leaves as a salad or appetizer course or with crackers as a before-meal spread. Garnish with grated egg yolk, chopped parsley or scallions.

GREEN BEANS IN SAVORY CHEESE

2 pkgs. frozen green beans
2 tbs. butter
2 tbs. flour
1 cup chicken or vegetable
  bouillon

1 bay leaf
½ cup grated sharp cheese
  Salt and pepper
  Dash Tabasco

Cook beans in bouillon with bay leaf until just tender. Melt butter and blend in flour. Slowly add to bean pan, stirring constantly and simmering until bean sauce thickens. Remove bay leaf. Add cheese. Continue stirring over lowest heat until cheese melts. Season and serve.

MAGYAR BEANS

2 *pkgs. frozen green beans or*
  2½ *cups fresh cooked beans*
1 *tbs. fat or oil*
1 *tbs. flour*
1 *tbs. chopped onion*
¼ *cup fresh chopped parsley*
1 *tsp. vinegar*

¼ *tsp. paprika*
1 *tsp. sugar*
⅔ *cup dairy sour cream*
¼ *cup water from cooked*
  beans
1 *clove garlic, minced (opt.)*
  Salt

Melt fat in skillet. Sauté onion in fat till soft but not brown. Add flour and stir until paste is free of lumps and golden in color. Add garlic, parsley, paprika and water from beans along with beans. Cook over moderate heat, stirring from time to time, until mixture is thick and has reached boiling point. Turn heat down to lowest point. Add sugar, vinegar, dash of salt and sour cream. Do not allow dish to boil after cream is added. Serve hot.

MENNONITE GREEN BEANS

2 *pkgs. frozen green beans*
½ *cup water*
1 *clove garlic, split (opt.)*
1 *bay leaf*
1 *small onion, chopped*
2 *cloves*

1 *tsp. vinegar*
1 *tsp. sugar*
1 *tbs. butter*
  Dash salt
  Dash cinnamon powder

Bring bay leaf, garlic, onion and water to a slow boil. Allow to boil a few minutes. Add beans and cook, covered, till tender. Remove beans. Discard bay leaf and garlic from cooking water. Add vinegar, sugar, cloves, salt and cinnamon. Boil for about 5 minutes, uncovered. Remove cloves. Pour sauce over beans. Add butter and serve.

FLAMENCO BEANS

2 pkgs. frozen cooked green beans
2 tbs. olive oil
1 red or green pepper, slivered
2 ozs. blanched, slivered almonds
1 tbs. chopped parsley
  Salt and pepper

Sauté pepper and almonds in oil, shaking pan from time to time, until pepper is soft and nuts are lightly toasted. Pour hot over hot green beans and toss through. Season, sprinkle with chopped parsley and serve.

DILL BEANS

1 lb. fresh wax beans (or green beans), trimmed and cut
2 tbs. fat or oil
1 green pepper, diced
1 small onion, diced
1 tomato, diced
½ cup water
  Salt and pepper
  Juice of ½ lemon
1 tsp. dry dillweed or 1 tbs. fresh chopped dill

Put all ingredients, except lemon and salt, in a heavy bottom saucepan. Bring to a boil, reduce heat to simmering, cover pot and cook for about 30 minutes. Add lemon, salt and pepper and serve.

CLAM DIGGER BEANS

2 pkgs. frozen cooked green beans or 2½ cups fresh cooked
1 can New England-style clam chowder
1 small can minced clams
2 tbs. Sherry (opt.)
  Dash onion salt
¼ tsp. thyme

Heat chowder, clams, onion salt and sherry in top part of double boiler. Mix in beans, and thyme. Heat but do not boil. Serve.

MUSHROOM PICKER BEANS

2 *pkgs. frozen green beans, cooked*
1 *can mushroom soup*
1 *small can button mushrooms*
1 *can French fried onions*
¼ *tsp. crumbled dry sage (opt.)*

Combine all ingredients in a buttered casserole dish. Bake in pre-heated oven at 325° for about 20 minutes or until top is bubbly. Serve.

ACROPOLIS GREEN BEANS

1 *lb. raw green beans,*
  trimmed and cut
1 *lb. lamb chunks (from*
  shoulder of lamb)
1 *can tomato sauce (8 oz.)*
1 or 2 *cloves garlic, minced*

2 *tbs. chopped fresh parsley*
2 *tbs. fresh chopped dill*
2 *onions, sliced*
2 *tbs. olive oil*
1 *cup water*
  Salt and pepper

Sauté onions in oil in large skillet until golden. Add lamb and brown slightly on all sides. Combine all ingredients in skillet except salt and pepper and simmer, covered, for about 1 hour or until beans are quite soft and liquid has cooked down to sauce consistency. Season to taste. Serve with lamb cubes as an entree or appetizer.

ARTHUR'S FAVORITE GREEN BEANS

2 *cups Italian style broad cut green beans, cooked*
1 *cup dairy sour cream*
  Dash MSG
3 *tbs. fine white bread crumbs, toasted**
3 *tbs. grated sharp cheese*
  Salt and pepper

---

* To toast bread crumbs, melt 2 tbs. butter in a skillet. Add bread crumbs and sauté till crumbs cease to bubble and foam in the pan. When crumbs are fairly dry and browned, remove from skillet and cool.

Butter a baking dish. Mix together sour cream, 2 tbs. toasted crumbs, 2 tbs. cheese, MSG and salt and pepper. Toss beans evenly through mixture. Pour into baking pan. Top with 1 tbs. crumbs mixed with 1 tbs. grated cheese. Bake for about 20 minutes (or until cheese bubbles on top) in 325° oven.

YUGOSLAV GREEN BEANS

1 *lb. fresh green beans, trimmed and cut*
3 *tbs. olive oil*
1 *large sweet onion, sliced thin (Spanish type, if possible)*
3 *tomatoes, diced*
  Dash garlic powder
  Dash sugar
½ *cup hot water*
  Salt and pepper

Sauté onion in oil till soft. Add tomatoes and water and cook till tomatoes begin to disintegrate in liquid. Add beans and garlic powder, sugar and some salt, cover, and cook over low heat for 2 or 3 hours. Season at the end of cooking period. This dish can be served hot as a side course or cold as a spread for crackers and breads.

DIXIELAND BEANS

½ *lb. spicy meat, such as corned beef, sausage or ham bone with meat*
  Water to cover
1 *lb. fresh green beans, trimmed and cut*
  Salt and pepper

Simmer meat and water in soup pot for about 1½ hours. Remove any scum that forms on top. Add beans. Cover pot and simmer for about ½ hour or until beans are tender. Stir occasionally to prevent sticking. Season with salt and pepper. Remove beans from meat liquid and serve.

TRICOLOR BEANS

2 *pkgs. frozen green beans*
3 *tbs. butter*
1 *tbs. chopped parsley*
3 *medium scallions, chopped, white and green parts*
¼ *cup cooking water from beans*
2 *egg yolks*
¾ *cup half & half*
  Juice of 1 lemon
  Salt and pepper, dash nutmeg

Cook green beans as directed in lightly salted water to which 1 tbs. butter has been added. Drain beans and set aside but reserve cooking liquid. Melt 2 tbs. butter in a skillet. Add drained beans, parsley and scallions. Sauté for about 1 minute. Add water to skillet. Mix egg yolks with half & half. Add slowly to pan, stirring constantly, till sauce thickens. Add lemon juice, salt and pepper to taste and nutmeg. Serve.

❧ BEAN CAKE

Bean cake is the cheese-like product of pressed soy bean curd. As a high-protein vegetable product, it makes a nutritionally sound substitute for meats. Its calorie content is moderate. Its bland flavor allows it to mix readily in saucy and/or spicy dishes. Chinese and Japanese people prize it for its food and flavor value.

WHERE TO FIND IT: The cakes can be bought fresh or canned. Fresh cakes (sold from a wooden tub) are infinitely better in flavor. Both kinds should be available in large markets of Chinese or Japanese neighborhoods.

TO PREPARE IT: Bean cake needs little time or trouble in preparation. Cut it into bite-size pieces and either braise it or stir-fry with other foods no more than 5–10 minutes.

TO KEEP IT: Place bean cake (canned, drained and rinsed or fresh) in a refrigerator container. Cover with cold, clear water and chill. Change water once each day till used. Bean cake will keep in your refrigerator a maximum of 4 days.

BEAN CAKE AND MUSHROOMS

1 *lb. fresh mushrooms, sliced*
4 *bean cakes, diced*
3 *tbs. corn or peanut oil*
1 *clove garlic, split*
2 *slices fresh ginger, minced**
1 *tbs. Chinese-style canned brown beans*
1 *tbs. dry Sherry*
2 *tbs. soya sauce*
½ *cup diced scallions*
1 *tsp. cornstarch and 1 tsp. water*
¼ *cup bouillon (chicken)*
¼ *tsp. MSG*

Heat oil in large skillet. Add garlic and minced ginger and sauté till brown. Remove from skillet. Sauté mushrooms and scallions in oil for about 5 minutes, stir-frying. Add bouillon, Sherry, soya sauce, MSG, brown beans, diced bean cake. Cover and simmer for about 5 minutes more. Uncover, mix corn starch and water and add slowly to pan. Stir until sauce thickens slightly (a few moments). Serve.

❧ BEAN SPROUTS

WHERE TO FIND FRESH: Available in Chinese-style green groceries.

WHERE TO FIND CANNED: In most supermarkets and large groceries.

TO PREPARE FRESH SPROUTS FOR COOKING: Rinse well under cold, running water.

---

* In place of fresh ginger, substitute ¼ tsp. powdered ginger and add with cornstarch.

To PREPARE CANNED SPROUTS: Drain, rinse under cold water.

To COOK FRESH SPROUTS: Drop into boiling water to cover sprouts half-way. Cook, covered, for just a few minutes or until sprouts are tender but still crisp. Season and serve or incorporate into stir-fry cookery.

CHINESE BEAN SPROUTS

1 *can bean sprouts, rinsed and drained*	1 *onion, chopped*
3 *tbs. corn or peanut oil*	1 *green pepper, chopped*
2 *slices fresh ginger root minced or ¼ tsp. dry powder*	2 *tbs. soya sauce*
	1 *tsp. sesame oil*
	¼ *tsp. salt*

Heat oil. Sauté bean sprouts, onion and peppers. Stir-fry for about 2 minutes. Add ginger, soya sauce and sesame oil, cover and simmer for 5 minutes. Serve.

✿ *LIMA BEANS**

To PREPARE: Fresh beans should be removed from pods shortly before cooking, whenever possible. If you must shell them early, keep them in a covered, refrigerated dish till needed. Wash and drain them after shelling.

To BOIL: Cook in a small amount of lightly salted, boiling water in a covered pot. Cooking time will be 20–30 minutes.

LIMAS BAKED WITH CHEESE

2½ *cups cooked limas*	1 *#2 can tomatoes*
1 *onion, chopped*	2 *tbs. butter*
1 *green or red pepper, chopped*	1 *can French fried onions*
2 *stalks celery, diced*	½ *cup grated Swiss cheese*
	Salt and pepper

* For dry beans, peas and lentils see heading: Lentils, Dry Beans And Peas.

Drain cooked limas but reserve 2 ozs. of cooking liquid. Sauté onion and celery in butter. Add to limas along with tomato sauce and cooking water. Season to taste. Pour into greased baking dish. Combine French fried onions and grated cheese. Pour over top of casserole. Bake until cheese is melted and bubbly, about 25 minutes at 350°.

LIMA BEANS ROMANO

1 *pkg. frozen limas*
¼ *cup chicken bouillon*
1 *tbs. fresh chopped parsley*
4 *strips bacon or beef fry*

1 *clove garlic, split*
1 *bay leaf*
Grated cheese (opt.)

Simmer limas in broth until tender with bay leaf and garlic. Drain beans. Discard garlic and bay leaf. Fry out bacon, drain and crumble. Combine with bacon and parsley. Season. Serve hot with grated Italian cheese on the side, if desired.

LIMA BEAN SCALLOP

2½ *cups firm cooked lima beans*
1 *cup firm cooked, diced carrots*
1 *cup sliced onions*
4 *tbs. butter*
1 *cup medium white sauce*
¾ *cup fine white bread crumbs*
   Seasoned salt

Fry onions in 2 tbs. butter until golden. Pour crumbs into pan and toast slightly. Stir crumbs till they absorb all apparent pan oil. Set aside. Combine limas and carrots. Butter a baking dish. Place a layer of vegetables, some sauce and a layer of onions, crumbs and dash of seasoned salt, and so on, till ingredients are used up. Top with crumbs and dot with 2 tbs. butter. Bake at 300° for about 10–15 minutes.

HEARTHSTONE LIMAS

2 *pkgs. frozen limas*
1 *cup firm-cooked soup macaroni*
2 *cups chopped escarole (or spinach)*
4 *sausages or 2 frankfurters, diced*
  Seasoned salt to taste
½ *cup water*

Boil water in saucepan. Add all ingredients. Bring to a boil once more. Reduce heat and simmer for about 15 minutes. Serve hot.

LIMAS ORIENTALE

2 *pkgs. frozen limas*
¼ *cup chicken stock*
¼ *tsp. MSG*

Dash garlic powder
2 *tbs. soya sauce*

Combine in a saucepan and simmer 15 minutes. Add salt, if needed, and serve.

GLOCKENSPIEL LIMAS

2 *tbs. butter or margarine*
2½ *cups cooked limas**
4 *strips fried out bacon or beef fry*
1 *tbs. sharp mustard*
2 *tbs. molasses*

3 *tbs. brown sugar*
2 *tbs. catsup*
1 *tbs. flour and 1 tbs. water*
½ *cup bouillon (onion or beef)*

Combine mustard, molasses, brown sugar, catsup and bouillon. Heat in top part of double boiler until all is well mixed. Add flour and water mixture and stir till sauce thickens. Place limas in buttered, heavy casserole. Stir in crumbled meat. Pour over sauce. Dot with butter or margarine. Bake in 300° oven till beans are browned. (1 hour or more for cooked dry beans.)

* Recipe is equally successful with dry or fresh beans.

SIMPLICITY SUCCOTASH

1 *pkg. frozen baby limas, partially cooked*
1 *medium can creamed corn*
2 *tbs. dehydrated vegetable flakes*
  Salt to taste

Cook limas only until thawed. In the top part of a double boiler, combine creamed corn, limas, flakes and salt. Simmer for 15 or 20 minutes.

✌ *BEETS*

To PREPARE: Cut the tops from beets but leave a short piece of stem on vegetable. Wash them thoroughly. Root end need not be cut nor skin removed for cooking.

To BOIL: Immerse whole and in skin in boiling salted water, to which the juice of 1 lemon or 2 tbs. vinegar has been added. Water should half cover beets. Cover pan and simmer till tender. Cooking time depends on age and type of beets. It can vary from $\frac{1}{2}$ hour to 2 hours. After cooking, drain, plunge in cold water, remove skin (skin should slip off easily between your fingers) and re-heat to serve.

BEETS IN WINE SAUCE WITH RAISINS

1 *#2 can sliced beets, drained*	2 *tbs. flour*
$\frac{3}{4}$ *cup beet liquid*	$\frac{1}{8}$ *tsp. salt*
$\frac{1}{4}$ *cup dry red wine*	$\frac{1}{3}$ *cup raisins or currants*
2 *tbs. butter*	$1\frac{1}{2}$ *tbs. brown sugar*
	$\frac{1}{8}$ *tsp. powdered allspice*

Melt butter in top part of double boiler. Stir in flour until smooth paste is formed. Pour in raisins and simmer with flour and butter for about 3 minutes or until they are soft. Combine beet liquid, wine, salt and sugar. Pour into pan slowly, stirring constantly.

Stir until mixture thickens. Add allspice and beets. Simmer till beets are warm. Serve.

BEET RAITA

2 medium cooked beets, grated
1½ cups yoghurt
1 small onion, grated
¼ tsp. chili powder
Salt to taste
Pinch sugar

Mix together. Chill at least 1 hour before serving. Use as a relish-style accompaniment to your entrees.

CELERY BEETS

2 cups cooked beets, cut julienne and drained
  Grated rind of 1 lemon
1 tbs. lemon juice
1 tsp. celery seed
¼ tsp. salt
½ tsp. sugar
⅓ cup dairy sour cream
  Dash nutmeg

Combine all ingredients in top part of double boiler. Add beets last. Heat but do not boil. Serve warm.

APPLE BEET PUDDING

2 cups cooked beets
4 tart apples, peeled and cored
4 eggs, well beaten
3 tbs. brown sugar
1 tsp. salt
3 tbs. melted butter
1½ tbs. cornstarch and 1½ tbs. water
1 pint light sweet cream
  Grated rind of 1 lemon
½ tsp. lemon extract
  Cinnamon sugar

Purée beets and apples. Add beaten eggs to mixture. Blend well. Incorporate sugar, salt, melted butter, lemon rind and lemon extract. Blend cornstarch and water to a smooth paste. Add to mixture and stir in. Blend in cream. Beat till frothy. Pour into greased large casserole dish. Place in pan of hot water. Bake in preheated oven at 350° for about 45 minutes. Sprinkle top with cinnamon sugar.

GINGER BEETS

1 onion, chopped
2 tbs. butter
2 tbs. flour
⅓ cup ginger ale
⅓ cup beet juice
1 #2 can sliced beets, drained

¼ tsp. salt
½ tsp. brown (or white) sugar
   Dash pepper, fresh nutmeg
1 tsp. red wine vinegar

Sauté onion in butter in a skillet until golden. Add flour and stir till golden paste is formed. Carefully add ginger ale and beet juice. Combine and stir until thickened. Add all seasonings except vinegar. Add beets and toss through sauce. Remove from heat, add vinegar and stir through. Serve hot. (Re-heat in double boiler.)

PINEAPPLE BEET CHIFFON

1 cup beet purée, canned or fresh
1½ cups pineapple purée, canned or fresh
1½ envelopes unflavored gelatin
⅓ cup water
   Pinch allspice, cardamom (opt.)
   Rind of 1 lemon
3 tbs. honey (or more to taste)
1 tbs. lemon juice
1½ cups sweetened whipped cream (heavy cream and 3 tbs. sugar)

Dissolve gelatin in water for 5 minutes. Heat pineapple purée and lemon rind and lemon juice until at boiling point. Add gelatin and mix over heat until gelatin melts. Add to beet purée. Combine with other ingredients except for cream. Chill until mixture starts to thicken, approximately $\frac{1}{2}$ hour in freezer. Then, whip cream and fold gelatin mix into it. Pour into mold or parfait glasses and refrigerate until set. (3 to 4 hours.) This dish makes an excellent party dessert surprise because of its pretty color and good taste.

Beets: Cook whole beets in boiling salted water for 20–40 minutes, until tender. Remove peeling, purée by mashing or in blender.

Pineapple: Purée canned crushed pineapple by mashing or in blender.

For dieters: Substitute sucaryl for honey; and yoghurt for cream.

✿ *BROCCOLI*

To PREPARE: Soak in salted, cold water for 5–10 minutes. Drain. Cut off tough parts of stem and any large leaves around flowers. Broccoli can be cooked whole, separated into flowerettes, chopped or cut into small serving pieces.

To COOK: Early or young heads are best steamed over water. Larger, more mature heads are better cooked in small amounts of boiling water, covered, for 10–25 minutes.

BRAISED BROCCOLI IN OYSTER SAUCE

1 *bunch broccoli*	2 *slices fresh ginger**
3 *tbs. corn or peanut oil*	$\frac{1}{4}$ *cup chicken bouillon*
1 *tbs. soya sauce*	2 *tbs. Chinese oyster sauce*
1 *tbs. gin*	$\frac{1}{4}$ *tsp. MSG*
1 *clove garlic, split*	

* In place of fresh ginger, substitute $\frac{1}{4}$ tsp. powdered ginger and add with soya sauce.

Remove any tough stalks. Cut broccoli into 2 inch strips, $\frac{1}{2}$ inch in diameter, cut on the bias (on the diagonal). Blanch in boiling water and allow to cool in water. Remove, drain. Heat oil in a large skillet. Sauté ginger and garlic in oil until they start to brown. Remove them. Add broccoli to pan and stir-fry for about 5 minutes. Add chicken broth, gin, oyster sauce, soya sauce and MSG. Cover and simmer for about 5 minutes more. Serve hot.

BROCCOLI CUSTARD

1 *package frozen chopped broccoli, cooked and drained*
1 *cup cheese sauce*
$\frac{1}{4}$ *tsp. powdered mustard (opt.)*
3 *eggs*
  Salt, pepper and paprika

Beat eggs well. Add cheese sauce, mustard, salt and pepper to taste and a good dash paprika. Incorporate broccoli. Pour into well-greased baking dish (ring mold is particularly good) and set in pan of hot water. Bake in preheated oven at 350° for about 45 minutes.

BROCCOLI SESAME

2 *tbs. sesame seeds, toasted**   1 *tbs. lemon juice*
2 *packages frozen broccoli or* $\frac{1}{4}$ *cup liquid from cooked*
  1 *fresh head*   *broccoli*
2 *tbs. fat or oil*   *Salt, if needed*
2 *tbs. soya sauce*

Boil or steam broccoli till half-done. Drain. Melt butter in a skillet. Separate broccoli flowerettes and cut stalks in $\frac{1}{2}$ inch diameter pieces. Stir-fry broccoli in fat or oil for 2 minutes. Add cooking liquid and soya sauce, cover and simmer for about 5 minutes. Add lemon juice and sesame seeds. Serve.

---

* To toast sesame seeds, place them in a skillet over moderate heat. Shake pan continually from the time they start to brown. Do not allow to burn.

BROCCOLI INDIENNE

2 *packages frozen chopped*
  broccoli
¼ *cup chicken bouillon*
1 *bay leaf*

¼ *tsp. thyme (opt.)*
  Salt to taste
2 *tbs. lemon juice*
1 *tbs. butter*

Cook broccoli in bouillon with bay leaf till done. Discard bay leaf. Add thyme, lemon juice and salt to taste. Serve.

ITALIAN BROCCOLI

¼ *cup water*
2 *pkgs. frozen broccoli*
1 *cup firm cooked elbow*
  macaroni
2 *tbs. olive oil*

¼ *tsp. garlic powder*
  Salt to taste
½ *cup chopped stuffed olives*
  (opt.)

Cook broccoli in water with oil and garlic powder. In final cooking moments, add macaroni and olives. Serve hot.

BROCCOLI DIVAN

2 *pkgs. frozen cooked broccoli*
2 *medium cans tuna, drained*
1 *can creamed mushroom soup*
½ *cup dairy sour cream*
⅓ *cup grated cheese*
  Salt to taste, paprika

Butter a baking dish. Place layer of broccoli stalks on the bottom. Break up tuna into chunks and make a layer over broccoli. Whip together condensed soup and sour cream. Pour a portion over tuna. Repeat layers, ending with soup-cream sauce. Top with grated cheese. Sprinkle with paprika. Bake at 375° for about 20–25 minutes, or until browned on top.

Variation: 1 lb. thin sliced turkey or chicken can be substituted for tuna.

BROCCOLI WITH TOMATOES

1 *bunch cooked broccoli or 2 pkgs. frozen cooked broccoli*
2 *onions, chopped*
4 *slices ham or pastrami, diced*
3 *tbs. olive oil*
1 *#2 can Italian-style plum tomatoes*
2 *tbs. fresh chopped parsley*
¼ *tsp. crushed marjoram (opt.)*
2 *tbs. dry red wine*
  Salt and pepper
1 *clove garlic, minced*

Sauté onions in oil till soft. Add all other ingredients. Simmer about 20 minutes. Place firm-cooked broccoli in sauce to heat. Simmer, covered, for just a few moments. Serve.

৯ৄ *BRUSSELS SPROUTS*

To PREPARE: Pull off any tough or discolored outer leaves. Cut off stems. Make a deep criss-cross gash on stem end with a sharp knife to quicken cooking time.

To COOK: Sprouts may be placed in rapidly boiling water to cover and simmered, uncovered, for 10–20 minutes.

The delicacy of flavor in this vegetable demands the least amount of cooking and rewarming. The flavor disappears in over-cooking and a strong, cabbage-like taste replaces it. For that reason I do not include any but quick-cooking recipes for sprouts. Always cook them gently.

BRUSSELS SPROUTS IN CARAWAY CREAM

2 *cups firm cooked Brussels*
  sprouts, drained
  Grated rind of 1 lemon
1 *tbs. lemon juice*

1 *tbs. butter*
1 *tsp. caraway seed*
½ *cup dairy sour cream*

Melt butter in top part of double boiler. Toss in seeds and sauté for a few minutes. Add sprouts, lemon rind, lemon juice, salt, pepper, and sour cream. Mix thoroughly but do not allow to boil. Serve hot.

SPROUTS IN CARROT CHEESE

2 *pkgs. frozen cooked*
   Brussels sprouts, drained
1½ *cups grated carrots*
3 *tbs. butter*
   Salt and pepper
2 *ozs. water*

1 *tbs. flour*
¼ *tsp. dry mustard*
4 *ozs. Velveeta-type*
   processed cheese, diced
1 *cup milk*
   Dash cinnamon

Simmer grated carrots, butter and water in top part of double boiler till carrots soften. Add salt, pepper, and flour. Stir in flour till mixture thickens. Add mustard and cinnamon. Slowly add milk and continue stirring till mixture thickens. Dice in cheese and stir until it melts. Add halved Brussels sprouts and heat briefly. Serve. Serves 6–8.

BRUSSELS SPROUTS AND CHESTNUTS

2 *cups cooked Brussels sprouts*
1 *lb. fresh chestnuts*
3 *tbs. butter*
   Salt and pepper
1 *small onion, chopped*

Cook Brussels sprouts, drain and keep warm. Shell chestnuts* and cook in boiling, salted water to cover, for about 20–30 minutes, until tender. Drain thoroughly. Melt butter in skillet. Stir-fry onion and chestnuts in pan until golden. Pour over warm Brussels sprouts. Serve.

* Before cooking, making a criss-cross on flat top of chestnut with a sharp knife. If shell does not come off easily, boil in shell and remove after cooking.

SPROUTS IN APPLE CREAM

2 *cups cooked Brussels sprouts*
4 *ozs. cream cheese*
6 *ozs. milk*
½ *cup dehydrated apples, diced*
½ *tsp. salt, pepper*
¼ *tsp. grated nutmeg*

Melt cheese and milk in top part of double boiler. Add apples, salt, pepper and nutmeg. Simmer for about 10 minutes. Pour over hot sprouts and serve.

TOMATO-DRESSED SPROUTS

1 *#2 can tomatoes*
1 *tbs. light oil*
1 *bay leaf*
1 *diced garlic clove*
1 *tsp. brown sugar*
¼ *tsp. salt*
2 *pkgs. frozen sprouts*

Cut up canned tomatoes. Add all ingredients except sprouts. Simmer for 15 minutes over low heat. Add sprouts, cover and cook till tender. Serves 6–8.

✿ *CABBAGE*

To PREPARE FOR COOKING: Remove coarse or discolored outer leaves. Halve. Cut out thick white stem. Either shred cabbage with a knife or a coarse grater or cut in quarters.

To BOIL: Place in water to cover and simmer till tender. (7–15 minutes for shredded green or red cabbage and 20 minutes for Savoy.)

OTHER COOKING METHODS: Shredded cabbage may be sautéed in a small amount of oil or steamed over boiling water. Cabbage wedges can be steamed or parboiled and baked in a sauce.

DILLED CABBAGE

1 *tbs. salad oil (corn or peanut)*
1 *medium head green cabbage*
¼ *lb. thin sliced ham or smoked salmon*

1 *medium sweet onion*
6 *sprigs fresh dill*
Salt
Peppercorns
2 *tbs. butter*

Select a medium size saucepan. Oil bottom. Slice cabbage into pieces ½ inch thick. Place 1 slice on the bottom of pot. Add a few slivers of ham or salmon, 1 slice of onion, 2 peppercorns, and a few dots of butter. Repeat layers until all ingredients are used. Add ⅓ cup boiling water and some salt. Cover and steam till tender.

CHEESE-FILLED CABBAGE LEAVES

1 *large head green cabbage*
½ *lb. bulk sharp cheese (Cheddar, Gouda, etc.)*
2 *tbs. butter*

Separate cabbage leaves. Drop in boiling salted water to cover and cook for about 5 minutes or until leaves soften somewhat. Drain and cool. Cut thick sticks from cheese. Place one in center of each leaf and roll leaf around cheese. Secure roll with a toothpick. Melt butter in a skillet. Place cabbage rolls in pan in a single layer, sprinkle with salt, pepper and sauté on both sides till leaves are lightly browned and cheese is melted within. Serve hot.

FRENCH CABBAGE STEW

1 *medium head cabbage*
2 *pkgs. onion soup mix*
2½ *qts. boiling water*
1 *cup dry white wine*
½ *tsp. caraway seeds*

9 *slices stale bread (any kind)*
½ *lb. thin sliced Swiss cheese*
Salt to taste
1 *tbs. oil*

Separate cabbage leaves. Rinse in cold water. (Do not drain completely.) Oil bottom of a large soup pot. Place ¼ of leaves over bottom. Make a thin layer of Swiss cheese on top of cabbage. Place 3 slices of stale bread on top of cheese. Repeat layers till all ingredients are incorporated. Combine onion soup mix, boiling water, wine, salt and seeds. Pour over cabbage layers. Bring to a boil. Reduce heat and simmer for about 1 hour or until cabbage is cooked. Serve in soup plates.

CABBAGE, CHINESE-STYLE

1 *medium cabbage or 2 heads Chinese cabbage*
4 *tbs. melted, strained chicken fat*
1 *tsp. sugar*
1 *tbs. salt*
½ *cup chicken bouillon*
¼ *tsp. MSG*
  Dash garlic powder, powdered ginger
1 *tsp. cornstarch and 1 tbs. water*

Cut cabbage leaves into serving size pieces. (Large leaves may be cut four ways.) Heat oil in large skillet or heavy bottomed soup pot. Add cabbage and coat evenly with fat. Cook over moderate heat, uncovered, till cabbage wilts, stirring frequently. Add broth, cover pot and simmer for another 10 minutes. Stir occasionally. Uncover, (cabbage should be fully tender) add MSG, garlic and ginger powders, sugar, salt. Slowly add cornstarch mixed with water. Stir over moderate heat until sauce thickens. Serve.

HOT SLAW

1 *cabbage, shredded and cored*
1 *onion, chopped*
2 *tbs. butter*
1 *tsp. salt*
3 *tbs. honey*
3 *tbs. wine vinegar (red)*
½ *cup water*
  Dash cinnamon
1 *diced tomato (opt.)*
1 *tsp. dry mustard*
1 *cup dairy sour cream*

Melt butter in large sauce pan. Sauté onion in butter until softened. Add cabbage, toss until well coated with butter and onion. Cook over moderate low heat, stirring from time to time, until softened. (About 15 minutes.) Combine water, vinegar, honey, cinnamon, tomato, salt, mustard powder. Pour over cabbage and simmer for 4 or 5 minutes. Add sour cream. Remove from heat, mix well and serve.

DUTCH-STYLE RED CABBAGE

1 *medium red cabbage, shredded*
$\frac{1}{4}$ *cup boiling water*
2 *large tart apples, peeled, cored and chopped*
1 *tbs. sugar*
3 *cloves*
2 *tbs. butter*
2–3 *tbs. cider or wine vinegar to taste*
1 *tsp. cornstarch and 1 tbs. water*

Place shredded cabbage in boiling water to cover. Let stand till water cools. Drain. Melt fat in large skillet. Add cabbage, apples, cloves and boiling water. Toss cabbage through mixture and allow to cook, stirring from time to time, until cabbage is tender (20–25 minutes). Add vinegar, cornstarch mixture and toss through. Simmer a few more minutes, till sauce thickens slightly. Serve.

CABBAGE LASAGNA

1 *medium cabbage*
$\frac{1}{2}$ *cup oil*
$\frac{1}{4}$ *tsp. garlic powder*
1 *can spaghetti sauce, plain*
  or mushroom

1 *cup ricotta*
2 *ozs. milk*
2 *egg yolks*
  Salt and pepper
$\frac{1}{4}$ *cup grated cheese*

Halve cabbage head. Wash and drain thoroughly. Cut halves into slices, $\frac{1}{2}$–$\frac{3}{4}$ inches thick. Add garlic powder to oil and heat in skillet. Fry cabbage slices till lightly browned on both sides. Remove from pan and drain on absorbent paper. Oil baking pan. Mix ricotta and milk till smooth. Add egg yolks and seasoning and blend well. Place a layer of fried cabbage, followed by a layer of ricotta mixture in pan. Continue alternating layers till you finish with cabbage. Add sauce. Sprinkle top with grated cheese. Cover pan with foil or waxed paper fitted snugly. Bake in hot oven (400°) for 15 minutes. Uncover and bake an additional 10 minutes, or place under broiler briefly. Serve hot.

SAUERKRAUT WITH APRICOTS

1   #2½ can sauerkraut,   1½ tsps. poppy seeds (opt.)
      rinsed and drained   Dash salt
½   cup beef bouillon   2   tbs. brown sugar
2   tbs. butter or oil   1   cup diced dry apricots
1   cup dry white wine

Combine all ingredients in a large skillet. Bring to a boil, reduce heat and simmer for 30–40 minutes. Serve hot as an accompaniment to meat or fowl entrees.

CABBAGE FILLING FOR STRUDEL

1 *medium head cabbage,*   1 *cup white raisins*
   cored and chopped   2 *cups sugar*
1 *large onion, chopped*   *Dash salt*
¼ *lb. sweet butter*   1 *tsp. powdered cinnamon*

Melt butter in a skillet. Sauté onion in it till softened but not brown. Add cabbage, toss through onion-butter mixture till well coated. Cook over moderate heat until cabbage is tender, stirring frequently. Cool mixture. Add sugar, raisins, salt and cinnamon. Mix well. Spread on favorite strudel dough* and roll up. Follow baking directions for ordinary strudel.

* Hungarian-style strudel leaves are available in refrigerated packages at many fine food stores. Simple directions for preparing leaves and baking are included in package.

VEGETARIAN STUFFED CABBAGE

2 medium cabbages	4 ozs. sugar
1 cup raisins	1 tbs. salt
1 cup raw rice, soaked 2 hours or more	1¼ sticks butter or margarine
	4 ozs. honey
3 tart apples, pared and chopped	½ tsp. cinnamon (opt.)
	Juice of 1½ lemons
3 onions, chopped	

Place whole cabbages in boiling water and cook for 5–10 minutes. Drain. Remove large leaves from cabbage. Cut out any coarse, thick veins from stem ends. Combine rice, apples, onions, sugar, salt, ¾ cup of raisins, and cinnamon. Place 2 tbs. of mixture in center of each leaf with a walnut-size piece of butter. Roll into cigar shapes and tuck ends under. Chop the cabbage hearts and place at the bottom of a large soup pot which has been lightly greased at the bottom. (Use corn or peanut oil.) Put cabbage rolls over chopped leaves in snug layers covering bottom of pot. Add 2 cups of water and ¼ cup raisins to pot. Cover and cook 3 to 4 hours over lowest heat. Transfer rolls to a pyrex baking dish. Pour over top, ½ cup honey, ½ cup water and lemon juice. Bake in oven at 350° for 2 hours.

"CASBAH" STUFFED CABBAGE

1 large head green cabbage
2 or 3 lamb bones
1 qt. water
8 ozs. rice, soaked for 1 hour
½ lb. ground lamb (not too lean)
3 ozs. melted fat or oil
½ tsp. allspice
  Juice of 1 lemon
  Salt and pepper

Combine ground lamb, soaked rice, fat or oil, allspice, salt and pepper. Set aside for stuffing. Simmer bones in water for 2 hours to make broth. Separate cabbage leaves. Parboil in rapidly boiling water till softened (but not cooked) 5–10 minutes. Remove leaves, drain and cool. Cut largest leaves in half. Put about 1 tbs. of filling in each leaf and roll up, tucking down the ends. In a large soup pot, place bones at the bottom. Arrange stuffed, rolled leaves across the bones, making successive layers. Add lamb broth to cover and salt to taste. Cover pan and simmer for about ½ hour. Add the juice of 1 lemon a few minutes before the end of cooking. Serve hot.

ALPINE KRAUT

1 #2½ can sauerkraut, rinsed and drained
1 tbs. oil
4 strips bacon or beef fry, diced
1 onion, chopped
1 green pepper, diced
1 clove garlic, minced

½ tsp. paprika
Salt and pepper
1 cup water
1 tsp. chopped dill (½ tsp. dry dillweed)
½ cup tomato sauce
2 tbs. oil and 2 tbs. flour, browned

Sauté onion, bacon, oil and pepper till bacon is crisp and vegetable is soft. Add kraut, broth, garlic, paprika, salt and pepper, tomato sauce, dillweed. Cover and simmer for about 1 hour. Thicken with mixture of 2 tbs. butter and 2 tbs. flour browned.

Either place in a casserole with boiled potatoes, topped with franks or sausages, and broil under flame till sausages are grilled, or serve with boiled potatoes, carrots and sausages prepared separately.

❧ CARROTS

To PREPARE: Carrots may be pared, scraped or simply brushed under running water. Most of the vitamins are near the skin so it is advisable to take off as little as possible. Root and stalk ends should be trimmed.

To BOIL: Simmer carrots whole, slivered, cut into sticks, sliced in rounds, diced or chopped in a small amount of water or stock until tender.

OTHER METHODS: Carrots maintain the most flavor steamed over boiling water until tender. Carrots can be stir-fried in a small amount of oil, as well.

Unless carrots are quite young and fresh, you may prefer them cut julienne-style for cooking. This method will protect the more tender, flavor-rich carrot centers from overcooking.

CARROT LOAF

3 *cups cooked carrots*
4 *eggs*
1 *tsp. salt*
3 *tbs. sugar*
1 *tbs. cornstarch and 1½ tbs.*
  water

1 *pint light cream*
¼ *tsp. nutmeg*
3 *tbs. oil or melted butter*
Dash ginger

Purée cooked carrots by mashing through sieve or in a blender. Beat eggs till frothy and add to carrots. Blend with sugar, salt and butter. Combine cornstarch and water. Add to purée mixture. Pour in cream and nutmeg. Blend well. Pour into greased baking dish and place in pan of hot water. Bake at 350° for about 45 minutes. Serve hot.

FRENCH CARROTS

2½ *cups fresh carrots, diced*
⅔ *cup white raisins*
½ *cup lightly salted water*

⅛ *tsp. nutmeg*
¼ *tsp. sweet basil*
1 *tbs. butter*

Combine all ingredients in a heavy bottomed skillet or saucepan. Bring to a boil, reduce heat and simmer, covered, for about 15 minutes.

CARROTS, BREAD AND CHEESE

3   cups firm-cooked carrots,　　2   eggs, beaten
　　cut into slices or pieces　　　¼　cup milk or cream
3   ozs. melted butter　　　　　1   cup grated sharp cheese
1½ cups seasoned bread　　　　　　Salt and pepper
　　croutons　　　　　　　　　　　Paprika

Beat eggs, butter, milk and cheese together. Mix in croutons and carrots. Grease a baking pan. Pour in mixture. Season. Sprinkle with paprika. Bake at 400° for 20 minutes, or until browned on top.

KID-STUFF CARROTS

2   cups firm-cooked carrots, drained
2   tbs. butter
2   tbs. flour
1½ cups milk
3   tbs. chunk-style peanut butter
　　Dash Tabasco
1   tbs. onion flakes
2   tbs. chopped peanuts
　　Salt

Melt butter in skillet. Add flour. Mix to smooth paste. Add onion flakes. Allow to cook over moderately slow heat for a few minutes or until paste begins to bubble. Slowly add milk. Stir until smooth and thickened. Add peanut butter. Blend smooth. Add chopped nuts, Tabasco, and salt to taste. To heat, place carrots in greased casserole. Pour sauce over top. Heat briefly and serve.

MARMALADE CARROTS

1½ lbs. half-cooked carrots, sliced or cut into strips
3   tbs. butter
1   cup orange marmalade
½   cup water

Arrange half-cooked carrots in a lightly greased baking pan. In a saucepan, combine and heat butter, marmalade and water. Blend and heat over low heat till marmalade is thoroughly melted. Pour over carrots. Bake in preheated 350° oven, basting occasionally, for 15 or 20 minutes, until carrots are well glazed.

CARROT AND POTATO WHIP

1 *lb. carrots, trimmed, pared and cubed*	*Salt and pepper*
3 *medium potatoes, pared and cubed*	3 *tbs. butter*
	1 *egg*
1 *medium onion*	¼ *cup dairy sour cream*
	Chopped parsley

Place carrots, potatoes and onions and 1 tbs. butter in cold, lightly salted water to cover. Bring to a boil, reduce heat and simmer till done. Drain off water. Return waterless pan to low heat to evaporate off any excess remnants of moisture in vegetables. (2 or 3 minutes.) Place vegetables in blender. Add raw egg, sour cream and 2 tbs. butter. Purée. Season with salt and pepper. Pour into greased casserole and brown briefly in oven before serving or serve as is.

Variations: White turnips may be substituted for potatoes. 3 tbs. of grated cheese may be added as topping to purée before browning.

BERTHA'S CARROT KUGEL

2 *cups raw grated carrots*	1 *tsp. baking powder*
¾ *cup brown sugar*	½ *tsp. baking soda*
½ *cup oil or shortening*	¼ *tsp. salt*
1 *egg*	*Juice of 1 lemon*
1 *cup flour*	1 *tsp. cinnamon*

Cream sugar and shortening. Add egg and mix well. Combine with dry ingredients, then with juice. Grease a 9 inch ring mold. Pour pudding in. Bake in a preheated 350° oven for 25 minutes. Serve hot.

HONEY CARROT CUSTARD

¾ *cup finely chopped carrots*
½ *cup honey*
¼ *tsp. salt*
2 *tbs. dry Sherry (opt.)*
4 *eggs, beaten well*
3 *cups scalded milk*
¼ *tsp. ground nutmeg or cinnamon*

Combine eggs, honey and salt. Beat till frothy. Pour in scalded milk slowly, stirring constantly. (Make sure milk does not set eggs.) Add carrots, wine. Pour mixture into buttered individual custard cups. Sprinkle each cup with cinnamon or nutmeg. Set cups in baking pan of hot water up to the level of the custard in the cups. Bake in a preheated oven at 325° for 1 hour or until custard is firm. Serves 8–10.

LEMONY CARROT COOKIES

1 *cup brown sugar*
¾ *cup shortening*
1 *well-beaten egg*
1 *tsp. baking soda*

1 *tsp. lemon extract*
1 *cup flour*
1 *cup chopped nuts*
2 *cups chopped (raw) carrots*

Cream sugar and shortening together. Add egg and blend in. Combine with all other ingredients. Spoon batter onto greased cookie sheets. Bake in 325° oven for about 15 minutes.

FRUIT CARROT CAKE

1 *lb. carrots*
1 *cup chopped walnuts*
1 *cup chopped raisins*
  Juice and rind of 1 lemon
  Juice and rind of 1 orange
1 *tsp. cinnamon*
1 *tsp. baking soda*

2 *tsps. baking powder*
2½ *cups flour, sifted*
2 *cups sugar*
4 *eggs*
¾ *cups oil or shortening*
  Pinch of salt

Sift flour, baking powder, baking soda, salt and cinnamon together. Beat eggs well. Add sugar, oil, lemon juice and rind, orange juice and rind, carrots, nuts and raisins. Stir flour mixture into egg mixture. Pour batter into well-greased baking pan. Bake in preheated 350° oven for 45 minutes.

NIAGARA CARROT CANDY

2½ *cups cooked carrots*	1 *tsp. powdered ginger*
1 *lb. honey*	2 *tbs. sweet red wine*
3 *ozs. ground almonds*	*Pinch salt*

Place cooked carrots in a strainer. Mash and drain all liquid out. Bring honey to a slow boil over low heat, taking care not to scorch pan. Add carrots and ground almonds. Cook over low fire, stirring constantly, until mixture browns. About 30 minutes. Select a bread or cheese board. Sprinkle wine and ½ tsp. of ginger over board. Turn out carrot mixture on board and spread out evenly to ¼ inch thickness. Sprinkle top of carrot candy with sugar and the rest of the ginger. When candy has cooled but before it is completely hard, cut into serving squares.

ꙮ CAULIFLOWER

To PREPARE: Cut off the stem and any leaves. Soak in salted water, head down, for 10 minutes to remove foreign matter. If you wish to cook it whole, cut slashes in thick stalks to insure even cooking. Cauliflower may be separated into flowerettes after cooking, if desired. White head may be rubbed with ½ lemon before cooking to keep it white.

To BOIL: Place whole cauliflower in enough water to cover thickest portions of stalk, head up. Steam, partly-covered, till stalk end is tender, 10–15 minutes.

CAULIFLOWER BAKE

1 *head cauliflower*	¼ *cup fine bread crumbs*
3 *tbs. olive oil*	¼ *cup grated cheese (your*
1 *large onion, thin sliced*	*favorite type)*
Salt, pepper	

Boil or steam cauliflower till almost tender. (Cook for ⅔ normal time.) Drain. Heat oil in a skillet. Add onions and sauté till golden. Pour in crumbs. Stir until oil is evenly absorbed. Place cauliflower (whole or in flowerettes) in a baking dish. Fold over it crumb-onion mixture. Season with salt and pepper and sprinkle cheese over top. Put under broiler until cheese melts and browns top lightly.

CREAMED CAULIFLOWER, DANISH

2   *pkgs. frozen cauliflower, firm-cooked or 2 heads cauliflower, flowers only, firm-cooked*
2   *tbs. butter*
2   *tbs. flour*
1½ *cups half & half or milk*
2   *tbs. dry white wine (opt.)*
¼   *lb. Blue cheese*
    Salt and pepper
    Dash Tabasco

Drain cauliflower. Make white sauce with butter, flour and milk. Crumble cheese and add to sauce. Stir until melted. Season. Add wine, if desired. Combine cauliflower and sauce, simmer briefly. Pour into serving dish. Trim with minced celery.

MORAVIAN CAULIFLOWER AND EGGS

2 *pkgs. frozen cauliflower, firm-cooked*	4 *eggs*
	Salt and pepper
2 *tbs. butter or oil*	¼ *cup bouillon (chicken or*
1 *med. onion, thin sliced*	*vegetable)*
1 *tsp. caraway seeds*	

Heat fat in a skillet. Add caraway seeds, onion and cauliflower. Stir-fry for a few minutes till lightly colored. Beat eggs, bouillon and seasonings until frothy. Pour into skillet. Pull cooked egg away from sides and bottom of pan a few times. Reduce heat to lowest. Cover skillet and cook till eggs are set.

CAULIFLOWER IN TUNA SAUCE

1 head cauliflower, cooked	$\frac{1}{2}$ cup bread crumbs
3 tbs. butter	1 tbs. chopped parsley
$\frac{1}{4}$ cup chopped celery and leaves	Salt and pepper
	$1\frac{3}{4}$ cups milk
6 large stuffed olives, chopped	1 7 oz. can tuna, drained
2 canned pimientoes, chopped	

Melt butter in a skillet. Put in celery, olives, pimiento. Sauté until celery is softened. Add bread crumbs. Stir over low heat until all pan liquids are evenly absorbed by crumbs. Slowly add milk, stirring constantly. Season with salt, pepper and parsley. Add shredded tuna. Mix until well blended. Cook mixture, stirring frequently, over low heat for about 10 minutes. Serve over cooked whole cauliflower head. (An excellent dairy meal or Lenten entree.)

❧ CELERY

To PREPARE: Celery tops are excellent flavoring agents for soups, stew, roasts, and baked meats, poultry and fish. In preparing celery for use as a hot vegetable, however, it is advisable that the tops be removed. The stem end of the celery should be trimmed, as well. Stalks may be separated and washed or brushed under water thoroughly to remove grit. The stalks may be cooked whole, halved, diced, sliced or chopped.

To BOIL: Celery should be cooked in very little water or bouillon (about ¼ cup to each 1 cup of vegetables) till tender. (7–10 minutes.)

CELERY À LA CRÈME

6 *cups celery, cut into crescents*
2 *eggs, well beaten*
1 *cup chicken stock (or vegetable bouillon)*
1 *cup cream or half & half*
½ *cup blanched, slivered almonds*
½ *cup buttered crumbs*
    Salt and pepper

Blanch celery by placing in cold, lightly salted water and bringing it to a boil. Simmer for 3 or 4 minutes and drain. Combine eggs, stock, cream, almonds and seasoning. Mix well. Place celery in buttered oven dish. Pour egg mixture over top. Sprinkle with buttered crumbs. Bake at 350° for ½ hour. Serves 8–10.

CELERY STUFFED WITH CELERY

3 *bunches celery*
2 *ozs. fat or oil*
1 *onion, minced*
2 *cups bread crumbs*
½ *cup chopped celery*
1 *chopped carrot*

Dash garlic powder
Salt and pepper, paprika
¼ *tsp. sage (powdered)*
¼ *cup bouillon or hot water*
1 *tbs. chopped parsley*

Combine melted fat, onion, crumbs, celery, carrot, seasonings and liquid. Set aside. Trim the widest celery stalks, cut them to convenient lengths (5 or 6 inches) and place them in a pot of cold, salted water. Bring to a slow boil and drain. When cooled, stuff with above mixture, dust with paprika and dot with butter, place in broiler pan and brown under heat. Serve hot or cold.

SWEET AND SOUR CELERY

4 *cups diced celery*	*Dash pepper*
1 *cup boiling water*	2 *tbs. sugar*
1 *tsp. salt*	3 *tbs. vinegar*
1 *bay leaf*	2 *tbs. butter or oil*
3 *whole cloves*	1 *tsp. cornstarch*

Combine celery, water, salt, bay leaf, cloves, and pepper in a saucepan. Bring to a boil, reduce heat and cook, covered, until firm-tender, about 15 minutes. Remove bay leaf. Drain thoroughly. Add sugar, butter and vinegar. Cook together over low heat for 5 minutes, stirring constantly. Sprinkle with cornstarch. Stir until celery pieces are evenly coated.

CELERY WITH SMOKED SALMON

2 *lg. bunches celery, trimmed of leaves and sliced in crescents*
2 *tbs. butter*
⅓ *cup bouillon (chicken or vegetable)*
¼ *cup smoked salmon, chopped*
½ *cup grated cheese (American or Cheddar)*
   Salt and pepper to taste

Melt butter in a large skillet. Sauté celery until somewhat softened, about 5 minutes, stirring frequently. Add bouillon, salmon and seasonings. Simmer covered until tender, about 10 minutes. Drain thoroughly. Pour celery and salmon into greased baking dish. Top with cheese. Bake in hot oven (425°) until browned on top. (10–15 minutes.)

❧ *CORN*

To PREPARE: Remove shucks and all shreds of silk.

BOILED: Boil for 10 minutes in 3 quarts of lightly salted water, uncovered.

STEAMED: Steam for 20 minutes on rack over boiling water, covered.

ROASTED: Wet shucks and roast (in shucks) over fire.

BAKED: Strip off shucks, wrap tightly in foil, individually. Bake in 315° oven for about 40 minutes.

SEASONINGS FOR CORN ON THE COB

1. Seasoned salt.
2. Flavored butters: chive, garlic or onion.
3. Sour cream.
4. Grated cheese.
5. Baked corn may be rolled in French dressing or barbecue sauce before being wrapped in foil and cooked.

CORN KERNELS

Kernels may be stripped off cobs with a sharp knife and sautéed in a small amount of butter for a few minutes, or cooked in the top part of a double boiler in a small amount of milk, vegetable juice or water for a few minutes, till tender.

CORN CREOLE

¼ cup fat or oil
¼ lb. chopped, fried bacon or beef fry (opt.)
2 large onions, sliced
1 green pepper, diced
1 clove garlic
1 #2 can tomatoes, diced
3 cups corn kernels, drained

½ cup chopped cooked mushrooms (opt.)
1 bay leaf
1 tsp. chili powder
Pinch powdered cloves
1 tsp. sugar (brown, preferably)
Salt and Tabasco

Heat fat in skillet. Sauté onion, pepper, mushrooms and garlic till onions turn golden. Add tomatoes, bay leaf and seasonings. Cook until tomatoes disintegrate. Remove bay leaf. Add corn and simmer till corn is hot. Serve as side dish or main course with grilled sausages.

CORN SAUTÉ

1 *can corn kernels, drained*
½ *cup green pepper, chopped*
1 *onion, chopped*
4 *slices bacon or beef fry*
  (opt.)

Dash garlic powder
Salt and pepper
2 *tbs. fat or oil*

Heat oil in a skillet. Sauté pepper and onions until soft. Add corn and seasoning. Stir-fry until golden. Fry out bacon or beef fry in a separate pan. Drain well. Crumble and use as garnish.

COLONIAL STYLE CORN STUFFING

3 *cups bread croutons*
¼ *cup fat or oil*
1½ *cups chicken bouillon*
1 *#2 can creamed corn*
1 *#2 can corn kernels,*
  drained
1 *large onion, chopped*
2 *chopped carrots*

½ *tsp. garlic powder*
¼ *tsp. ground sage*
¼ *tsp. crushed oregano*
¼ *tsp. ground ginger*
2 *eggs, well beaten*
  Salt to taste, pepper
¼ *lb. chopped fried out*
  bacon or beef fry (opt.)

Sauté onion and carrots in fat until soft. Add croutons, stirring frequently, and fry until all pan oils are absorbed and croutons are lightly toasted. Remove to mixing bowl. Add bouillon and all other ingredients. Pour into buttered baking pan. Trim with thin raw carrot slices. Bake in 350° oven for about 1 hour.

CORN MEAL DUMPLINGS (KNAIDLECH)

4 *eggs, separated*
1 *cup corn meal*
½ *cup flour*
1 *tsp. baking powder*
½ *tsp. baking soda*

1 *heaping tbs. chopped*
  parsley
½ *tsp. powdered ginger*
  Salt to taste

Beat egg whites until stiff. Add yolks and blend in. Add other ingredients, one at a time, and blend thoroughly. Allow batter to chill (in the refrigerator) for about 20 minutes. Wet hands and form dough into small balls. Drop into 2 quarts slowly boiling, salted water. Simmer over moderately low heat until balls are fluffy and floating on top of pot. Serve in soup or with corn creole and sausages. Leftover cooked dumplings may be placed in a greased casserole and baked with a meat or tomato sauce on top. Dumplings will absorb liquid and take shape of pan.

MODERN DAY CORN PUDDING

1   *can corn kernels*
1   *can French fried onions*
1½ *cups grated Cheddar-type cheese*
1   *cup milk or half & half*

3   *eggs, well beaten*
1   *cup corn flakes, crushed*
    Salt, Tabasco
½   *tsp. mustard powder*

Blend well. Pour into greased baking mold. Place in pan of hot water in preheated oven. Bake at 350° for 1 hour.

AMERICAN CORN FONDUE

2   *tbs. butter*
2   *tbs. flour*
1   *cup mlk*
1½ *cups grated Swiss-style cheese*
1   *#2 can creamed corn*
1   *tsp. salt*
½   *tsp. sugar*

    Dash Tabasco
2   *tbs. dry white wine (opt.)*
¼   *cup chopped pimiento (opt.)*
¼   *cup frozen cooked green peas (opt.)*
¼   *tsp. ground nutmeg*

Melt butter in top part of double boiler. Mix in flour and blend to a smooth paste. Slowly add milk, mixing constantly. Continue stirring until thickened. Add corn and cheese. Stir frequently till cheese is thoroughly melted. Add seasonings and wine. Pour into a chafing dish. Garnish with pimiento and peas. Serve with cubes of Jubilation Corn Pone. Guests skewer cubes on forks, dip into fondue and eat. Excellent for teenage parties or as hors d'oeuvres with cocktails.

JUBILATION CORN PONE

3 *eggs, beaten*
½ *cup sugar*
1 *tsp. salt*
1 *cup dairy sour cream*
1 *cup corn meal*

1 *cup flour*
1 *tsp. baking soda*
1 *tsp. baking powder*
¼ *tsp. ginger*
  Dash nutmeg

Mix together all ingredients until well blended. Add baking powder last. Beat with rotary beater until frothy. Bake in a greased square baking pan at 350° for ½ hour. Cool in pan.

CORN PIE

1 *unbaked pie shell*
3 *cups corn kernels (fresh or canned), drained*
1 *tsp. salt*
½ *cup minced pimiento*

½ *tsp. sugar*
  Dash pepper
1 *tbs. butter, melted*
2 *tbs. flour and 2 tbs. water*
1 *cup thin white sauce*

Combine corn, salt, pimiento, sugar, pepper, butter, flour and water. Pour into pie shell. Pour white sauce over pie. Bake in 400° oven for about 45 minutes or until center is set. Serve hot or cold.

❧ CUCUMBERS

To PREPARE: Cucumbers may be eaten in the skin if no commercial wax coating has been applied. For cooking, I like to remove the center seeds. Cucumbers may be salted, drained and cooked, or simply boiled and baked, sautéed, roasted or stewed. Cucumbers can be used as flavoring for other cooked foods in the same manner as celery.

To BOIL: Cook cucumbers as you would summer squash (page 244).

CUCUMBERS WITH TOMATOES AND DILL

1 *tsp. salt*
3 *cucumbers*
1 *large onion*
2 *tbs. olive oil*
  Dash garlic powder (opt.)

½ *cup chopped olives*
3 *ripe tomatoes, diced*
½ *cup chicken or vegetable*
  bouillon
2 *tbs. chopped dill*

Pare and quarter cucumbers. Remove seeds and cut each quarter into 3–4 inch sticks. Heat oil in pan. Sauté onions until soft. Add tomatoes, dill, garlic, olives, bouillon and cucumbers. Simmer for 5–10 minutes or until cucumbers are firm but cooked.

BAKED STUFFED CUCUMBERS

6 *large cucumbers*
1½ *cups medium white sauce*
½ *cup grated Cheddar cheese*
1 *tbs. chopped parsley*
4 *hard-boiled eggs, diced*
¼ *cup buttered crumbs*
6 *anchovy fillets, cut in half*

Pare and halve cucumbers. Remove seeds. Drop in boiling salted water and allow to cool in water. Drain. Combine eggs, sauce, cheese, and parsley. Spoon into cucumber shells. Top with crumbs and ½ anchovy fillet each. Place stuffed shells on greased baking sheet or in pan and bake at 350° for about 20 minutes.

CUCUMBERS, CHINESE-STYLE

2 *tbs. corn or peanut oil*
3 *large cucumbers*
½ *cup chopped peanuts*
2 *onions, chopped coarsely*
1 *tsp. salt*

2 *tbs. soya sauce*
½ *cup beef bouillon*
1 *clove garlic, minced*
1 *tsp. cornstarch and water*

Pare and quarter cucumbers. Remove seeds from center. Dice. Place in a strainer or colander. Sprinkle with salt and toss so all pieces are coated. Allow to drain in sink for 15 minutes. Place oil, bouillon, soya sauce, cucumbers, peanuts, onions and garlic in skillet. Bring to a boil over high heat. Reduce heat to lowest and simmer for 2 or 3 minutes, covered. Add cornstarch and 1 tbs. water. Stir till thickened. Serve.

᠅ EGGPLANT

To PREPARE: Eggplants may be peeled and pared, sliced or cubed before cooking or baked in the skin, plunged in cold water and peeled after. The latter method is particularly efficient when you wish to incorporate cooked eggplant into a recipe. Eggplant absorbs water and fat readily. For this reason, in a dish where eggs, flour or starch will not thicken your recipe during cooking, eggplant should be cut and drained of surplus liquid before cooking. It is a good idea to drain eggplant before frying to cut down the amount of fat the eggplant will absorb. There are two methods you may use to drain peeled and cut eggplant. You may lightly salt eggplant pieces and place them on a rack (in the sink or over a pan) to drain. You may also stack eggplant pieces on a rack or in a colander, place a plate with a heavy object on it above vegetable and allow to drain. ½ hour should be adequate draining time. To prevent eggplant pieces from discoloring after cutting, rub pieces with lemon juice.

To STEW: Cook pared, cut eggplant in a small amount of lightly salted water, covered, for about 10 minutes. Drain well.

BAKED HALVED EGGPLANT

2 *medium eggplants*	½ *pkg. onion soup mix*
¼ *cup olive or corn oil*	*Salt and pepper*
2 *cloves garlic*	2 *tbs. chopped parsley*
½ *cup bread crumbs*	1 *tbs. butter or margarine*
¼ *cup hot water*	

Wash and dry eggplants. Cut in half, lengthwise. Cut the flesh side with deep, crisscross gashes over the entire surface. Heat oil in skillet. Sauté the halves, cut side down, in oil for 5–10 minutes or until soft and somewhat mushy. Purée by mashing or in a blender: garlic, bread crumbs, water, soup mix and salt and pepper. With a butter knife, spread this mixture over the surface of each eggplant face. Dust with parsley and dot with butter. Bake in a greased baking pan at 350° for about ½ hour.

EGGPLANT POTATO WHIP

2 cups leftover mashed
  potatoes
1 medium eggplant
½ cup minced, fried ham or
  smoked salmon
3 tbs. fat or oil

1 onion chopped
1 tbs. fresh chopped dill
¼ tsp. garlic powder (opt.)
¼ cup boiling water, salted
  Salt and pepper
2 eggs, well beaten

Peel and cube eggplant. Boil in small amount of water till soft. Drain well. Sauté onion, meat or fish in oil. When soft, add water and eggplant. Cook till mushy. Remove from heat. Combine potatoes, eggplant, dill, garlic powder, salt, pepper and eggs. Mix well. Pour into a greased casserole, reheat in oven till puffy. Serve hot.

BABA GHANOUJ

1 large eggplant
⅓ cup sesame seed dressing*
2 tbs. olive oil
1 clove garlic
  Juice of ½ to 1 whole lemon (to taste)
  Salt, pepper and paprika
2 tbs. chopped parsley
  Dash Tabasco (opt.)

* Sesame seed dressing, called Techina, is available at Near-Eastern food specialty shops.

Bake eggplant in skin in the oven at 400° for about 1 hour or until pulp is quite soft and eggplant has a collapsed appearance. Remove skin. Place eggplant meat and all other ingredients in a blender. Purée. Adjust seasoning. Pour into serving bowl. Garnish with additional chopped parsley, paprika, and 1 more tbs. olive oil drizzled over top. Serve on lettuce or as a dip with breads. (The traditional Arab bread to serve with this dish is Hibis.)

HOME-STYLE EGGPLANT SOUFFLÉ

3–4 *ozs. butter or oil*
1 *large eggplant*
6 *slices white bread, lightly toasted*
6 *slices Cheddar or American cheese*
1 *cup milk*
3 *eggs*
  Salt and pepper
  Dash Tabasco

Peel eggplant. Slice thin down the length. Place in dish with a weight above to drain for ½ hour. Heat 2 tbs. of oil at a time in skillet. Brown eggplant slices on both sides in oil. Drain on absorbent paper. Fry toast in a little oil briefly, till color deepens. Place 1 layer of eggplant slices in casserole pot. Cover with 2 slices fried bread and 2 slices cheese. Repeat layers, ending with bread and cheese. Combine eggs, milk and seasonings. (Be sure to season well.) Pour over dish. Set in pan of hot water and bake at 350° for 35–40 minutes.

BROILED EGGPLANT STEAKS

1 *eggplant, thick-sliced in*
  skin
2 *tbs. wine vinegar*
  Dash garlic powder

¼ *tsp. mustard powder*
  Pinch crushed dry basil
  Salt and pepper, paprika
6 *tbs. olive oil*

Salt eggplant slices lightly. Allow to drain. Combine dressing ingredients: vinegar, seasonings, and oil. Immerse eggplant slices in dressing, making sure both sides are coated. Marinate for ½ hour. Place in broiler pan. Broil for 15–20 minutes (turning once) under hot flame until done.

EGGPLANT WITH CHICK-PEAS IN OIL

2 *medium onions*	*Salt and pepper*
2 *medium eggplants, peeled*	1 *tsp. sugar*
1 *medium can chick-peas,*	¼ *cup olive oil*
drained	2 *tbs. fresh chopped parsley*
4 *ozs. tomato paste*	1 *clove garlic, crushed (opt.)*
2 *cups hot water*	

Heat oil in large skillet. Fry onions until soft. Add eggplant cut in chunks and allow to cook until soft, stirring frequently. Add chick-peas and allow to cook for 5 minutes. Combine paste, water, salt and pepper, parsley, garlic, sugar and pour over other ingredients. Cook over low heat for about ½ hour. Re-season and serve.

THE SHEIK'S FAVORITE EGGPLANT

2 *large eggplants*	½ *to 1 tbs. allspice (to taste)*
1 *lb. chopped beef or lamb*	3 *ozs. tomato paste*
2 *ozs. pine nuts (or chopped*	2 *cups boiling water*
peanuts)	*Salt and pepper*
3 *medium onions, chopped*	½ *tsp. sugar*
5 *tbs. fat or oil*	

Peel eggplants and slice them ½ to ¾ inches thick. Sprinkle them lightly with salt. Allow to drain for 5 minutes. Place 3 tbs. fat or oil in skillet. Sauté eggplant slices till golden on both sides. (Add more oil as needed.) Drain slices to eliminate excess oil. Place 2 more tbs. fat or oil in the skillet. Add meat, onions, pine nuts, allspice and some salt and pepper. Fry until onions are transparent and meat is cooked, stirring constantly. Make a layer of eggplant slices at the bottom of a large baking pan. Spread some of the meat-onion mixture over top. Repeat layers till all ingre-

dients are used. Combine tomato paste, hot water, sugar and salt
and pepper to taste. Pour over dish. Bake in 375° oven for about
30 minutes, or until eggplant is quite soft and most of liquid has
been absorbed.

EGGPLANT WITH EGGS, SPANISH STYLE

1 *eggplant, cubed*
1 *onion, coarse-chopped*
1 *green pepper, coarse-chopped*
2 *ripe tomatoes*
½ *cup Greek or Italian-style black olives (rinsed and drained),*
   chopped
3 *eggs, well beaten and seasoned*
5 *tbs. olive oil or corn oil*
½ *cup water*
   Salt and pepper

Stew eggplant in a covered saucepan containing 3 tbs. oil and
½ cup water. Sauté onion and pepper in 2 tbs. oil in a skillet.
When soft but not brown, add tomatoes and olives. Simmer until
tomatoes cook down, about 5 minutes. Add eggplant and cook
together for a few minutes. Season with pepper and salt. Pour
eggs over eggplant mixture. Cover pan and cook over lowest heat
until eggs set. (A few minutes.) Remove from heat and garnish
with fresh chopped parsley.

CREAMED EGGPLANT WITH MUSHROOMS

1 *large eggplant*
1 *onion, chopped*
½ *cup mushrooms, chopped (canned or fresh)*
3 *tbs. fat or oil*
¼ *cup grated Cheddar-type cheese*
2 *tbs. dry wine (red or white, or Sherry)*
1 *cup dairy sour cream*
   Salt and pepper

Peel and cube eggplant. Sauté onion and mushrooms in fat or oil until soft. Add the eggplant and wine. Stew until eggplant is thoroughly cooked. Stir frequently. Put mixture into a baking dish. Season with salt and pepper. Add sour cream and top with grated cheese. Heat in 350° oven until top is brown and cheese has melted. (15–20 minutes.)

CONFETTI STUFFED EGGPLANT

2 *medium eggplants*
1 *green pepper, diced*
1 *onion, coarse chopped*
1 *cup diced sausage meat*
  stripped of casings

1–3 *tbs. olive oil*
1 *tbs. celery flakes*
¼ *tsp. marjoram*
2 *cups cooked rice*
Salt

Place whole eggplants in boiling water for about 10 minutes. Remove and dry. Cut in half, lengthwise. Carefully scoop out eggplant flesh, making sure to leave enough meat on the shell to keep it firm. Heat 3 tbs. oil in a large skillet. Add eggplant meat, pepper, onion and sausage meat. Cook over moderate heat till eggplant is soft. Stir frequently. Combine eggplant mixture with rice. Add 1 tbs. more oil, and all seasonings. Salt to taste. Bake in 375° oven for 15–20 minutes, until sizzling hot.

Variation: Substitute ground beef or veal for sausage meat.

EGGPLANT POLENTA

4 *ozs. oil*
1 *large eggplant*
¾ *cup corn meal*
1 *6 oz. can tomato paste*
4 *cups hot water*
1 *medium chopped onion*

6 *rashers fried-out bacon or*
  beef fry
¼ *tsp. garlic powder (opt.)*
Salt and pepper, 1 tsp.
  sugar
Seasoned salt

Slice eggplant into ½ inch slices. Salt slices lightly and allow to drain for about 15 minutes. Place 1 tsp. oil on the bottom of a 2½ quart baking dish. Combine corn meal, fat or oil and chopped

onion. Spread a thin layer of meal mixture over eggplant. Sprinkle
with seasoned salt and place 1 rasher of bacon on each eggplant
piece. Repeat layers, ending with meal and bacon. Combine
tomato paste, hot water, garlic powder, salt and pepper to taste
and sugar. Pour over dish. Bake, covered, in 350° oven until most
of liquid is absorbed, about 1½ hours. Uncover, and brown ½ hour
in oven.

EGGPLANT SOUFFLÉ

1 *large eggplant*
1 *cup medium white sauce*
½ *cup grated sharp cheese*
¼ *tsp. onion powder*
2 *tbs. catsup*

¼ *tsp. marjoram (opt.)*
3 *eggs, separated*
  Salt to taste
  Dash Tabasco

Pare eggplant. Cut into 1 inch cubes. Cook till tender in lightly
salted, boiling water just covering cubes. Drain in a sieve, pressing out all excess liquid with the back of a tablespoon. Purée
through a sieve or in a blender. Add grated cheese to white sauce
and heat till melted in top part of double boiler. Combine with
onion, marjoram and egg yolks. Cool. Beat egg whites till stiff
and in peaks. Carefully fold into mixture. Pour into well-greased
baking dish. Place dish in a pan of hot water in the oven at 350°
for about 45 minutes, or until center is firm.

❧ FENNEL

Fennel is a celery-like plant usually seen in this country in
Italian markets. It has a characteristic anise (or licorice) flavor.
It can be served raw as part of a salad, stuffed or plain for an
hors d'oeuvre or added to cooked foods in place of celery where
anise flavor is desirable. The leaves, like celery, are excellent
flavoring agents. They should be used discreetly, however.

To PREPARE: Use as you would celery.

❧ GREENS

THESE ARE: Mustard, dandelion, beet, turnip greens, kale, escarole, spinach, chicory, Swiss chard.

To PREPARE: Greens must be cleaned carefully as they are likely to come to market full of grit and dirt. First, trim off the root end and any tough or overlarge stalks near the root. Remove all discolored or bruised leaves. Wash repeatedly by immersing in a large bowl of tepid water. Change water once and repeat. Separate leaves and run under cold water from faucet. Do not drain.

To BOIL: Each type of greens requires a different cooking period. (See boiling guide on page 14.) The water clinging to the leaves is usually sufficient liquid in which to cook greens.

NOTE: The recipes included here for greens are generally useful for all varieties unless otherwise indicated.

SAVORY GREENS

2 *tbs. fresh greens: turnip tops, beet tops, kale or chard, in combination or singly*
4 *rashers bacon or beef fry*
1 *large onion, chopped*
½ *cup croutons*
  Salt and pepper

Cook greens in small amount of water (according to boiling instructions) till tender. Drain. Fry out bacon or beef fry. Remove, drain and crumble. Fry onion in 2 tbs. fat (or substitute 2 tbs. light oil, if preferred). When onion is soft, add croutons and stir till all oil is absorbed and bread is lightly browned. (Stale rye bread with seeds makes excellent croutons for this dish.) Season with salt and pepper. Pour over greens. Add crumbled meat. Serve hot.

GREENS VINAIGRETTE

3 *cups cooked, drained*
  greens
¼ *cup wine vinegar*
¾ *cup olive oil*
1 *tsp. mustard powder*
1 *hard-boiled egg, chopped*

1 *clove garlic, split*
2 *tbs. pickle relish (opt.)*
2 *tbs. chopped pimiento*
  Salt and pepper to taste
1 *tbs. minced chives or*
  scallions

Place in a tightly covered container: oil, vinegar, mustard, chopped egg, pimiento, scallions or chives and pickle relish. Close container and shake well. Pour over greens. Add split garlic clove, season to taste and chill overnight or half a day. Drain and serve as a salad or appetizer.

SPICY GREENS

1 *lb. corned beef*
1 *clove garlic, split*
1 *bay leaf*

3–4 *juniper berries (opt.)*
1½ *lbs. greens*
  Salt and pepper

Boil meat with bay leaf, garlic, berries for about 1½ hours till soft. Skim off scum that forms on top. Remove meat, cool and slice. Set aside. Simmer trimmed greens in a small amount of meat water. Serve over sliced meat with potatoes and carrots that have also been cooked in meat water on the side. Serves 4.

SAVORY SPINACH CROQUETTES

2 *pkgs. frozen chopped spinach, cooked, or 2 cups chopped,*
  cooked fresh spinach
2 *eggs*
1 *small onion, chopped (or ½ medium)*
¼ *cup cooked mushroom pieces*
3 *eggs, well beaten*
4 *tbs. bread crumbs*
  Salt and pepper
¼ *tsp. marjoram*

Press par-cooked spinach through a sieve to eliminate all excess water. When dry, combine with all ingredients. Mix well. Season to taste. Spoon onto well-greased hot skillet. Brown on both sides. Drain on absorbent paper.

Variation: Use half chopped spinach and half corn or half spinach and half mashed potatoes. Substitute carrots for mushrooms. Substitute chopped peanuts for onion.

SPINACH CUSTARD

2 *cups chopped, cooked spinach, well drained*
2 *cups milk or light cream*
3 *eggs, well beaten*
1 *small grated onion*
¼ *tsp. grated nutmeg*
  Salt and pepper to taste

Combine ingredients. Beat together with a wooden spoon till frothy. Pour into a greased loaf pan. Place pan in a tray of hot water. Bake in preheated oven at 350° till custard is set, 45 minutes–1 hour. Slice and serve. Serves 6–8.

GREEN CUSTARD PIE

1 *baked pie shell**
2 *lbs. spinach or mixed greens*
3 *tbs. butter*
½ *cup milk*
  Salt and pepper
2 *tbs. onion flakes*
¼ *tsp. mace*
3 *egg yolks*
1 *cup half & half (or rich milk)*
⅓ *cup fine white bread crumbs*

Clean, remove stems and chop greens. Cook with milk, butter and salt and pepper over low heat till tender (5 to 15 minutes, depending on greens selected). Drain greens and onion thoroughly and put into pie shell or greased pie plate. Beat together milk or cream, yolks and seasonings. Pour over greens. Sprinkle top with crumbs. Bake in 350° oven until set, 30 minutes or more.

* This dish can be made in a greased pie plate without a shell, as well.

SPINACH, RICE AND CHEESE

2 *lbs. fresh spinach or 2 pkgs.*   1 *cup chopped tomatoes*
  frozen chopped   2 *tbs. grated onon*
1 *cup milk*   2 *tbs. catsup*
¾ *cup Cheddar cheese*   3 *eggs, well beaten*
2 *cups firm-cooked rice*   *Salt and pepper*

Thaw frozen spinach (don't cook) in boiling water. Drain, pressing out as much water as possible. For fresh spinach, remove stems after cleaning and chop leaves fine. Combine all ingredients. Season to taste. Pour into a baking pan. Dot top with butter. Place in pan of hot water and bake till set (30–40 minutes).

Variation: Substitute macaroni for rice.

CHARD WITH NUTS AND RAISINS

1 *small onion*
2 *bunches Swiss chard*
3 *tbs. butter or oil*
½ *cup raisins*
¼ *cup pignolas or chopped peanuts*
  Salt to taste
¼ *tsp. cinnamon or mace*

Clean and remove stems from chard. Cook for about 10 minutes, covered, in a small amount of water. Remove and drain well. Heat oil in skillet. Add onions, raisins and nuts. When nuts are lightly browned and onions are soft, add chard and cook, covered, over moderate heat for about 15 minutes or till tender. Serve.

CARAWAY GREENS WITH CRUMBS

2 *lbs. fresh greens*   1 *tbs. caraway seeds*
4 *tbs. olive oil or butter*   *Salt, paprika*
½ *cup fine bread crumbs*   *Sour cream (opt.)*

Clean greens. Remove stems and cut leaves into pieces. Remove excess water from leaves. Heat oil in skillet; when hot, add seeds and crumbs. When they are brown, add greens, stirring until they cook down. If they are long-cooking greens, cover and allow to simmer till tender. Season. Serve with sour cream on the side.

Variation: Add garlic (remove it when it turns brown) or onion or sesame seeds in place of caraway. Serve with lemon juice (fresh) instead of sour cream.

CHINESE GREENS

2 *lbs. greens, well drained*
3 *tbs. oil*
1 *clove garlic, split*
1 *tbs. gin*
¼ *tsp. MSG*
  Salt to taste

⅓ *cup chicken, beef or*
  vegetable bouillon
1 *tsp. cornstarch and 1 tbs.*
  water
1 *tbs. soya sauce*
  Dash powdered ginger (opt.)

Heat oil and garlic in skillet, when garlic starts to brown, remove. Add cut up greens and stir-fry for a few minutes. Add all other ingredients except cornstarch and water. Cook, stirring constantly, until greens cook down. Add cornstarch and water. Mix in and cook uncovered till liquid thickens. (Particularly good with mustard greens.)

MEDITERRANEAN SPINACH

1½ *lb. fresh spinach*
1-2 *cloves garlic, split in half*
4 *tbs. olive oil*

  Salt and pepper
  Lemon wedges
2 *tbs. chopped scallions*

Wash spinach thoroughly. Drain off excess moisture but allow some water to cling to leaves. Heat oil in skillet. Sauté onion till soft and garlic till browned. Remove garlic cloves. Add ⅓ spinach to skillet. As this wilts, add more and stir up cooked part from bottom of skillet. Continue until all is cooked down. When leaves are limp but still deep green in color, remove to serving dish. Serve with lemon wedges and a sprinkling of scallions on top.

CREAMED SPINACH

2 pkgs. frozen chopped spinach or 2 lbs. fresh spinach
3 ozs. sweet butter
2 tbs. minced celery (or celery flakes)
¼ tsp. chervil or tarragon
½ tsp. sugar
½ cup cream (sweet or sour)
1 egg yolk
    Salt and pepper

If fresh, clean and drain spinach. Remove stems and chop leaves. If frozen, cook as directed but 2 minutes less than package indicates. Place fresh chopped leaves in skillet with melted butter. Cook until moisture evaporates and spinach is cooked. Stir frequently. Add all other ingredients and season to taste. (Do not boil after addition of cream.) Simmer gently for 5–10 minutes.

Variation: Substitute onion for celery. Add 1 tbs. dry Sherry to final cooking moments. Serve with hard-boiled eggs.

COUNTRY SPINACH COOKED IN MILK*

2 lbs. spinach
½ cup milk
1 tbs. butter (opt.)

Salt and pepper
¼ tsp. mace or nutmeg

Wash fresh spinach in many waters. Blot leaves between 2 kitchen towels. (The traditional way is to place leaves in a cloth bag and whirl the bag of spinach around your head outdoors repeatedly until the leaves are dry.) Bring the milk to a boil. (Remove any scum that forms on top.) Add spinach leaves and mace or nutmeg. Cook over moderate heat briefly, until leaves begin to wilt. Remove from milk, cut into bite-size pieces, season with salt and pepper and serve. Butter may be added before serving, if desired.

* The value of this cooking method is that most of the spinach acids are removed in the process and the flavor is mellow and smooth.

SPINACH PASTRIES

2 *cans refrigerated crescent roll dough*
1½ *cups chopped, cooked spinach*
1 *cup grated Cheddar or American cheese*
   Salt and pepper
2 *scallions, chopped*
1 *egg*

Follow directions and roll out dough. Combine well-drained spinach, cheese, scallions, salt and pepper and egg. Mix well. Place 2 or 3 tbs. of filling mixture in center of triangle and close dough around center securely. Place on cookie sheets. Bake 10 minutes longer than roll packages direct, or until well browned on top. Serve hot.

❧ *KOHLRABI*

To PREPARE: Trim tops and pare bulbous roots. Cook them whole or cubed.

To BOIL: Cook in boiling salted water, uncovered, till soft. (About ½ hour for cubed kohlrabi and longer for whole ones.)

STUFFED KOHLRABIS

2 *bunches medium size*
   kohlrabis
1 *lb. ground veal*
4 *ozs. fine white bread*
   crumbs
½ *cup thick white sauce*
½ *tsp. sugar*
1 *egg*
½ *tsp. nutmeg*

1 *tbs. chopped parsley*
1 *tbs. minced onion*
2 *tbs. lemon juice*
   Salt
3 *ozs. butter or oil*
½ *cup light broth or bouillon*
   (chicken or vegetable)
2 *tbs. fat and 2 tbs. flour*

Pare and trim kohlrabis. Scoop out insides and reserve, leaving thick enough shell not to collapse in cooking. Parboil shells in lightly salted water for 10 minutes. Drain. Combine meat, crumbs, sauce, salt, nutmeg, parsley, onion, 1 tbs. lemon juice and 1 oz. fat. Stuff kohlrabis. Place 2 ozs. fat in wide-bottomed pan. Layer pan with stuffed kohlrabis, tiering them if necessary. Add ½ cup broth, 1 tbs. lemon juice, salt, sugar and nutmeg. Cover pan and simmer until kohlrabis are tender. Remove from pan and set aside. Heat liquids in pan. Add flour and 1 tbs. fat. Cook till thickened. If desired, you may add 1 cup sweet or sour cream to pan. Use as a sauce to serve over kohlrabis. Serve hot. Serves 6–8.

BRAISED KOHLRABI AND TOMATOES

2 *bunches kohlrabi, cubed*	½ *cup light bouillon*
5 *ripe tomatoes, diced, or*	1 *onion, chopped*
1 #2 *can tomatoes*	*Salt, pepper, paprika*
¼ *cup fat or oil*	¼ *tsp. cumin powder (opt.)*

Heat oil in skillet. Sauté onion till soft. Add tomatoes and cook about 5 minutes over moderate heat. Add kohlrabi, bouillon, salt, pepper, paprika and cumin. Cover and simmer till tender, about 25 minutes.

MASHED KOHLRABI

2 *cups diced, cooked kohlrabi*
⅓ *cup rich milk or sour cream*
   Salt and pepper
2 *tbs. butter*

Boil according to boiling directions, page 14. Mash with a fork. Add butter and milk or sour cream, salt and pepper, grated onion or celery (if desired), caraway, poppy seeds or nutmeg.

KOHLRABI PANCAKES

2 *cups mashed kohlrabis*
⅓ *cup rich milk and 5 tbs.*
  bread crumbs
2 *eggs*
1 *small onion, chopped*

1 *celery stalk, chopped*
½ *cup dry curd cheese*
2 *tbs. fat*
  Salt and pepper to taste

Combine all ingredients. Fry in hot fat in skillet till brown on both sides.

❧ LEEKS

To PREPARE: Remove roots and wilted green leaves. Wash thoroughly as sand is likely to have penetrated to the innermost leaves. Cook whole, split in half or cut into 1 inch pieces.

To BOIL: Cook, uncovered, in boiling salted water to cover for about 20 minutes.

OTHER METHODS: Leeks may be prepared in much the same way as celery and asparagus.

LEEKS IN LEMON CREAM

10 *leeks, sliced in 1 inch pieces, green leaves removed*
½   *cup chicken or vegetable bouillon*
    Juice of ½ lemon
2   *tbs. butter*
2   *tbs. dry Sherry*
1   *egg*
¼   *cup cream or milk substitute*
    Salt to taste

Simmer leeks in bouillon, lemon juice, butter and Sherry for 12–15 minutes, until tender. Beat together egg and cream. Add ½ cup hot cooking liquid to egg mixture, gradually, stirring constantly. Slowly pour onto leeks and blend well. Simmer for a few moments to thicken cream. Serve hot as a side dish. Excellent with fish and poultry.

  Variation: Add 1 cup sliced fresh mushrooms and cook with leeks.

BRAISED LEEKS WITH MUSHROOMS

10–12 *leeks, sliced in 1 inch pieces, greens removed*
¼ *cup olive oil*
¼ *cup light broth or boiling water*
1 *tbs. lemon juice*
½ *lb. fresh or canned mushrooms, sliced or diced*
2 *cloves garlic, split*
  Salt and pepper
1 *bay leaf (opt.)*

Simmer to boiling point: oil, broth, juice, garlic, bay leaf. Add sliced leeks and mushrooms and reduce heat. Cover and cook for about 15 minutes over moderate heat. Remove bay leaf and garlic and serve.

LEEK PIE

1 *recipe leeks in lemon cream (page 208)*
2 *cups ricotta or dry curd cottage cheese*
3 *eggs*
  Salt to taste

Grease a pie plate. Dust plate with bread crumbs. Combine recipe with cheese and additional eggs. Beat together well. Salt to taste. Bake in 375° oven till set. (About 40 minutes.)

❧ LENTILS, DRY BEANS, PEAS

THESE INCLUDE: Dry limas, cream and orange lentils, favas, white mottled and red kidney beans, pea beans, chick-peas, split peas, etc.

TO PREPARE: Wash and sort through for foreign particles. Remove these. Dry beans should be soaked overnight to soften and then cooked in water to cover till tender. Each variety of beans requires a different cooking. Naturally, the smaller the bean, the less cooking required. After cooking, drain and use for recipes.

LENTIL CUTLETS

1 *cup lentils*
1 *cup water*
¼ *tsp. powdered ginger*
1 *medium onion*
  Dash cayenne pepper
1 *tsp. crushed mint leaves*
  (opt.)

Salt and pepper
⅓ *cup bread crumbs*
1 *beaten egg*
  Hot oil

Soak lentils in water for about 1 hour. Boil the lentils in the same water till soft. Add hot water as lentils dry down in cooking. Drain. Pour into a blender with onion, mint leaves, pepper and salt. Purée. Pour into mixing bowl. With wet hands, shape patties. Dip first in egg and then in crumbs. Fry in hot oil till brown on both sides.

PEA OR BEAN PURÉE

2 *cups dry beans, soaked overnight*
1 *bay leaf*
1 *medium onion, quartered*
½ *cup dairy sour cream or plain yoghurt*
  Salt and pepper
¼ *tsp. hot paprika or regular*
  Good dash Tabasco

Simmer beans, onion and bay leaf in water to cover until beans are tender. Drain and remove bay leaf. Purée in a blender beans, onion and seasonings. Fold into sour cream. Re-season if necessary. Heat in oven briefly and serve.

LEBANESE BEAN APPETIZER

2 *cups dry beans (your choice), soaked overnight*
2 *cloves garlic, pressed*
2 *tbs. chopped parsley*
1 *tsp. dry crushed mint leaves*
  Juice of 2 lemons
1 *sweet onion, sliced fine*
  Salt and pepper

Cook beans in water to cover for about 1½ hours or until soft. Pour the hot beans into a serving dish. Combine pressed garlic, parsley, mint, lemon juice and salt and pepper. Mix beans with onion slices. Pour dressing over beans. Serve hot or chilled.

DAHL OR INDIAN BEANS

1½ *cups yellow split peas or lentils*
3 *tbs. butter or light oil*
1 *bay leaf*
1 *tsp. caraway seeds (or fennel)*
2 *tbs. minced onion (dry flakes or fresh)*
1 *quart and 1 cup water*
¼ *cup lemon juice*
  Rind of ½ lemon
1 *tbs. curry powder*
1 *tsp. salt or more to taste*

Wash peas or lentils. Melt butter in deep soup pot. Add peas, bay leaf and caraway. Stir-fry for 2 minutes. Add 3 cups water and bring to a boil. Reduce heat and add onion, curry, lemon juice, rind and salt. Simmer, uncovered, till water is absorbed, stirring frequently. Add 2 cups more hot water. Cook until water is gone and peas are purée consistency. Remove bay leaf and lemon rind. Serve over rice and with other braised vegetables.

HUMMOUS

1 *medium can chick-peas*
  with liquid
1 *clove garlic*
¼ *cup Techina (sesame seed*
  dressing)
  Juice of ½–1 lemon (to taste)

2 *tbs. olive oil*
  Salt, pepper
1 *tbs. chopped parsley*
  Paprika
  Additional olive oil

Heat chick-peas in liquid from can for 5 minutes. Cool and pour into blender (liquid and peas). Add garlic, Techina, lemon juice, oil, salt and pepper. Blend to purée consistency. Pour into wide, flat serving dish. Dribble some oil over top (to retard hardening of surface on standing). Sprinkle with chopped parsley and paprika. Serve as a spread for crackers or a dip with Arab or other breads.

CREAMED LENTILS WITH CHEESE AND WINE

1 *cup lentils, soaked overnight*
2 *tbs. butter*
1 *heaping tbs. flour*
¾ *cup milk or half & half*
1 *cup grated Cheddar cheese*
¼ *cup dry white wine*
¼ *tsp. allspice (powdered)*
¼ *cup chopped celery*
  Salt to taste

Drain lentils. Pour into saucepan with fresh cold water to cover. Simmer till soft. (15–20 minutes.) Drain. Melt 2 tbs. butter in top of a double boiler. Add flour and blend well. Gradually stir in milk, cheese, wine, salt, and allspice. Combine lentils, chopped celery and cheese sauce. Butter a baking dish. Pour mixture into it. Bake in oven at 350° for ½ hour.

Variation: Substitute dry yellow split peas for lentils.

BAKED BEANS LUISE

2 cups red or white kidney beans, soaked overnight	1 large onion, sliced
	2 tbs. olive oil or fat
1 medium can tomatoes	1 bay leaf
1½ cups catsup	2 tbs. chopped parsley (opt.)
1 cup dry red wine	1 tsp. garlic powder
½ cup hot water (or beef bouillon)	Dash Tabasco
	Salt to taste

Cook beans in water to cover for about 1½ hours. Add more water as it cooks down. Drain. Put oil or fat at the bottom of a baking dish. Combine all ingredients. Bake in a moderately slow oven for 2 hours or longer. Remove bay leaf and serve. (This is a dish that tastes better with long cooking. Reheating the day after it is made improves the flavor.) Serves 8–10.

Variation: Beef cubes dredged in seasoned flour and sautéed in a little fat till brown may be added to baking dish to make entree out of recipe. Flavor will be heartier with the addition of meat.

CHOLENT OR OVERNIGHT BEANS AND MEAT

2 lbs. brisket or beef, cut in ½ lb. pieces
2 beef bones (opt.)
2 cups dry kidney beans (white or red), dry lima beans or other medium size dry beans
2 onions, chopped
1 bay leaf
2 cloves garlic, minced
Salt
1 tsp. chili powder (opt.)

Combine in a large soup pot: meat, bones, beans, onions, bay leaf, garlic, chili powder, some salt. Cover with water. Simmer on top of the range, uncovered, for 3 or 4 hours. Remove bones. Place pot in oven on lowest heat for 3 or 4 more hours. Traditionally, this dish is kept in the oven overnight. Serve the next day as a hearty main course.

HONEY BEANS

2 *cups dry beans*   ½ *cup honey*
2 *tbs. fat or oil*   2 *tsp. salt*
½ *cup water*

Soak beans overnight. Drain. Boil and cook for 1–2 hours, till tender. Mix all ingredients together and pour into a baking dish. Bake at 350° till browned, about 40 minutes.

❧ LETTUCE

THESE INCLUDE: Head and leaf lettuces. (See vegetable buying guide for varieties.)

To PREPARE: Remove wilted leaves. Cook or steam whole. To cook head lettuce, place in saucepan with small amount of water, covered for first half cooking time, uncovered for latter half. Turn heads frequently during cooking. Lettuce will be tender cooked this way in 5–10 minutes. Leaf lettuce requires no more cooking water than the moisture clinging to the leaves.

BELGIAN LETTUCE AU GRATIN

2 *heads lettuce, quartered*   ¼ *cup dry white wine*
4 *slices boiled ham cut in half* ¼ *tsp. grated nutmeg*
  or 8 strips smoked salmon   *Salt and pepper*
2 *cups medium white sauce*   2 *tbs. bread crumbs*
1 *cup grated Swiss-type*   1 *tbs. butter, melted*
  cheese

Cook lettuce as in boiling instructions. Drain. Grease a baking pan. Lay 1 slice ham or smoked salmon over each quarter. Heat white sauce in top part of double boiler. Add cheese and stir till melted. Pour in wine, nutmeg, seasonings. Pour sauce over lettuce. Combine crumbs and butter. Sprinkle over top of dish. Brown under moderate heat in broiler. Serve.

ENDIVES WITH EGGS, DUTCH STYLE

8 *medium endives* $\frac{1}{4}$ *tsp. nutmeg*
2 *hard-boiled eggs*   *Salt and pepper*
3 *tbs. melted butter*

Cook endives in water to cover until tender, about 25 minutes. Drain. Discard cooking water. Chop eggs finely. Combine butter, nutmeg, salt and pepper and stir into eggs. Pour over endives and serve.

BRAISED LETTUCE

2 *medium heads lettuce, trimmed and quartered*
1 *bay leaf (opt.)*
2 *medium scallions, split*
2 *tbs. butter or oil*
$\frac{1}{4}$ *cup dry white wine*
$\frac{1}{2}$ *cup light bouillon or boiling water*
  Salt and pepper
  Dash nutmeg

Bring bouillon or water, wine, scallions, butter or oil to a boil in a wide skillet. Lay in lettuce quarters. Spoon over some of the cooking liquid, lower heat, cover pan and simmer for 5–10 minutes. Serve with 1 tbs. cooking liquid spooned over vegetable. Add salt, pepper, and nutmeg. Serve hot.

LETTUCE WITH MUSHROOMS AND OLIVES

2 *heads or bunches lettuce* $\frac{1}{4}$ *tsp. crushed tarragon leaves*
2 *tbs. butter or oil*   *Salt and pepper*
$\frac{1}{2}$ *lb. chopped mushrooms*   1 *tbs. flour*
$\frac{1}{4}$ *cup chopped olives* $\frac{1}{2}$ *cup light bouillon*
  Dash Tabasco   1 *tbs. lemon juice*

If heads are used, quarter and cook in 1 cup water for 5 to 10 minutes, covered, part of the time. If leaf lettuce is used, separate leaves and cook in moisture clinging to leaves only—adding no additional water, in the same manner as for heads. Melt butter in a separate pan. Add mushrooms and olives and sauté lightly. Add flour and blend well. Mix in bouillon, tarragon, salt and pepper, Tabasco. Stir until thickened. Add lemon juice and pour sauce over lettuce and serve.

❧ MUSHROOMS

To PREPARE: Brush mushrooms or wipe with a damp cloth to clean. Some people peel the skin off; it is not advisable to do so from a nutritional point of view. Tough, woody stems should be cut off (not too close to cap) and saved for flavoring stews or soups. Mushrooms may be used whole, sliced or chopped. Lemon juice sprinkled over cut mushrooms or incorporated in recipe will keep mushrooms white.

Dry mushrooms should be soaked in lots of warm water from $\frac{1}{2} - 4$ hours, depending on size and variety. After soaking, they may be used like fresh.

Mushrooms need little cooking. They may be incorporated into many recipes or served by themselves. Canned mushrooms can be used in place of fresh, cooked mushrooms.

MUSHROOMS AND PEPPERS

Excellent with hearty meats.

1 *lb. mushrooms, sliced*
2–3 *red or green peppers, sliced*
2 *tbs. salad oil*
1 *tbs. Marsala (dry) or dry Sherry*
1 *clove garlic, minced*
$\frac{1}{8}$ *tsp. oregano*
  Salt and pepper

Sauté mushrooms and peppers lightly (until wilted) in hot oil. Add garlic, salt and pepper, wine, and simmer for 10–15 minutes, covered. Add oregano in final cooking moments.

SAVORY MUSHROOM PANCAKES

½ pkg. onion soup mix
1 cup dairy sour cream
¼ cup cottage cheese
6 ozs. chopped, cooked
 mushrooms

3 eggs, well beaten
½ cup flour
½ tsp. baking powder
Dash salt, if desired

Combine all ingredients. Mix well, till batter is quite smooth. Spoon batter onto well-greased hot skillet. Brown on both sides. Serve. Pancakes can be served with lemon butter or sour cream. Serves 4.

MUSHROOMS IN HOME-STYLE SAUCE

1 lb. button mushrooms
1 medium can plum tomatoes
2 tbs. chopped fresh parsley
1 clove garlic, minced
4 rashers bacon or beef fry

2 medium onions, sliced
Salt and pepper
¼ tsp. oregano
¼ tsp. basil

Fry out bacon or beef fry. Remove and drain. Sauté onions in 2 tbs. bacon fat or olive oil (as desired) until soft. Add tomatoes, garlic, salt, and pepper and fried, crumbled bacon. Simmer for ½ hour. Add herbs and mushrooms. Cover pan and simmer till mushrooms are soft. (10–15 minutes.)

SERBIAN MUSHROOM PUDDING

3 tbs. butter, melted
½ medium loaf French or
 Italian bread
3 eggs
1 cup milk or half & half
1 tbs. farina

1 cup canned chopped
 mushrooms, drained
¼ tsp. poppy seeds
Salt
¼ tsp. nutmeg or mace

Beat together eggs and milk. Slice bread into thin slices. Combine bread, cereal, salt in egg mixture. Soak for 1 hour. Add mushrooms, seeds and seasoning. Pour melted butter into a baking dish. Mix batter thoroughly, till bread disintegrates. Pour into dish. Bake at 350° for about ½ hour. Cut into slices and serve.

MUSHROOMS STUFFED WITH MUSHROOMS

Juice of ½ lemon
24 large mushrooms
2 tbs. butter or light oil
¼ tsp. poultry seasoning
2 tbs. chopped scallions

2 tbs. chopped parsley
Salt and pepper
¼ cup bread crumbs
2 tbs. dry Sherry

Clean and remove stems from mushrooms. Sprinkle caps and stems with lemon juice. Combine stems, poultry seasoning, scallions, parsley, bread crumbs, oil and salt and pepper. Purée in a blender. Mix in wine. Set caps on an oiled baking pan, cup sides up. Fill caps with purée. Bake at 350° for about 15 minutes. Remove and set under the broiler to brown. (5–10 minutes.) Serve.

Variations: 1. Stuff mushrooms with: chopped stems, ¾ cup crumbs, ½ cup grated cheese, ¼ tsp. nutmeg, salt and pepper. Dot with butter and bake-broil as directed.

2. Sauté caps on cap side lightly in 2 tbs. butter or oil. Stuff mushroom caps with the following: ½ cup bread crumbs, ¼ cup sautéed celery, 1 cup cottage cheese, salt and pepper. Place on greased cookie sheet. Place under broiler till stuffing is quite hot. Serve.

MUSHROOMS, CARROTS AND BARLEY

1½ cups thin sliced
    mushrooms
1 cup thin sliced carrots
¼ cup butter or oil
1 cup pearl or medium
    barley

2 cups chicken bouillon
¼ tsp. powdered ginger
Salt and pepper
½ cup raisins

Heat oil in skillet. Add mushrooms and carrots and sauté till they soften. Pour in barley. Fry till all fat is absorbed and barley is slightly browned. Fold into a greased baking dish. Add bouillon and seasonings and raisins. Stir through. Cover dish snugly, and bake at 350° for about 40 minutes. Uncover and bake until all liquid is gone and barley is quite fluffy.

WHITE RUSSIAN MUSHROOMS

1 *lb. fresh mushrooms, sliced*	*Salt and pepper*
1 *medium onion, chopped*	$\frac{1}{4}$ *tsp. nutmeg*
2 *tbs. fat or oil*	1 *cup dairy sour cream*

Sauté onion in hot oil till soft. Add mushrooms, salt and pepper and nutmeg. Braise till cooked. Remove from heat. Add cream. Adjust seasoning. Serve on toast points, with croutons, in patty shells, etc. Serves 4.

MUSHROOMS WITH CHEESE

2 *cups button mushrooms*
2 *tbs. butter or oil*
1 *cup medium white sauce*
$\frac{1}{2}$ *cup grated Swiss-style cheese*
1 *tbs chopped chives or* $\frac{1}{2}$ *tsp. French mustard*
2 *tbs. chopped parsley*
$\frac{1}{4}$ *cup brandy*
   Salt and pepper
$\frac{1}{4}$ *tsp. nutmeg*

Sauté mushrooms in hot fat until wilted. Drain. Combine all other ingredients in the top of a double boiler, adding brandy last. Cook for 5 minutes after brandy is added. Add mushrooms to sauce. Pour into a buttered oven dish and bake at 350° for about 20 minutes.

MUSHROOM AND EGGPLANT CUSTARD

2 tbs. butter or oil
2 cups chopped mushrooms
1 small to medium eggplant
1 onion
2 tbs. dry white wine or
   Sherry

$\frac{1}{4}$ tsp. basil
Salt and pepper
2 tbs. flour
1 cup light cream or half &
   half
3 eggs, well beaten

Pare and cube eggplant. Cook in lightly salted water till soft. Drain and press out all moisture through sieve. Sauté onion in butter. Add mushrooms. Sauté till mushrooms are cooked, stirring frequently. Add eggplant and wine and seasonings. Cook till liquids reduce. Stir in flour and continue stirring till pan liquids thicken. Slowly add milk and cook, stirring constantly, until a thick sauce is made. Cool slightly. Re-season to taste. Beat 3 eggs very well. Combine thoroughly with mushroom mixture. Pour into well-greased baking dish. Bake at 350° for about 1 hour.

MUSHROOMS AND KASHA*

1   cup cooked mushrooms or 1–8 oz. can mushroom pieces
1   cup groats
2   eggs
1   clove garlic, crushed or $\frac{1}{4}$ tsp. garlic powder (opt.)
4–5 tbs. fat or oil (combination olive oil and corn oil is
   suggested)
   Salt and pepper to taste
$2\frac{1}{3}$ cups hot liquid (broth from can plus boiling water)

Combine groats, mushrooms (drained), garlic, eggs, salt and pepper and mix well. Heat oil in skillet. Add groat mixture. Stir constantly till all of oil is absorbed. (Groats and mushrooms should have an eggy coating.) Add hot liquid. Stir till it is evenly distributed in pan. Lower heat. Cover. Simmer till groats and mushrooms are quite dry and browned on top, $\frac{1}{2}$ hour or more.

* Variations and Note: Kasha is commercially known here as buckwheat groats. Cracked wheat (Borghul) can be substituted for Kasha in this recipe with equally good results.

MUSHROOM RICE

$\frac{1}{2}$ *lb. sliced mushrooms*
1 *large onion, diced*
2 *tbs. fat or oil*
1 *cup raw rice*

1 *can beef consomme*
  concentrate
1 *can cold water*
  Salt and pepper

Sauté onions and mushrooms in hot oil until soft. Combine in a baking dish: rice, consomme, water, seasoning and sautéed vegetables. Cover snugly. Bake in a preheated, 350° oven for about 45 minutes. (The addition of meats or fish turns this dish into a main course.)

❦ *OKRA*

Small pods are the most tender. Large ones are stronger flavored but are favored for stuffing. Stews using okra require little thickening as okra contains its own thickening agent.

To PREPARE: Wash and remove stems. Medium size okra may be sliced thick. Smaller ones may be left whole for cooking.

To BOIL: Cook in boiling salted water to cover until tender, 15–25 minutes, depending on size.

OKRA VINAIGRETTE

1 *lb. medium okra*
  Juice of 1 lemon
  Salt and pepper
1 *clove garlic, split (opt.)*

2 *scallions, chopped, or 1 tbs.*
  fresh chopped dill
2 *tbs. chopped parsley*
$\frac{2}{3}$ *cup olive oil*

Wash and remove stems from okra. Slice into $\frac{1}{2}$ inch pieces. Cook in salted water to cover in a covered pan until tender, 15 to 20 minutes. Drain. Place in refrigerator dish. Cover with marinade ingredients above. Chill at least 4 hours. Serve as an appetizer, drained of marinade, or as part of antipasto. You may garnish with anchovies.

OKRA SAUTÉ À LA CRÉME

1 *lb. small okra firm-cooked*	1 *medium can creamed corn*
1 *medium onion, chopped*	2 *tbs. chopped pimiento*
1 *green pepper, chopped*	*Salt and pepper*
4 *rashers bacon or beef fry*	¼ *tsp. marjoram (opt.)*

Fry out bacon and remove from pan to drain. Pour off all but 2 tbs. bacon fat. Sauté onion and pepper in fat. Add creamed corn, seasonings and okra. Simmer till bubbly. Pour into serving dish. Sprinkle with chopped pimiento and crumbled bacon. Serve.

OKRA GUMBO

1   *frozen pkg. okra or 1½ cups fresh sliced okra*
1   *#2 can tomatoes or 2 cups fresh diced*
1   *medium onion, chopped*
2   *tbs. fat or oil*
1½ *cups baby lima beans*
    Salt
    Dash Tabasco
½   *tsp. sugar*
¼   *tsp. allspice*

Heat fat in skillet. Sauté onion until transparent. Add tomatoes and stew for about 5 minutes over moderate heat. Add all other ingredients. Cover and simmer till vegetables are tender. (About 20 minutes.) If mixture is too thick, add ¼ cup bouillon after first 10 minutes of cooking. You may add cooked fish or poultry in cooking. Serve over rice.

ARABIAN OKRA (BAMIYA*)

1 *lb. okra, trimmed, whole*	*Salt to taste*
2 *tbs. olive oil*	1 *cup tomato purée*
2 *onions, chopped*	2 *cups water*
¼ *tsp. garlic powder*	

* This recipe resembles the dish I speak of in the Introduction served at the Workman's Cafe in the old Market of Jerusalem.

Fry okra in oil until wilted but not brown. Remove from pan. Add chopped onions and sauté until golden. Toss in garlic powder and some salt. Return okra to pan. Add juice and water. Simmer on lowest heat for about ½ hour or until liquid thickens.

❧ ONIONS

To PREPARE: Peel under water or drop into rapidly boiling water and leave for less than a minute. Drain, chill and slip off skin. Onions become strong-flavored and foul-smelling when over-cooked. Steaming is recommended, as is baking in the skin in the oven. (1½ hours to bake medium size onions.)

To BOIL: Cook, covered, in boiling, salted water to cover. Small or cut onions require about 20 minutes. Larger or whole onions: 30–40 minutes.

BAKED ONIONS WITH PEAS

2 *cups small white cooked onions*
1 *cup cooked green peas*
2 *cups medium white sauce (made with milk)*
  Salt and pepper
½ *tsp. curry powder or allspice*
1 *cup crushed corn flakes*
2 *tbs. melted butter*

Combine peas, onions, white sauce, seasonings and pour into buttered baking dish. Mix melted butter with crushed flakes. Sprinkle over top of dish. Bake in moderate oven until hot and bubbly. (About 25 minutes.) Serve.

Variation: Substitute cheese sauce for white sauce.

ONIONS IN WINE SAUCE

2 *cups white pearl onions*
¼ *cup (2 oz.) butter*
2 *tbs. flour*
2 *tbs. chopped parsley*
1 *small bay leaf*

Good dash nutmeg
½ *cup stock*
¼ *cup Madeira or dry Sherry*
Salt to taste

Melt butter in skillet. Sauté onions until well coated with butter, shaking pan. (A few minutes.) Add flour, parsley, bay leaf, salt, nutmeg and stock. Mix well. Cook, stirring constantly until onions are tender. Add wine. Cook an additional few moments. Serve.

FRENCH FRIED ONIONS

4 *medium onions*
1 *cup favorite pancake batter*
  Salt and pepper

Peel onions. Slice thin and separate into rings. Place rings in batter. Remove them one at a time, drain off excess batter and fry in deep fat till brown. Remove from fat, drain on absorbent paper and serve.

STUFFED ONIONS

4 *large Spanish or Bermuda*
  onions
⅔ *cup chopped leftover*
  cooked meat, tuna or other
  fish
1 *tbs. toasted bread crumbs*

2 *tbs. butter or oil*
  Salt and pepper
¼ *tsp. thyme or basil*
1 *tbs. chopped parsley*
1 *egg, lightly beaten*

Peel skin from onions. Cut in half across diameter. Poach in salt water to cover till firm-cooked. Drain. Remove center portion of onions leaving many-layered shell. Chop centers and sauté till golden in 2 tbs. fat. Combine sautéed onions and all other ingredients. Fill onion shells with mixture. Place in a buttered baking pan. Cover securely with foil. Bake at 350° for about 20 minutes. Remove cover and bake uncovered for 10 more minutes. Serve. Stuffed onions may be sauced with white or tomato sauce before serving.

ONION-CHEESE PIE

1½ *cups crushed white crackers*
½ *cup melted butter*
2 *tsp. salt, pepper*
2½ *cups onions, sliced*
2 *tbs. butter*
1½ *cups milk or light cream, scalded*

¼ *tsp. dry mustard or 1 tsp. French mustard*
3 *eggs, lightly beaten*
1 *cup grated Swiss-style cheese*
2 *tbs. dry Sherry (opt.)*

Combine crumbs, melted butter and 1 tsp. salt. Press into 9″ pie plate. Sauté onions in butter until golden. Place on pie crust. Slowly beat milk into eggs. Add cheese, seasonings and wine, if desired. Pour mixture over onions. Bake in moderately slow oven (325°) for about 45 minutes. Cool and slice into pie-shaped wedges. Serve as appetizer.

ONIONS IN COCONUT CREAM

1½ *lbs. small white onions, peeled and cut in quarters*
2 *tbs. butter*
2 *cups milk or half & half*
⅛ *tsp. powdered cloves*
¼ *tsp. nutmeg or mace*
1 *tsp. salt*
   Dash ground pepper
1 *3½ oz. can flaked, sweetened coconut*
1 *tbs. cornstarch and 1½ tbs. water*

Poach onions in milk, butter, nutmeg and cloves for about 5 minutes. Remove from pan and set aside. Rinse coconut in 2 cups boiling water. Drain. Add salt, pepper and coconut to milk broth.

Simmer till milk thickens slightly, stirring frequently. Adjust seasonings to taste. Add cornstarch mixed with water. Stir till sauce thickens. Return onions to pan. Simmer till hot but do not boil. Serve.

BAKED ONION GUMBO

2 *lbs. yellow onions, sliced*
1 *green pepper, chopped*
2 *tbs. chopped celery tops*
6 *ozs. canned tomatoes*
  Salt, pepper
½ *tsp. chili powder*
1 *clove garlic, minced (opt.)*
  Dash cayenne or Tabasco
1 *tbs. butter*
⅓ *cup buttered crumbs*

Place onions in greased baking dish. Add green peppers, celery, tomatoes, garlic, and other seasonings. Top with buttered crumbs and dot with butter. Bake at 350° for 1 hour.

SWEET ONION PUDDING CAKE

1 *recipe onions in coconut cream made with diced yellow*
  onions instead of white
6 *ozs. stale French or Italian bread*
3 *eggs*
1 *tbs. sugar*
¼ *cup orange juice*
1 *tbs. cornstarch*

Soak bread in water till soft. Squeeze out as much moisture as possible. Combine with onion recipe. Beat eggs with juice and sugar. Add to batter. Mix till bread is evenly distributed. Pour into buttered round casserole. Bake at 350° for about 1 hour. Cool in oven. Serve warm. (At its best soon after cooking. This dish loses flavor on standing.)

ONION STEW

2 *lbs. onions, diced*
½ *lb. cubed (1 in. pieces) lean beef*
2 *tbs. tomato paste*
1 *small nut of sour salt (to taste)*
1 *tbs. apricot jam*
2 *tbs. honey*
2 *tbs. sultana raisins (opt.)*
½ *tsp. salt*

Place onions and beef in heavy-bottomed saucepan. Cover with cold water. Bring to a boil. Skim off any meat scum that forms on top. Add all other ingredients. Reduce heat to lowest, cover pot and simmer for 2 hours. Stir from time to time. If not sufficiently thick (stewy) after this cooking period, cook uncovered for an additional ½ hour. Serves 6–8.

❦ *PARSNIPS*

To PREPARE: Scrape, peel or simply wash, as preferred. Cut into dice, sticks, or leave whole. Tough or woody cores should be removed. Cook, covered, in boiling salted water to cover till tender, 30–40 minutes.

PARSNIP FRITTERS

2 *cups mashed parsnips*
1 *egg, beaten*
½ *cup milk*
1 *cup flour*
½ *tsp. salt*
1 *tbs. sugar*
¼ *tsp. nutmeg*

Add ingredients, one at a time, to beaten egg. When well blended, drop spoonfuls of batter into hot fat. Fry till golden on both sides.

NUTTED PARSNIP PUFFS

12 *small parsnips*
3 *eggs, well beaten*
5 *tbs. flour*
½ *tsp. salt, pepper*

½ *tsp. baking powder*
¼ *tsp. allspice*
12 *walnut meats*

Clean parsnips, but do not peel. Cook in salted water as preceding recipes direct. Remove skins and mash vegetables. Combine with other ingredients. Form into small balls. Indent center with your thumb and insert 1 nutmeat into each ball. Close puff balls around nutmeats. Fry balls in hot fat until brown. Drain. Sprinkle with chopped parsley and serve.

GLAZED PARSNIPS

1½ *lbs. small or medium parsnips*
2 *tbs. melted butter*
1 *tsp. cornstarch and 1 tbs. water*
¼ *cup cinnamon sugar*
½ *tsp. salt*

Peel or scrape parsnips. Slice or cut into 2–3 inch sticks. If central cores seem tough and woody, remove. Cook in salted water to cover in covered pan for about ½ hour, until tender, or steam like amount of time. Drain. Heat butter in a skillet. Add cornstarch and water and salt. Add parsnips. Cook, turning frequently, till parsnips are browned and glazed. Sprinkle with cinnamon sugar and serve.

❧ PEAS

To PREPARE: Do not shell till ready to cook. Shell and wash peas. (If necessary to shell in advance, place in covered refrigerator container and chill.) Cook covered, in small amount of water till tender, about 15 minutes.

PEAS WITH DILL CREAM*

1 *pkg. frozen cooked peas, well drained*
2 *tbs. butter*
  Salt, pepper
1 *egg yolk*
2 *tbs. dairy sour cream*
1 *tbs. chopped fresh dill or ½ tsp. dry dillweed*

Melt butter in the top of a double boiler. Place over hot water. (Do not allow water to reach bottom of upper pan.) Add egg yolk and stir until well blended. Slowly add sour cream and stir until sauce is thick. Toss in peas, dill and salt and pepper. Heat but do not allow to boil.

Variation: Diet-conscious vegetable lovers should substitute plain yoghurt for sour cream.

PEAS AND PASTA

1 *pkg. frozen peas, cooked or 1½ cup fresh, cooked peas*
½ *cup soup macaroni (small tubbati style suggested)*
1 *tbs. vegetable flakes*
1 *tbs. butter or oil*
1 *bouillon cube (any type)*
2 *cups boiling water*
2 *tbs. grated Parmesan cheese*
  Salt to taste

In a wide skillet, combine butter, bouillon cube, water and vegetable flakes. Add ½ tsp. salt and bring to a boil. Toss in macaroni and boil, stirring frequently with a fork, until macaroni is soft. (About 8 minutes.) Water should be almost totally evaporated by end of cooking period. Add cooked peas and stir through macaroni. Pour into serving dish, top with grated cheese and blend well. Serve hot.

---

* This dish is recommended as an accompaniment to fish entrees.

PEAS WITH EGG DUMPLINGS

$2\frac{1}{2}$ cups fresh peas or 2 pkgs.
frozen peas
2 cups chicken bouillon
1 bay leaf
2 hard-boiled eggs

1 raw egg yolk
Dash salt
$\frac{1}{8}$ tsp. powdered ginger
$\frac{1}{2}$ tsp. fat or oil

Combine hard egg yolks, salt, ginger, melted fat or oil and minced egg whites. Mash together. Add raw egg yolk and mix well. Form into tiny balls. Cook in boiling bouillon (to which bay leaf has been added) for 1 or 2 minutes. Remove. Cook raw peas in just enough bouillon to cover, in covered pan, until tender. Add dumplings and heat briefly. Pour into serving dish.

ARABIAN PEAS

1 pkg. frozen peas, thawed or
$1\frac{1}{2}$ cups fresh peas
1 small onion, chopped
$\frac{1}{4}$ cup pine nuts
$\frac{1}{4}$ tsp. allspice

$\frac{1}{2}$ tsp. crushed mint leaves
$\frac{1}{4}$ cup bouillon (beef or
vegetable)
Salt, pepper
2 tbs. fat or oil

Heat oil in skillet. Sauté onions and pine nuts till onions are soft and nuts are lightly browned. Add bouillon and seasonings and bring to a boil. Add peas, reduce heat and simmer, covered, till tender. You may serve peas with yoghurt or sour cream to be added at the table.

PEAS WITH TOMATO

1 pkg. frozen peas
1 ripe large tomato, diced
$\frac{1}{4}$ tsp. garlic powder (opt.)
$\frac{1}{4}$ tsp. ginger powder
1 tbs. onion flakes
1 tbs. celery flakes

$\frac{1}{4}$ tsp. sugar
Salt and pepper
$\frac{1}{4}$ cup bouillon (chicken or
vegetable)
2 tbs. oil or butter

Heat oil in skillet. Add garlic, ginger, onion, celery and tomato. Simmer for about 5 minutes. Add broth and simmer for 5 minutes more. Add peas and sugar. Separate frozen block with fork over high heat. Reduce heat. Cover and simmer for a few minutes, or until tender. Add salt and pepper and serve.

Variation: Beat 4 eggs. Drain off all liquid from peas with tomato recipe and add to eggs. Beat again. Oil an omelet pan and heat. When hot, pour eggs into pan. Pull away cooked egg from bottom and sides a few times. Add peas and tomatoes from preceding recipe. Cover omelet pan and cook till done.

OLD-STYLE CREAMED PEAS

2 *cups fresh peas*	2 *oz. butter*
4 *lettuce leaves*	1 *egg yolk*
¼ *tsp. chervil or marjoram*	¼ *cup cream or half & half*
¼ *tsp. salt*	½ *tsp. sugar*
¼ *cup water*	*Dash pepper*

Place lettuce at bottom of saucepan. Add water, herbs, seasonings, peas and butter. Bring to a boil, reduce heat and simmer, covered, till tender. Remove lettuce. Pour into serving dish. Mix in cream mixed with yolk, sugar and pepper. Serve.

❧ *STUFFED PEPPERS*

GENERAL PREPARATION: Slice off the stem ends of peppers. Remove core, white ribs, and rinse to eliminate all seeds. If peppers are large, cut in half from end to end. Parboil by tossing in boiling water and allowing to cool in water. Drain well. Stuff with your favorite filling and according to directions.

STUFFING IDEAS

1. Combine leftover chicken, turkey or white-meated fish with medium white sauce that has been well seasoned. (2 cups sauce to 1½ cups leftovers.) Grate cheese over top and bake in medium oven for about 20 minutes.

2. See Confetti Stuffed Eggplant (page 198) and use stuffing for peppers. Substitute ground beef, veal or other meats for sausage, if desired. Place in a greased casserole dish and pour over top 1 cup hot tomato sauce. Bake ½ hour.

3. 1 cup cooked rice, 4 tbs. butter or oil, 3 tbs. grated Parmesan cheese, ½ cup diced mozzarella or grated Swiss cheese, salt, pepper and parsley. Bake ½ hour.

4. 1 cup hot mashed potatoes, 6 ozs. stale French or Italian bread soaked in water and squeezed dry, 1 well-beaten egg, small minced onion, ½ tsp. poultry seasoning, ¼ cup diced celery, salt and pepper. Bake 20 minutes.

5. 2 cups corn kernels sautéed in butter and seasoned with seasoned salt and chopped parsley. Bake 20 minutes.

PEPPERS WITH TOMATOES AND POTATOES

4 *large red or green peppers,*
    sliced thin
2 *large ripe tomatoes, diced*
1 *cup firm-cooked potatoes,*
    diced
3 *tbs. oil or fat*

1 *bay leaf*
    Dash paprika
    Salt
2 *tbs. chopped parsley*
    Dash garlic powder
1 *small onion, chopped*

Remove core and seeds of pepper. Heat oil in skillet. Sauté onions with garlic powder till soft. Add peppers and cook till wilted, about 5 minutes. Add tomatoes and bay leaf. Simmer for an additional 5 minutes. Add potatoes. Toss through to coat with pan liquids. Simmer till potatoes are hot. Garnish with parsley, remove bay leaf and serve.

SWEET PEPPER APPETIZER

3 *red or green peppers, cored,*
    seeded and diced
2 *tbs. olive oil*
¼ *tsp. curry powder*

½ *cup plain yoghurt*
1 *tbs. celery flakes*
    Salt

Heat oil in skillet. Add curry powder and peppers. Sauté peppers, stirring frequently, until soft. Remove from skillet and drain. Combine with yoghurt. Chill for a few hours or overnight. Serve on tomato slices.

❧ POTATOES

TO PREPARE: These may be boiled in their skins or pared. Their skins should be brushed well to clean for cooking; cut out any deep eyes or deep discolor marks.

TO BOIL: Cook in boiling, salted water, covered, for 20–40 minutes.

NOTE: It is always best to make potatoes fresh. The texture and flavor is lost rapidly on standing.

Sweet potatoes are treated in the same way as plain potatoes.

BAKED POTATOES

Clean skins. Dry well. Rub all over with fat or oil. Bake in oven for 45 minutes to 1 hour, depending on size. Or, you can wrap oiled potatoes in foil and bake. Or use a potato baker on top of stove to bake potatoes. When tender, remove from oven or baker. Make 2 crisscrossed cuts on one side. Pinch potato open. Place fat, oil or sour cream (1 tbs.) within and salt and pepper. Serve.

BAKED STUFFED POTATOES

Proceed as directed above. When cooked, cut in half down the length. Scoop out potato flesh, leaving substantially fleshed shell intact. To mashed potato centers, add the following:

1. Leftover creamed meats, fish or vegetables. Moisten with fat, season, sprinkle with paprika and return to shell and brown in oven.

2. Mix with ground meats, onion and/or garlic, parsley, herbs or spice and salt, pepper. Continue as directed above.

3. Stuff potatoes with ½ cup small curd creamed cottage cheese, potato meat, 1 egg, salt and pepper and chopped scallions (if desired). Recipe is for 2 medium size potatoes.

4. Moisten with fat, milk or vegetable cooking water and beat until fluffy. Return to shell, top with grated Cheddar or Swiss-style cheese.

5. Mix with commercial Blue cheese or Cheddar cheese spread.

HOMEMADE POTATO CHIPS

Pare potatoes. Slice as thin as possible. Soak in cold water for 1–2 hours. Drain well on absorbent paper. Fry in deep hot fat till golden. Remove and drain. Salt and serve.

GLOCKENSPIEL POTATOES

3 *cups leftover, seasoned and creamed mashed potatoes*
3 *rashers bacon or beef fry*
1 *small onion, chopped*
1 *cup toasted croutons*
2 *tbs. minced celery*
Salt, paprika, pepper

Fry out bacon. Add onion and sauté till soft and yellow. Add croutons and brown. Pour into mashed potatoes. Season. Garnish with chopped celery and paprika.

LUCERNE POTATOES

4 *medium potatoes*
1 *medium onion*
4 *tbs. corn or peanut oil*
Salt and pepper
2 *tbs. milk*

Clean and grate potatoes with skin on a medium grater. Grate onion and mix with potatoes. Heat oil in an omelet pan until quite hot. (Test with a droplet of water dripped into pan. It should sizzle fiercely.) Pour potato mix into pan and smooth with a fork into an omelet shape. Season. Sprinkle milk over top. Cook on medium high heat until underside of potatoes is golden brown.

Invert potato pancake on a dish and slide back into pan to brown on opposite side. Serve hot.

HUNGARIAN SOUR POTATOES

$2\frac{1}{2}$ lbs. tiny new potatoes
2 tbs. butter or oil
2 tbs. flour
2 tbs. chopped onion
1 tbs. dry white wine or lemon juice

$\frac{1}{4}$ tsp. sugar
2 tsp. dairy sour cream
   Salt and pepper
1 tsp. caraway seeds (opt.)

Cook potatoes covered, in boiling, salted water to cover until tender. (About 20–30 minutes.) Drain but reserve cooking liquid. Shake potatoes in their saucepan over low heat until they are quite dry. (Steam will cease to appear.) Heat fat in a fry pan. Add flour and mix until it makes a brown paste. Add onions and cook till soft. Add 1 cup liquid from cooking potatoes (or whatever liquid remains plus cold water to equal 1 cup) and stir until thickened. Add potatoes and caraway. Simmer for a few minutes. Add wine or juice, sugar, cream and seasonings. Bring to a boil. Serve.

POTATOES IN TOMATO SAUCE

6 medium potatoes, cooked and sliced
1 cup tomato sauce (canned)
$\frac{1}{2}$ cup bouillon, any kind
1 bay leaf
$\frac{1}{4}$ tsp. celery seed
1 tbs. butter or oil
2 tbs. flour
  Salt and pepper
1 tbs. sugar

Heat oil in a skillet. Stir in flour and continue mixing till lightly browned. Add bouillon and bay leaf and stir till thickened. Pour in sauce and blend. Add potatoes and season. Heat and serve.

BAKED MUSTARD POTATOES

2 *cups par-cooked, thick-sliced potatoes*
1 *cup chicken bouillon*
3–4 *tbs. French-style mustard (to taste)*
2 *tbs. bread crumbs*
1 *tbs. fat or oil*
1 *tbs. flour*
  Salt and pepper

Grease a baking dish. Make layers of potato slices. Melt 1 tbs. butter in a saucepan. Add flour and brown. Slowly add bouillon, stirring until well blended and thickened. Add mustard and salt and pepper. Pour over potatoes. Sprinkle top with bread crumbs and dots of additional butter or margarine. Cook at 425° until crusty and browned. (About 20 minutes.)

Variation: 1. Substitute peanut butter, chunk-style, for mustard.

2. Use ¾ cup chicken bouillon and ¼ cup dry white wine.

STUFFED POTATO DUMPLINGS

DOUGH:
3 *large raw potatoes, peeled*
1 *large cooked potato, peeled and mashed*
1 *small minced onion*
5 *tbs. cracker meal*
2 *lightly beaten eggs*
  Salt and pepper
½ *tsp. powdered ginger*

FILLING:
1 *lb. ground beef or veal, lean*
1 *small chopped onion*
1 *tbs. chopped parsley*
  Salt and pepper
¼ *tsp. marjoram and basil*
1 *carrot, chopped*

Grate potatoes on medium grater. Allow to stand 10 minutes. Pour off any liquid that rises to top. Add mashed potato and combine. Add other dough ingredients. Make 2 large balls out of dough. Hollow out centers. Mix together filling ingredients and stuff ½ into each large dumpling. Close dough around filling. Cook the dumplings in meat gravy or with macedoine of vegetables and bake with meats.

POTATO PIE

1 *lb. cooked, pared potatoes*
2 *tbs. cornstarch and 2 tbs.*
 milk
1 *small onion, minced*
2 *tbs. minced celery*

¼ *tsp. marjoram, rosemary or*
 poultry seasoning
 Salt and pepper, paprika
2 *tbs. buttered crumbs*

Grate potatoes. Add all other ingredients and fold into greased baking pan. Dot top with buttered crumbs and paprika. Bake at 400° for 30 minutes.

SCALLOPED POTATOES #1

2 *cups pared potatoes, thin-sliced*
1 *large onion, chopped*
1 *tbs. flour*
1 *cup milk*
2 *tbs. butter*
1 *can cream of chicken or cream of mushroom soup, condensed*
¼ *cup grated Cheddar-type cheese*
 Salt and pepper

In a well-greased casserole, place 1 layer of potatoes. Sprinkle with chopped onions, salt, pepper, flour, and dot with butter. Repeat till all ingredients are used. Pour over condensed soup. Bake at 350° for about 1 hour. In final 10 minutes of cooking, add grated cheese to top. Serves 6–8.

POTATO SCALLOP #2

8 *medium raw potatoes,*
 sliced thin
2 *onions, sliced thin*
¾ *cup bread crumbs*

¼ *tsp. garlic powder*
 Salt and pepper
2 *cups chicken broth*
¼ *tsp. marjoram or thyme*

Butter a wide, flat baking dish. Make a layer of potatoes, a layer of onions, cover with a thin coat of crumbs, dash of garlic powder and salt and pepper. Continue till all ingredients are used. End with potatoes. Pour broth blended with herbs over top. Bake at 350° for 1 hour.

POTATO PUDDING #1

4 *medium to large raw potatoes, pared*
1 *medium onion*
2 *eggs, lightly beaten*
1 *tsp. salt*
2 *slices stale white or rye bread*
2 *tbs. chicken fat, bacon or beef fry dripping or olive oil*
   Dash pepper

Grate potatoes into cold water. Drain thoroughly. Grate onion and add to potatoes. Soak bread in water. Squeeze out well and add to potatoes. Combine all other ingredients except fat. Pour mixture into a blender and purée for a few minutes on a slow speed. (Do not eliminate all texture.) Melt fat in a baking dish. Pour in potato batter. Bake at 350° till set, about 1½ hours.

POTATO PUDDING #2

6 *medium potatoes, raw*   ½ *tsp. baking powder*
1 *small onion*   3 *tbs. flour*
½ *tsp. celery seed*   1 *tsp. salt*
2 *eggs, lightly beaten*   *Pepper*

Grate potatoes and onion. Allow to stand till liquid surfaces. (10–15 minutes.) Drain well. Add beaten eggs and all other ingredients. Bake in shallow pan, well greased, at 350° for 1 hour. Serve with apple sauce or sour cream.

   Variations: Bake raw recipe in well-greased muffin tins to make potato muffins, 350° for about 45 minutes or until tops are brown. You may use the same recipe for potato pancakes. Simply drop spoonfuls of batter onto well-greased griddle or skillet and brown on both sides.

QUICK DUCHESSE POTATOES

1½ *cups leftover mashed potatoes*
1   *beaten egg and ¼ cup milk or broth*
    Salt and pepper, paprika
2   *tbs. chopped onions*
¼   *cup chopped, cooked mushrooms*
    Butter

Combine ingredients (except butter) and blend well. Drop by spoonfuls on greased cookie sheet. Indent with the bowl of a spoon. Dot in the hollow with butter and sprinkle with paprika. Bake till top is brown.

SWEET POTATO PIE

3 *sweet potatoes, mashed*
1 *cup mashed cooked carrots*
¾ *cup milk or half & half*
¼ *cup orange marmalade*
¼ *tsp. mace*
¼ *tsp. powdered ginger (opt.)*

1 *large banana, mashed*
2 *ozs. butter, melted*
2 *eggs*
1 *cup corn flakes, crushed*
2 *tbs. dry Sherry (opt.)*

Combine all ingredients. Mix thoroughly. Pour into greased casserole or loaf pan and bake at 350°. (45 minutes, or until set.)

BAKED SWEET POTATOES

Follow directions for baked potatoes.

BAKED STUFFED SWEETS

Open large, baked sweets as you would regular potatoes. Hollow out and mix mashed potato center with cream, butter, honey and/or brown sugar. Peanut butter, orange juice, sweet fruit liqueurs, cherry juice, marmalade, wines, candied fruits can also be used as part or total of stuffing ingredients.

SWEET POTATO BAKE

8 *medium sweets*
¾ *cup brown sugar or honey*
¼ *cup orange juice*
  Grated rind of 1 orange and
  1 lemon
¼ *tsp. powdered cloves*

¼ *tsp. cinnamon*
  Dash mace
¼ *cup bourbon or brandy*
½ *cup diced dry apricots*
¼ *cup butter*

Boil potatoes until tender. Pare and halve. Place in greased baking dish. Heat together juice, sugar, 3 tbs. butter and spices. Pour over sweets. Add other ingredients. Bake at 350° for about 1 hour.

BAKED SWEETS OR YAMS

1 *can sweet potatoes*
½ *cup orange juice*
2 *tbs. honey*

¼ *tsp. salt*
¼ *tsp. nutmeg*

Cook canned sweets till hot. Drain. Place in greased baking pan. Heat together honey, orange juice, salt. Pour over sweets. Add nutmeg. Dot with butter. Bake.
  Variation: Substitute pineapple or apple juice for orange.

CRANBERRY SWEETS

8 *sweet potatoes, cooked*
¼ *tsp. salt*
  Pinch powdered cloves or ginger
½ *cup whole cranberry sauce*
2 *tbs. butter*
¼ *cup chopped walnut meats*
1 *small can crushed pineapple and liquid*

Heat together cranberries, butter and crushed pineapple. Add salt, cloves. Pour over sweets that have been sliced in buttered casserole. Top with nuts. Bake in oven 1 hour in moderate heat.

SWEET POTATO BALLS

Make balls of mashed buttered sweets. Insert nut meats, raisins or dry prunes in center. Roll balls in crushed corn flakes. Fry in deep hot fat. Drain.

❧ *RUTABAGAS AND TURNIPS*

The following recipes can be used for either vegetable. Actually, turnips are at their best in stews, soups or combination vegetable dishes. Rutabagas are delicious prepared independent of other foods.

Rutabagas can be baked whole in the skin, like potatoes or squash and then peeled and incorporated into recipes.

To PREPARE: Wash vegetables. Pare and slice, dice, quarter or julienne-cut them.

To BOIL: Cook in boiling salted water to cover for 20–30 minutes.

RUTABAGAS JULIENNE

1 *small rutabaga (2 lbs.)*
  Cinnamon sugar
2 *tbs. butter*

Pare rutabaga. Cut into julienne strips. Place in boiling salted water to cover and cook 15–20 minutes, or until firm but tender. Drain. Sprinkle with cinnamon sugar. Toss butter through and serve.

GLAZED TURNIPS

6 *medium turnips, diced and* $\frac{1}{4}$ *cup water*
  par-cooked $\frac{1}{4}$ *tsp. mace or nutmeg*
2 *tbs. butter* $\frac{1}{4}$ *tsp. salt*
$\frac{1}{4}$ *cup honey*

Combine honey, water and seasonings. Place turnips in large, flat baking dish that has been well greased. Pour syrup over vegetables. Bake in 350° oven for about ½ hour or until vegetables are browned. Serve.

RUTABAGA STEW

1 *small rutabaga (1½–2 lbs.)*
1 *can French fried onions*
1 *cup chicken broth*
1 *cup hot water*
½ *pkg. onion soup mix*
1 *fresh tomato, diced*

1 *clove garlic, crushed*
Dash Tabasco
Pinch each: basil, thyme,
marjoram (opt.)
2 *tbs. butter*
Salt

Peel and cut rutabaga into 1 inch cubes. Melt butter at the bottom of a soup pot and sauté rutabaga till partially wilted. Add all ingredients except wine and herbs. Simmer until turnips are tender. Add wine and seasonings. Simmer 5 minutes longer. Serve. Excellent with chicken or meat.

TURNIPS WITH APPLE

6   *small white turnips*
1½ *cups milk*
1   *tbs. butter*
1   *tbs. flour*
¾   *cup chicken bouillon*

1   *large tart apple*
½   *tsp. salt, pepper*
1   *tbs. sugar or honey*
2   *tbs. raisins*
¼   *tsp. nutmeg*

Peel and dice turnips into 1 inch pieces. Cook in boiling water to cover about 5 minutes. Drain. Return to pan and cover with milk. Simmer gently till tender. Drain again. (Milk may be used in soups, gravies or cream sauces.) Melt butter in pan. Add flour and stir to form a paste. Stir in bouillon and mix till thickened. Add pared, cored, diced apple and seasonings. Cook for 5 or more minutes to blend. Pour sauce over turnips and serve.

TURNIP RING

1 cup mashed cooked turnips
½ cup mashed cooked
   potatoes
½ cup mashed cooked carrots
1 cup crushed cheese crackers
1 small onion, minced

2 eggs, well beaten
2 tbs. butter
¼ cup light cream
   Salt to taste
   Dash cayenne pepper

Combine mashed vegetables and eggs. Crumb the crackers in a blender. Add to vegetable mixture. Sauté onion in hot butter until soft. Add to batter. Add all other ingredients. Season to taste. Pour into well-greased ring mold. Bake at 350° until firm. (About 1 hour.) Turn out on platter. Set creamed fish in the center. Serve. Serves 6.

SHREDDED TURNIPS, ORIENTALE

1½ lbs. small or medium
   turnips
1 small onion, chopped
1 medium carrot, thin sliced
2 tbs. corn or peanut oil
⅔ cup light chicken broth

2 tbs. minced scallion greens
2 tbs. soya sauce
   Dash garlic powder
   Salt, pepper
¼ tsp. MSG

Clean, pare and grate turnips. Heat oil in a skillet. Sauté turnips, onion and carrot for 2 minutes or until partially wilted. Add MSG, dash salt, pepper and broth. Cover and simmer about 5 minutes. Remove cover. Add soya sauce, garlic powder, and cook over low heat 2 more minutes. Top with scallion greens and serve.

SCANDIA RUTABAGA PUDDING

2 large rutabagas, peeled and
   diced
½ cup half & half
¼ cup fine white bread
   crumbs
3 eggs, well beaten

2 tbs. molasses or honey
3 ozs. melted butter
¼ tsp. mace
1 tsp. salt
   Dash pepper
   Cinnamon sugar

Cook rutabagas, covered, in boiling, lightly salted water about 20–30 minutes, or until tender. Drain. Soak crumbs in milk. Mash vegetable with butter. Combine seasonings and eggs. Beat into mashed rutabagas. Add milk and crumbs. Mix well. Pour into greased baking dish. Sprinkle top with cinnamon sugar. Bake at 375° for about 1 hour.

SOUTHERN MEDLEY

1 *cup mashed cooked rutabagas*
½ *cup mashed cooked carrots*
½ *cup chopped cooked onions*
4 *rashers bacon or beef fry*
2 *tbs. drippings*
  Salt and pepper

Combine vegetables. Fry out bacon or beef fry. Drain. Add 2 tbs. drippings to medley, season and crumble bacon on top.

⚘ SQUASH

To PREPARE SUMMER SQUASH: Wash and slice, dice, quarter or cut in sticks. If skin is quite thin and not bitter (taste and judge), squash need not be peeled. Mature or large seeds should be removed. Young, underdeveloped seeds need not be.

To BOIL: Place in smallest amount of lightly salted water. Cover and simmer till tender, 10–15 minutes.

To PREPARE WINTER SQUASH: Wash or brush under cold water. Cut in half. Remove seeds and stringy membranes. Remove peel. Cut meat into serving size pieces.

To BOIL: Boil over medium high heat in small amount lightly salted water for 20–30 minutes, or until tender.

SIMPLE SUMMER SQUASH

1½ *lbs. young green or yellow squash*
1   *medium onion, chopped*
½   *cup boiling water*
¼   *cup chopped fresh parsley*
    Salt and pepper
2   *tbs. olive oil*

If green squash is used, cut in medium size slices. Quarter yellow squash and remove center seeds. Cut in 1 inch dice. Heat oil in skillet. Sauté onion till soft. Add squash and boiling water. Cover and simmer till tender, 10–15 minutes. Toss through with chopped parsley. Serve.

STUFFED SUMMER SQUASH

To prepare squashes for stuffing and baking:

METHOD 1: Wash squashes. Steam or cook them in very little water till firm but tender. Drain and cool. Either split squash in half down the length or cut off stem end. Scoop out squashes, being careful to leave enough meat on shell to keep firm through further cooking. Stuff squashes with one of stuffings suggested below. Place in baking pan with very little water or broth and bake at 400° until hot, 10–15 minutes.

METHOD 2: Scoop out raw squash (as above) either through stem end or after cutting in half down the length. Rub stuffed shells with oil or fat. Bake as above.

STUFFINGS FOR SQUASH

1. For 2 lbs. squash: 1 cup cottage cheese, 2 tbs. chopped cooked pimiento, ¼ tsp. celery seed, 2 beaten eggs. Combine. Spoon into squash. Dot with butter or sprinkle with buttered crumbs. If desired, you may grate sharp cheese over top. Or, 1 tbs. of sour cream may be spooned on top in last 5 minutes of cooking.

2. Chopped scooped-out centers of squash, 3 tbs. chopped walnuts, 1 tbs. butter, 1 tbs. bread crumbs, 4 tbs. grated yellow cheese, salt, pepper, paprika, dash Worcestershire.

3. Arabic style: Scoop out squash from stem end. Fry whole shells in 2 tbs. of oil till lightly browned; drain. Fry in same oil $\frac{1}{2}$ lb. ground meat, 2 medium chopped onions. When onions are golden, add $\frac{1}{4}$ cup pine nuts, 1 tsp. allspice, salt and pepper. Stir through and remove from heat. Stuff squash and place in baking pan. Cover with 1 cup tomato juice and 1 cup water. Bake at 300° for about 40 minutes.

PROVINCIAL STEW

1 *lb. yellow or green squash, cubed*
1 *large onion, sliced*
2 *tomatoes, diced*
1 *green or red pepper, sliced*
3 *tbs. olive oil*
1 *clove garlic, minced (or $\frac{1}{4}$ tsp. garlic powder)*
  Salt and pepper
$\frac{1}{2}$ *cup pitted, green olives, cut in half*

Heat oil in large skillet. Add onions and stew over moderate heat until soft. Add pepper, squash, tomatoes, garlic and salt and pepper. Cover and stew for 10–15 minutes. Uncover, and add olives and simmer till most pan liquids are absorbed.

GLAZED ZUCCHINI

1 or 2 *medium zucchini*
$\frac{1}{4}$ *cup dairy sour cream*
  Cinnamon sugar
  Salt

Slice zucchini very thin. Place in a flat, large, lightly greased baking dish. Make a single layer of slices. Sprinkle lightly with salt and coat thinly with sour cream. Repeat till all slices are incorporated. (It is not advisable to use more than 3 layers.) Bake in a 350° oven for about ½ hour. Remove to heat-proof serving dish. Sprinkle slices with cinnamon sugar and place under broiler for a moment to melt sugar. Serve.

HUNGARIAN-STYLE SQUASH

2 *medium squash (seeded, if yellow)*
2 *medium onions, chopped fine*
3 *tbs. butter*
1 *tsp. paprika*
1 *cup dairy sour cream*
1 *tbs. chopped fresh dill or 1 tsp. dillweed*
1 *tbs. chopped parsley*
Salt to taste
Pepper
Dash garlic powder, if desired

Grate squash, unpeeled. Salt lightly and allow to drain through strainer or cloth. Heat butter in frying pan. Sauté onions till golden. Add squash, lower heat and simmer, covered, for 10 minutes. Combine garlic, paprika, sour cream and dill. Pour over squash. Season and heat but do not boil. Serve garnished with chopped parsley.

ZUCCHINI ITALIENNE

4 *medium zucchini, cubed*
1 *medium onion, chopped or thin-sliced*
1 *small clove garlic, minced (opt.)*
1 *small can Italian plum tomatoes*
¼ *tsp. basil*
Salt and pepper
2 *tbs. olive oil*

Heat oil in skillet. Add onion and sauté until soft. Add tomatoes and garlic, salt and pepper. Simmer for 5–10 minutes. Add cut squash and cook slowly, covered, for 15–20 minutes. Serve.

LAURIE'S SUMMER SQUASH

1½ *lbs. summer squash, peeled, seeded and cubed*
¼ *tsp. garlic powder (opt.)*
1 *tbs. soya sauce*
1 *small can Italian eggplant appetizer (Caponata)*
  Salt and pepper
1 *tbs. butter*

Cook squash in small amount of water containing garlic and soya sauce, covered, till tender. Drain. Pour into serving plate. Add butter, salt and pepper and eggplant appetizer. Toss through. Serve.

Variation: Add 1 tsp. crushed oregano instead of Caponata.

ZUCCHINI PATTIES

3–4 *small zucchini squash or 2*   ½ *tsp. oregano*
  large ones   1 *egg, lightly beaten*
1 *cup bread crumbs*   *Oil for frying*
¼ *tsp. garlic powder*   *Salt, pepper*

Wash and grate unpeeled zucchini. Salt slightly and drain in a cheesecloth till excess moisture has run out. Combine all ingredients. Mix well. Shape into flat cakes. Brown in hot oil on both sides. Drain and serve.

BATTER FRIED ZUCCHINI

1 or 2 *large zucchini*
1 *cup pancake mix*
¾ *cup milk or* ½ *cup half & half plus* ⅓ *cup dry white wine*
½ *cup grated Cheddar cheese*
  Salt
  Good dash pepper
1 *egg*

Combine pancake mix, milk or cream and wine, cheese, egg and seasonings. Beat to a smooth batter with egg beater. Slice zucchini quite thin. Dip individual pieces in batter and toss into hot oil or fat in skillet. Brown on both sides. Drain on absorbent paper, salt and serve as snacks, hors d'oeuvres or vegetable side dish.

BAKED WINTER SQUASH

Cut acorn or Danish squash in half. Remove seeds. Pumpkin, banana, Hubbard and butternut squashes should be seeded and cut into serving chunks or squares. Score squares with a sharp knife and lay pieces at the bottom of a greased baking dish. Fill center wells or sauce cut squash with the following:

(Recipes are for 2 halves.)

1. 1 tbs. butter, 1 tbs. lemon juice, 2 tbs. dry Sherry (opt.), 2 tbs. honey (or maple syrup), dash salt. Sprinkle rims with nutmeg.

2. 2 tbs. brown sugar, rind of 1 lemon, $\frac{1}{4}$ tsp. ginger or mace, 4 tbs. condensed milk.

3. 2 tbs. maple syrup, dash salt, 2 rashers crisp bacon, crumbled.

Cover baking dish with foil for cut squash.

Wrap halves securely in aluminum foil. Bake in preheated oven at 350° for about 1 hour. Uncover. Mash pulp together with sauce in center well and serve.

WINTER SQUASH SCALLOP

2 medium acorn squash	Salt and pepper
2 tbs. butter, melted	Paprika
1 small onion, chopped	$\frac{1}{4}$ cup buttered crumbs

Bake squash in skin till soft. (1 hour at 350°.) Halve, remove seeds and scoop out flesh. Fry onion in butter. Add to squash. Season to taste. Pour into buttered baking dish. Top with crumbs and paprika. Bake at 350° for 20–25 minutes, or until top browns.

FLAMING SQUASH PUDDING

2 *cups cooked mashed winter*
  squash
$\frac{1}{3}$ *cup molasses or honey*
2 *tbs. butter, melted*
1 *tsp. cinnamon*
$\frac{1}{2}$ *tsp. powdered cloves*

$\frac{1}{4}$ *cup chopped walnuts*
1 *tsp. salt*
2 *tbs. orange or unsweetened*
  pineapple juice
2 *tbs. warmed rum*

Combine squash, butter, spices, salt and juice. Pour into a greased casserole. Pour molasses over top. Sprinkle with chopped nuts. Bake at 425° for 15 minutes. Pour warmed liquor over dish. Ignite and bring to table.

SQUASH FESTIVAL PUDDING

2 *cups cooked, mashed*
  butternut squash (1 large
  squash)
2 *tbs. melted butter*
$\frac{1}{2}$ *tsp. salt*
$\frac{1}{2}$ *tsp. powdered ginger*

$\frac{1}{2}$ *cup chopped nutmeats*
  (opt.)
$\frac{1}{3}$ *cup sweet red wine*
2 *grated tart apples*
  Honey to taste
1 *egg*

Combine all ingredients. Fold into a greased oven dish. Top with $\frac{1}{2}$ cup corn flakes, crumbled and dotted with butter. Bake at 350° for about 40 minutes.

∙ঞ় *TOMATOES*

    This fruit can be cooked in myriad ways: stuffed and baked, stewed, fried, scalloped, incorporated into sauces, used for flavoring. The one method of preparation we do not recommend is boiling.

    The recipes included here contain instructions for preparation appropriate to the dish discussed.

STUFFED TOMATOES

GENERAL METHOD: Select firm-ripe tomatoes. If you wish to bake them peeled, scald in hot water and plunge immediately in cold. Skin will slip off easily. (You may find that tomatoes keep their shape better in baking with shell intact.)

Place stuffed tomatoes in greased baking pan. Bake in moderate oven. (Time is listed for each stuffing.) Stuffings listed below fill 4 medium tomatoes: Cut off top slice at stem end. Scoop out pulp, reserve for soups and salads. You may add a small amount of chopped pulp to stuffing. Reserve top slice. Salt inside of tomato shells lightly. Turn upside down on rack and drain.

FILLING #1: 2 cups bread crumbs, 2 tbs. chopped scallions, $\frac{1}{2}$ tsp. salt, 1 tbs. butter, 1 well-beaten egg, pepper, 2 tbs. tomato pulp. Combine and stuff into tomato cases. Replace top. Bake at 400° for 20–25 minutes.

FILLING #2: 2 cups grated Swiss-style cheese, 1 cup milk, 2 beaten egg yolks, 6 tbs. bread crumbs, 2 tbs. melted butter, $\frac{1}{3}$ cup chopped ripe olives, 2 tbs. chopped parsley, $\frac{1}{4}$ tsp. marjoram and/or thyme. Combine and stuff into tomatoes. Sprinkle with paprika or top with buttered crumbs. Bake in moderate oven for 25 minutes.

FILLING #3: Pan-fried corn (see stuffed peppers with pan-fried corn, page 232).

FILLING #4: 1$\frac{1}{2}$ cups leftover vegetables, meat, poultry or fish, diced. Combine with $\frac{1}{2}$ cup medium white sauce and stuff tomatoes. Top with buttered crumbs. Bake in moderate oven till filling is hot.

FILLING #5: Try cottage cheese stuffing under "Stuffed Summer Squash" (page 245) for tomatoes.

FILLING #6: Chopped tomato pulp, $\frac{1}{4}$ cup cooked rice, 1 tsp. cinnamon, $\frac{1}{4}$ lb. chopped beef, 1 small chopped onion, 2 tbs. olive oil, salt and pepper, 2 tbs. pine nuts. Sauté onion in oil till soft. Add meat and sauté till cooked, add nuts and cook 2 more minutes. Combine all ingredients, stuff and bake $\frac{1}{2}$ hour in moderate oven. (Tomatoes may be placed under moderate heat in broiler for last 10 minutes of cooking time.)

BAKED TOMATOES IN CREAM

4 *medium, firm ripe tomatoes*   *Seasoned salt, pepper*
¼ *cup minced onion*   ½ *cup white sauce (medium)*
¼ *cup minced green pepper*   *made with light cream*
4 *tbs. butter*   ½ *tsp. chili or curry powder*
½ *tsp. sugar*

Peel tomatoes. Cut off 1 thin slice at stem end. Place in greased
pie plate. Dust each top lightly with sugar, sprinkle with seasoned
salt and pepper. Place combination of 1 tbs. onion and 1 tbs.
green pepper on each tomato head. Top each with 1 tbs. butter.
Bake at 350° until soft, about 25 minutes. Make sauce. Pour in
tomato pan juices and chili or curry. Cook over low heat till
combined. Place tomatoes on bed of rice, noodles, toast points
or croustades. Pour sauce over them. Serves 4.

PAN-FRIED TOMATOES

4 *medium green tomatoes*   ½ *cup flour*
2 *tbs. fat or oil*   ¼ *tsp. garlic powder (opt.)*
1 *tsp. curry powder*   1 *tsp. sugar*
   Salt and pepper

Combine flour, curry, sugar, salt and pepper and garlic powder.
Slice green tomatoes thick. (¼ inch.) Dip in flour. Fry in hot fat
till browned on both sides. Garnish with fresh chopped parsley
and serve with lemon wedges on the side.

GRILLED TOMATOES

2 *large, firm-ripe tomatoes*   3 *tbs. melted butter*
1 *cup bread crumbs*   ½ *tsp. sugar*
½ *tsp. oregano, basil,*   *Salt and pepper*
   marjoram and/or thyme

Wash tomatoes. Dry thoroughly. Cut in half lengthwise. Salt and
pepper cut surfaces. Dust lightly with sugar. Combine crumbs,
butter, herbs. Spread approximately 2 tbs. on each tomato half.

Place halves in greased casserole. Broil under moderate heat 350° for about ½ hour, until tomatoes are soft but not collapsed.

Variation: Add any of the following: ¼ tsp. garlic powder, 2 tbs. minced onion, ½ tsp. powdered ginger, ½ tsp. celery seed, 1 tbs. fresh chopped dill, 2 tbs. scallion greens, 2 rashers minced fried bacon or other spicy meat to crumb mixture. Or add ½ tsp. poultry seasoning in place of herbs. Broil under moderate heat.

TOMATO-CHEESE PIE

1 *cup bread crumbs*
2 *tbs. butter*
2 *tbs. grated cheese (Swiss or Cheddar)*

Combine and line pie plate with crumbs to make shell. Bake in 400° oven for 10 minutes or until lightly browned. Cool.

1 *tsp. butter*	½ *tsp. crushed basil*
2 *beefsteak tomatoes,*	*Ground pepper*
firm-ripe	2 *tbs. minced onion or 1 tbs.*
½ *tsp. sugar*	*onion flakes*
1 *tsp. salt*	

Layer tomatoes in pie plate. Dust with sugar, sprinkle with salt, pepper, basil and onions. Dot with butter.

2 *beaten eggs*	½ *cup grated yellow cheese*
1 *cup rich milk*	*Salt and pepper*

Beat together. Pour over tomatoes. Place in 375° oven for 30–40 minutes, until set.

TOMATO PUDDING

1 *large can tomatoes*	1 *tbs. flour*
(1 lb., 12 ozs.)	1 *tsp. salt*
2 *cups (herb) seasoned bread*	1 *tbs. sugar*
stuffing	*Dash cayenne or Tabasco*
1 *tbs. onion flakes*	1 *tsp. mustard powder*
3 *tbs. melted butter*	*Additional salt*

Either purée canned tomatoes in a blender or chop in a bowl. Combine tomatoes, stuffing and onion. Melt butter. Mix with flour, seasonings and mustard. Add to tomato mixture. Pour into a well-greased casserole. Sprinkle with additional salt. Bake at 400° for ½ hour. (You may sprinkle top with 2 tbs. grated yellow cheese in last ten minutes of baking.)

STEWED TOMATOES AND PEPPERS

4 *ripe tomatoes, quartered*
2 *bell peppers, in strips (red, if possible)*
1 *medium onion, sliced thin*

2 *tbs. salad oil*
1 *clove garlic, split (opt.)*
1 *tsp. crushed oregano*
  Salt and pepper

Heat oil in a skillet with garlic clove. Remove clove when it starts to brown. Sauté onion and peppers till soft over moderate heat. Add tomatoes. (Tomatoes may be peeled, if you prefer. See instructions under Stuffed Tomatoes, page 251.) Simmer over low heat for about ½ hour. Serve garnished with oregano.

Index

Acropolis Green Beans, 157
Adapting recipes to reducing diets,
  141–42
Alpine Kraut, 178
American Corn Fondue, 190
Appetizer, Lebanese Bean, 211
Appetizer Salad, Eggplant, 131
Appetizer, Sweet Pepper, 232–33
Apple Beet Pudding, 165–66
Apple Cream Sauce, Hot, 54–55
Apple Cream, Sprouts in, 172
Apple, Turnips with, 242
Apricots, Sauerkraut with, 176
Arabian Peas, 230
Arabic Sesame Seed Dressing, 57
Arthur's Favorite Green Beans,
  157–58
Artichoke Hearts, 22–23, 26, 27,
  36, 61, 101, 106, 146–47
Artichoke Hearts, Creamed, 146–
  47
Artichoke Hearts Provençal, 146
Artichoke Hearts Salad, 61
Artichoke Potatoes Italienne, 106
Artichoke Salad, 61
Artichokes, 4, 61, 62, 106, 145–48
Artichokes, Dressing for Plain
  Boiled, 147
Artichokes, Stuffed Baked, 147–48
Artichokes with Chicken, Greek-
  Style, 148
Asparagus, 4–5, 12, 14, 22–23, 23–
  24, 24–25, 26, 27, 28, 36, 61, 62,
  75, 101, 105, 107–08, 149–53,
  208
Asparagus à la Ratatouille, 152–53
Asparagus Au Gratin, 150
Asparagus, French Fried, 152
Asparagus Omelet, 151
Asparagus Salad, 75
Asparagus Salad, Cold, 61
Asparagus, Syrian, 152

Asparagus Tips, French-Style,
  150–51
Asparagus with Eggs, Italienne,
  149–50
Asparagus with Leeks, 151
Aspic, Tomato, 130
Aspic, Vegetable, 77
Athens Salad, 74
Au Gratin Asparagus, 150
Au Gratin, Belgian Lettuce, 214
Au Gratin, Cabbage, 108
Au Gratin Potatoes and Tomatoes,
  104
Austrian Caraway Marinade, 65–
  66
Avocado Salad, 75
Avocado Salad, Grapefruit, 73
Avocado Sauce, 58

Baba Ghanouj, 194–95
Bacon or Beef Fry Sauce for
  Greens, 52
Bamboo Shoots, 152–53
Bamiya, 222–23
Basic preparation and definitions,
  13–17
Batter Fried Zucchini, 248–49
Bean Appetizer, Lebanese, 211
Bean Bowl, The, 72
Bean Cake, 159–60
Bean Cake and Mushrooms, 160
Bean Purée, 210–11
Bean Soup, Kidney-Navy, 85–86
Bean Soup, Yankee Baked, 90
Bean Sprouts, 160–61
Bean Sprouts, Chinese, 161
Beans (See Green Beans, Lentils,
  Lima Beans, Snap Beans)
Beans, Baked Luise, 213
Beans, Cholent or Overnight, and
  Meat, 213
Beans, Dahl or Indian, 211–12

Beans, Dill, 156
Beans, Dried, 210–14
Beans, Honey, 214
Béchamel Sauce, 49
Beet Chiffon, Pineapple, 166–67
Beet Green (*See also* Greens), 7, 200
Beet Pudding, Apple, 165–66
Beet Raita, 165
Beet Salad, 61, 65
Beet Salad Mold, 131
Beet Salad, Scandinavian, 69
Beets, 5, 13, 14, 21, 24–25, 27, 36, 53, 55, 61, 62, 65, 66, 69, 131, 164–67
Beets, Celery, 165
Beets, Ginger, 166
Beets in Wine Sauce with Raisins, 164–65
Belgian Grape Sauce, 54
Belgian Lettuce Au Gratin, 214
Bertha's Carrot Kugel, 181
Blue Cheese Dressing, 65
Borghul, 67
Borscht, Cold Meatless, 96–97
Borscht, Jellied, 97–98
Borscht, Russian Meat, 84–85
Braised Broccoli in Oyster Sauce, 167–68
Braised Kohlrabi and Tomatoes, 207
Braised Leeks with Mushrooms, 209
Braised Lettuce, 215
Broccoli, 5, 7, 12, 14, 22–23, 23–24, 24–25, 26, 27, 28, 37, 62, 64, 70, 101, 102–03, 105, 108, 129–30, 167–70
Broccoli, Braised in Oyster Sauce, 167–68
Broccoli Custard, 168
Broccoli Divan, 105, 169
Broccoli Indienne, 169
Broccoli, Italian, 169
Broccoli Sesame, 168
Broccoli with Tomatoes, 170
Brown Sauce, Classic, 46
Brown Stock, Favorite, 83
Brussels Sprouts, 5, 12, 14, 22–23, 23–24, 24–25, 26, 27, 28, 37, 101, 105, 108, 129–30, 170–72
Brussels Sprouts and Chestnuts, 171
(Brussels) Sprouts in Apple Cream, 172
Brussels Sprouts in Caraway Cream, 170–71

(Brussels) Sprouts in Carrot Cheese, 171
(Brussels) Sprouts, Tomato-Dressed, 172
Butter Sauce, Herb, 49
Buttermilk Hollandaise, Quick, 55

Cabbage, 5, 12, 22–23, 23–24, 25, 27, 28, 37, 60, 65, 93, 108, 115, 172–78
Cabbage Au Gratin, 108
Cabbage, "Casbah" Stuffed, 177–78
Cabbage, Chinese-Style, 174
Cabbage, Dilled, 173
Cabbage, Dutch-Style Red, 175
Cabbage Filling for Strudel, 176
Cabbage Lasagna, 175–76
Cabbage Leaves, Cheese-Filled, 173
Cabbage Soup, Polish, 93
Cabbage Stew, French, 173–74
Cabbage, Stuffed, 177–78
Cabbage, Vegetarian Stuffed, 177
Cake, Fruit Carrot, 182–83
California Vegetable Ring, 102–03
Candy, Niagara Carrot, 183
Caraway Cream, Brussels Sprouts in, 170–71
Caraway Marinade, Austrian, 65–66
Caraway Sauce, 52
Carrot and Potato Whip, 181
Carrot Cake, Fruit, 182–83
Carrot Candy, Niagara, 183
Carrot Cheese, Sprouts in, 171
Carrot Cookies, Lemony, 182
Carrot Custard, Honey, 182
Carrot Kugel, Bertha's, 181
Carrot Loaf, 179
Carrot Scallop, 106–07
Carrot Soup, Cream of, 87–88
Carrots, 6, 13, 14, 22–23, 23–24, 24–25, 26, 27, 28, 37, 53, 55, 60, 61, 62, 66, 87–88, 101, 102–03, 106–07, 107–08, 109, 115, 129–30, 137, 139, 162, 171, 178–83, 218–19
Carrots, Bread and Cheese, 180
Carrots, French, 179
Carrots, Kid-Stuff, 180
Carrots, Lemony, 139
Carrots, Marmalade, 180–81
Carrots, Mushrooms and Barley, 218–19
Casseroles, 99–109

Cauliflower, 6, 12, 14, 23–24, 24–25, 25–26, 27, 28, 38, 60, 62, 101, 105, 108, 115, 129–30, 183–85
Cauliflower à la Grecque, 129–30
Cauliflower and Eggs, Moravian, 185
Cauliflower Bake, 184
Cauliflower, Danish Creamed, 184
Cauliflower in Tuna Sauce, 185
Celery, 6, 12, 14, 22–23, 23–24, 24–25, 26, 27, 28, 38, 55, 60, 62, 101–02, 102–03, 107–08, 110, 129–30, 135, 137, 165–66, 185–87, 208
Celery à la Crème, 186
Celery Beet Pudding, 165–66
Celery Beets, 165
Celery, Creamed Corn and, 110
Celery, Curried Stewed, 135
Celery Stuffed with Celery, 186
Celery, Sweet and Sour, 137, 187
Celery with Smoked Salmon, 187
Chard, 7
Chard with Nuts and Raisins, 203
Cheese and Wine, Creamed Lentils with, 212
Cheese, Baked Tomatoes with, 134
Cheese Balls, Cucumber, 129
Cheese, Carrots, Bread and, 180
Cheese Dressing, Blue, 65
Cheese, Green Beans in Savory, 154–55
Cheese, Limas Baked with, 161–62
Cheese, Mushrooms with, 219
Cheese Pie, Onion, 255
Cheese Pie, Tomato, 253
Cheese Salad, 77
Cheese Salad, Vegetable, 132
Cheese Sauce, 51
Cheese Sauce, Cold, 57
Cheese Sauce, Low Calorie, 134
Cheese, Spinach, Rice and, 203
Cheese, Sprouts in Carrot, 171
Chick-Peas (Hummous), 212
Chick-Peas in Oil, Eggplant with, 197
Chicory (See also Greens), 6–7, 60, 200
Chinese Bean Sprouts, 161
Chinese Greens, 204
Chinese Hot and Sour Soup, 95
Chinese Hot Vegetable Salad, 74
Chinese Radish Salad, 70
Chinese-Style Cabbage, 174
Chinese-Style Cucumbers, 192–93
Chinese Vegetables, 22–23

Cholent or Overnight Beans and Meat, 213
Chowder, Potato, 88–89
Chowder, Vegetable, 86–87
Chutney Dressing for Fruit Salads, 133
Clam Digger Beans, 156
Cocktail, Diet, 130
Coconut Cream, Onions in, 225–26
Cold Soups, 96–98
Cole Slaw, 65
Collards, 7
Colonial-Style Corn Stuffing, 189
Confetti Stuffed Eggplant, 198
Cookies, Lemony Carrot, 182
Cooking terms, glossary of, xix
Corn, 7, 12, 14, 22–23, 23–24, 25–26, 27, 28, 38, 60, 62, 101–02, 110, 188, 189–90, 191
Corn and Celery, Creamed, 110
Corn Creole, 188
Corn Fondue, American, 190
Corn Kernels, 188
Corn Meal Dumplings, 189–90
Corn Pie, 191
Corn Pone, Jubilation, 191
Corn Pudding, Modern Day, 190
Corn Sauté, 189.
Corn Stuffing, Colonial-Style, 189
Country Spinach Cooked in Milk, 205
Cracked Wheat Salad, 67
Cranberry Sweets, 240
Cream of Carrot Soup, 87–88
Cream of Yam Soup, 87–88
Creamed Artichoke Hearts, 146–47
Creamed Corn and Celery, 110
Creamed Eggplant and Mushrooms, 197–98
Creamed Green Beans, Dill-Style, 139
Creamed Lentils with Cheese and Wine, 212
Creamed Peas, Old-Style, 231
Creamed Spinach, 205
Crème Luise, 94
Creole Dressing, 63
Creole Sauce, 53
Creole Vegetables, 23–24
Croquettes, Savory Spinach, 201–02
Cucumber-Cheese Balls, 129
Cucumber Poppy Sauce, 56
Cucumber Salad, 65
Cucumber Salad, Marinated, 131
Cucumbers, 7, 12, 22–23, 23–24,

27, 28, 38, 56, 60, 65, 70, 129, 131, 135, 136, 139, 191–93
Cucumber, Baked Stuffed, 139–40, 192
Cucumbers, Chinese-Style, 192–93
Cucumbers, French Fried, 136
Cucumbers with Tomatoes and Dill, 192
Curried Stewed Celery, 135
Curry Cream, Greens in, 136
Curry Dessing, 64
Custard, Broccoli, 168
Custard, Honey Carrot, 182
Custard, Mushroom and Eggplant, 220
Custard Pie, Green, 202
Custard, Spinach, 202
Cutlets, Lentil, 210
Cutlets, Vegetable, Basic, 115

Dahl or Indian Beans, 211–12
Dandelion Greens (See also Greens), 7, 200
Danish Creamed Cauliflower, 184
Devilled Vegetable Sauce, 48
Diet Cocktail, 130
Diet Salad Dressing, French-Style, 133
Diet, Vegetable Lover's, 118–42
Different-Ingredient Soup, Ten-Minute, 96
Dill Beans, 156
Dill Cream, Peas with, 229
Dill, Cucumbers with Tomatoes and, 192
Dill Sauce, Cold, 56
Dill-Style Creamed Green Beans, 139
Dilled Cabbage, 173
Dixieland Beans, 158
Dressing, Another Yoghurt, 133
Dressing, Arabic Sesame Seed, 59
Dressing, Blue Cheese, 65
Dressing, Chutney, for Fruit Salads, 133
Dressing, Creole, 63
Dressing, Curry, 64
Dressing, Diet Salad, French-Style, 133
Dressing for Plain Boiled Artichokes, 147
Dressing, French, and Marinade with Variations, 62–63
Dressing, Honeyed Yoghurt, 65
Dressing, Lemon Butter, 66
Dressing, Lime, for Fruit and Lettuce Salads, 63

Dressing, Sesame Seed, 64
Dressing, Soya Sauce, 134
Dressing, Spinach Salad, 132–33
Dressing, Sweet and Sour Cream, 64–65
Dried Beans, 210–14
Dry Onions (See also Onions), 8–9, 13
Duchesse Potatoes, Quick, 239
Dumplings, Stuffed Potato, 236
Dutch Glunarensla, 76
Dutch Pea Soup, 92
Dutch-Style Endives with Eggs, 215
Dutch-Style Red Cabbage, 175

East-Indian Quick Soups, 92
Egg Dumplings, Peas with, 230
Egg Sauce, 51
Egg Sauce, String Beans in, 142
Eggs, Dutch-Style Endives with, 215
Eggs, Italienne Asparagus with, 149–50
Eggs, Moravian Cauliflower and, 185
Eggs, Spanish-Style Eggplant with, 197
Eggplant, 7, 12, 13, 22–23, 23–24, 24–25, 25–26, 27, 28, 39, 62, 101–02, 103–04, 131, 138, 193–99, 220
Eggplant Appetizer Salad, 131
Eggplant, Baked Halved, 193–94
Eggplant, Confetti Stuffed, 198
Eggplant Custard, Mushroom and, 220
Eggplant Fiesta, Baked, 103–04
Eggplant Polenta, 198–99
Eggplant Potato Whip, 194
Eggplant Salad, 70, 131
Eggplant Scallop, Tomato, 138
Eggplant Soufflé, 199
Eggplant Soufflé, Home-Style, 195
Eggplant Steaks, Broiled, 195–96
Eggplant, The Sheik's Favorite, 196–97
Eggplant with Chick-Peas in Oil, 196
Eggplant with Eggs, Spanish-Style, 197
Eggplant with Mushrooms, Creamed, 197–98
Endive (See also Greens), 6–7, 60
Endives with Eggs, Dutch-Style, 215

Escarole (*See also* Greens), 6–7, 60, 163, 200

Fennel, 199
Festival Pudding, Squash, 250
Festival Soup, Vietnamese, 94
Fiesta, Baked Eggplant, 103–04
Filling for Strudel, Cabbage, 176
Flamenco Beans, 156
Flaming Squash Pudding, 250
Fondue, American Corn, 190
French Carrots, 179
French Onion Soup, Quickie, 87
French Spinach Salad, 72
French-Style Asparagus Tips, 150–51
French-Style, Diet Salad Dressing, 133
French Vegetables, 23–24
Fritters, Parsnip, 227
Fritters, Vegetable, Basic, 114
Fruit Carrot Cake, 182–83
Fruit Salads, Chutney Dressing for, 133
Fruit Salads, Lime Dressing for, 63

Garlic, 7
Ginger Beets, 166
Globe Artichokes and Artichoke Hearts, 145–48
Glockenspiel Limas, 163
Glockenspiel Potatoes, 234
Glossary of cooking terms, xix
Glunarensla, Dutch, 76
Golden Glow Casserole, 109
Grape Sauce, Belgian, 54
Grapefruit-Avocado Salad, 73
Greek-Style Artichokes with Chicken, 148
Green Bean Salad, 61
Green Beans, (*See also* Snap Beans), 21, 22–23, 25–26, 61, 62, 64, 101–02, 102–03, 105, 107–08, 115, 139, 154–55, 156, 157–58, 159
Green Beans, Creamed, Dill-Style, 139
Green Custard Pie, 202
Green Onions (*See also* Onions), 9, 12,
Green Sauce, 56
Greens, 6–7, 12, 14, 22–23, 23–24, 25–26, 27, 28, 39, 52, 60, 64, 70, 136, 163, 200–06
Greens, Bacon or Beef Fry Sauce for, 52

Greens, Caraway, with Crumbs, 203–04
Greens, Chinese, 204
Greens in Curry Cream, 136
Greens, Salad, 12
Greens, Savory, 200
Greens, Spicy, 201
Greens, Vinaigrette, 201
Gumbo, Baked Onion, 226
Gumbo, Baked Vegetable, 103
Gumbo, Okra, 222

Hearthstone Limas, 163
Hearty Minestrone, 89
Hearty Tomato Soup, 84
Herb and Spice Guide, 29–32
Herb Butter Sauce, 49
Hollandaise Sauce, Classic, 48
Hollandaise Sauce, Quick Buttermilk, 55
Honey Beans, 214
Honey Carrot Custard, 182
Honeyed Yoghurt Dressing, 65
Hot Vegetable Salad, Chinese, 74
Hot Slaw, 174–75
Hummous, 212
Hungarian Mustard Sauce, 57
Hungarian Sour Potatoes, 235
Hungarian Squash, 137–38, 247
Hungarian Vegetables, 24–25

Indian Beans, 211–12
Indian Vegetables, 25–26
Italian Broccoli, 169
Italian Pepper Slaw, 71
Italian-Style Tomato Sauce, 48
Italian Vegetables, 26
Italienne, Artichoke Potatoes, 106
Italienne Asparagus with Eggs, 145–50
Italienne Zucchini, 247

Jellied Borscht, 97–98
Jellied Madrilène, 98
Jellied Salad, 77
Jubilation Corn Pone, 191

Kale (*See also* Greens), 7, 200
Kasha, Mushrooms and, 220
Keeping vegetables fresh, 12–13
Kidney-Navy Bean Soup, 85–86
Kid-Stuff Carrots, 180
Knaidlech, 189–90
Kohlrabi, 14, 23–24, 24–25, 27, 28, 39, 62, 138, 206–08
Kohlrabi and Tomatoes, Braised, 207

Kohlrabi, Mashed, 138, 207
Kohlrabi Pancakes, 208
Kohrabi, Stuffed, 206–07
Kraut, Alpine, 178
Kugel, Bertha's Carrot, 181

Lasagna, Cabbage, 175–76
Laurie's Summer Squash, 248
Lebanese Bean Appetizer, 211
Leek Pie, 209
Leeks, 9, 39, 62, 151, 208–09
Leeks, Asparagus with, 151
Leeks, Braised, with Mushrooms, 209
Leeks in Lemon Cream, 208–09
Leftovers, 111–17
Lemon Butter Dressing, 66
Lemon Butter Sauce, 47
Lemon Cream, Leeks in, 208–09
Lemony Carrot Cookies, 182
Lemony Carrots, 139
Lentil-Barley Soup, 85
Lentil Cutlets, 210
Lentils, 23–24, 25–26, 27, 28, 62, 85, 210–14
Lentils with Cheese and Wine, Creamed, 212
Lettuce, 7–8, 22, 23, 39, 214–16
Lettuce Au Gratin, Belgian, 214
Lettuce, Braised, 215
Lettuce Salads, Lime Dressing for, 63
Lettuce with Mushrooms and Olives, 215–16
Lima Bean Scallop, 162
Lima Beans, 5, 12, 14, 23–24, 26, 27, 28, 101–02, 161–64
Lima Beans Romano, 162
Limas Baked with Cheese, 161–62
Limas, Glockenspiel, 163
Limas, Hearthstone, 163
Limas Orientale, 163
Lime Dressing for Fruit and Lettuce Salads, 63
Literary Salad, 73
Liver Pâté, 154
Loaf, Basic Vegetable, 114
Low Calorie Cheese Sauce, 134
Lucerne Potatoes, 234–35

Macaroni, Mushroom, 109
Macaroni Salad, 68
Madrilène, Jellied, 98
Magyar Beans, 155
Marinade, Austrian Caraway, 65–66
Marinade, Curry Dressing and, 64

Marinade with Variations, French Dressing, 62–63
Marinades, 56, 57, 61–66
Marinated Cucumber Salad, 131
Marmalade Carrots, 180–81
Max's Man-in-the-Kitchen Soup, 95
Meat Borscht, Russian, 84–85
Mediterranean Spinach, 204
Medley, Southern, 244
Mennonite Green Beans, 155
Mennonite Salad, 71
Middle-Eastern Vegetables, 27
Mid-East Salad Platter, 75–76
Minestrone, Hearty, 89
Minestrone, Home-Style, 91
Mold, Party Salad, 132
Moravian Cauliflower and Eggs, 185
Mushroom and Eggplant Custard, 220
Mushroom Bisque with Brandy and Chives, 86
Mushroom Macaroni, 109
Mushroom Pancakes, Savory, 217
Mushroom Picker Beans, 157
Mushroom Pudding, Serbian, 217–18
Mushroom Rice, 221
Mushroom Sauce, 50
Mushrooms, 8, 22, 23–24, 24–25, 25–26, 27, 28, 40, 50, 60, 62, 86, 101, 102–03, 107–08, 109, 129–30, 136, 137, 157, 160, 216–21
Mushrooms and Kasha, 220
Mushrooms and Peppers, 216
Mushrooms, Baked, 136
Mushrooms, Bean Cake and, 160
Mushrooms, Carrots and Barley, 218–19
Mushrooms, Creamed Eggplant with, 197–98
Mushrooms in Home-Style Sauce, 217
Mushrooms, Stewed, 137
Mushrooms Stuffed with Mushrooms, 218
Mushrooms, White Russian, 219
Mushrooms with Cheese, 219
Mustard Greens (See also Greens), 7, 200

Navy Bean Soup, Kidney, 85–86
Niagara Carrot Candy, 183
Niçoise Salad, 61

Okra, 8, 14, 23–24, 25–26, 27, 28, 40, 62, 221–23
Okra, Arabian (Bamiya), 222–23
Okra Gumbo, 222
Okra Sauté à la Crème, 222
Okra Vinaigrette, 221
Omelet, Asparagus, 151
Omelets, 113
Onion-Cheese Pie, 225
Onion Gumbo, Baked, 226
Onion Pudding Cake, Sweet, 226
Onion Sauce, 50–51
Onion Soup, Quick French, 87
Onion Stew, 227
Onions (*See also* Dry Onions, Green Onions), 14, 22–23, 25–26, 27, 40, 50–51, 53, 60, 62, 87, 101–02, 137–38, 223–27
Onions, Baked, with Peas, 223
Onions, French Fried, 224
Onions in Coconut Cream, 225–26
Onions in Wine Sauce, 224
Onions, Stuffed, 224–25
Orientale, Limas, 163
Orientale, Shredded Turnips, 243
Overnight Beans and Meat, 213
Oyster Sauce, Braised Broccoli in, 167–68

Pancakes, Kohlrabi, 208
Pancakes, Savory Mushroom, 217
Parsley, 9, 60
Parsnip Fritters, 227
Parsnip Puffs, Nutted, 228
Parsnips, 9, 13, 15, 24–25, 27, 40, 62, 227–28
Parsnips, Glazed, 228
Party Salad Mold, 132
Pasta, Peas and, 229
Pastries, Spinach, 206
Pâté, Vegetarian Liver, 154
Patties, Zucchini, 248
Peanut Sauce Supreme, 54
Pea Purée, 210–11
Pea Soup, Dutch, 92
Peas, 9, 12–13, 15, 22–23, 23–24, 24–25, 25–26, 27, 28, 41, 55, 60, 62, 64, 66, 92, 101–02, 115, 210–11, 223, 228–31
Peas and Pasta, 229
Peas, Arabian, 230
Peas, Baked Onions with, 223
Peas, Old-Style Creamed, 231
Peas with Dill Cream, 229
Peas with Egg Dumplings, 230
Peas with Tomato, 230–31
Pennsylvania Dutch Vegetables, 27

Pepper Appetizer, Sweet, 232–33
Pepper Slaw, Italian, 71
Peppers, 9–10, 12, 22–23, 25–26, 27, 41, 60, 62, 101–02, 102–03, 107–08, 216, 231–33, 254
Peppers, Mushrooms and, 216
Peppers, Stewed Tomatoes and, 254
Peppers, Stuffed, 231–33
Peppers with Tomatoes and Potatoes, 232
Perishables, 12
Pie, Basic Vegetable #1, 116
Pie, Basic Vegetable #2, 116–17
Pie, Corn, 191
Pie, Green Custard, 202
Pie, Leek, 209
Pie, Potato, 237
Pie, Squash-Potato, 105–06
Pie, Sweet Potato, 239
Pineapple Beet Chiffon, 166–67
Polenta, Eggplant, 198–99
Polish Cabbage Soup, 93
Polonaise, Vegetables, 102
Poppy Sauce, Cucumber, 56
Potato Casserole, Spanish, 105
Potato Chips, Homemade, 234
Potato Chowder, 88–89
Potato Dumplings, Stuffed, 236
Potato Pie, 237
Potato Pie, Squash, 105–06
Potato Pudding #1, 238
Potato Pudding #2, 238
Potato Salad, 61, 65
Potato Scallop #2, 237–38
Potato Soup, Old-Fashioned, 88
Potato Whip, Carrot and, 181
Potato Whip, Eggplant, 194
Potatoes, 10, 13, 15, 22–23, 23–24, 24–25, 25–26, 27, 28, 41, 55, 61, 62, 64, 65, 66, 88–89, 101, 102–03, 104, 105, 106, 107–08, 115, 181, 194, 201–02, 233–40
Potatoes and Tomatoes, Au Gratin, 104
Potatoes, Baked Mustard, 236
Potatoes, Baked Stuffed, 233–34
Potatoes, Glockenspiel, 234
Potatoes, Hungarian Sour, 235
Potatoes in Tomato Sauce, 235
Potatoes Italienne, Artichoke, 106
Potatoes Lucerne, 234–35
Potatoes, Quick Duchesse, 239
Potatoes, Scalloped #1, 237
Provençal, Artichoke Hearts, 146
Provençal, Salade, 69
Provincial Stew, 246

Pudding, Apple Beet, 165–66
Pudding, Basic Vegetable, 115
Pudding Cake, Sweet Onion, 226
Pudding, Modern Day Corn, 190
Pudding, Potato #1, 238
Pudding, Potato #2, 238
Pudding, Scandia Rutabaga, 243–44
Pudding, Serbian Mushroom, 217–18
Pudding, Squash, 140
Pudding, Squash Festival, 250
Pudding, Tomato, 253–54
Puffs, Nutted Parsnip, 228
Purée, Pea, 210–11
Purées, 113

Quick Buttermilk Hollandaise, 55
Quick Duchesse Potatoes, 239
Quick East Indian Soups, 92
Quickie French Onion Soup, 87

Radish Salad, Chinese, 70
Radishes, 10, 12, 60, 62, 70
Raisin Sauce, 53
Red Cabbage, Dutch-Style, 175
Red Salad, 71
Reducing diets, adapting recipes to, 141–42
Rhubarb, 10–11, 15, 24–25, 27, 41, 140
Rhubarb Whip, 140
Rice and Cheese, Spinach, 203
Rice, Mushroom, 221
Rice Salad, 67–68
Rice, Vegetable, 107
Ring, California Vegetable, 102–03
Root Soup, Scandinavian, 91–92
Russian Meat Borscht, 84–85
Russian Mushrooms, White, 219
Russian Salad, 76
Rutabaga Pudding, Scandia, 243–44
Rutabaga Stew, 242
Rutabagas, 12, 13, 15, 23–24, 27, 28, 42, 53, 55, 62, 102–03, 241–44
Rutabagas Julienne, 241

Salad, Artichoke Hearts, 61
Salad, Asparagus, 61, 75
Salad, Athens, 74
Salad, Avocado, 73, 75
Salad, Beet, 61, 65, 69
Salad, Cheese, 77
Salad, Chinese Hot Vegetable, 74
Salad, Chinese Radish, 70

Salad, Cracked Wheat (Borghul), 67
Salad, Cucumber, 65
Salad, Cucumber, Marinated, 131
Salad, Eggplant, 70
Salad, Eggplant Appetizer, 131
Salad, French Spinach, 72
Salad, Grapefruit-Avocado, 73
Salad, Green Bean, 61
Salad greens, 12
Salad, Jellied, 77
Salad, Literary, 73
Salad, Macaroni, 68
Salad, Mennonite, 71
Salad Mold, Beet, 131
Salad Mold, Party, 132
Salad, Niçoise, 61
Salad Platter, Mid-East, 75–76
Salad, Potato, 61, 65
Salad, Red, 71
Salad, Rice, 67–68
Salad, Russian, 76
Salad, Vegetable Cheese, 132
Salad Dressing, French-Style Diet, 133
Salad Dressing, Spinach, 132–33
Salad dressings and marinades, favorite, 62–66
Salade, Provençal, 69
Salads, Chutney Dressing for Fruit, 133
Salads, Favorite, 66–77
Sandwiches, Grilled, 113
Sauce, Avocado, 58
Sauce, Bacon or Beef Fry, for Greens, 52
Sauce, Beets in Wine, with Raisins, 164–65
Sauce, Belgian Grape, 54
Sauce, Caraway, 52
Sauce, Cauliflower in Tuna, 185
Sauce, Cheese, 51
Sauce, Cheese, Cold, 57
Sauce, Cheese, Low Calorie, 134
Sauce, Classic Brown, 46
Sauce, Classic Hollandaise, 48
Sauce, Classic White, 46–47
Sauce, Cold Dill, 56
Sauce, Cold Yoghurt, for Hot Vegetables, 133
Sauce, Creole, 53
Sauce, Cucumber Poppy, 56
Sauce, Devilled Vegetable, 48
Sauce, Egg, 51
Sauce, Green, 56
Sauce, Herb Butter, 49
Sauce, Hot Apple Cream, 54–55

Sauce, Italian-Style Tomato, 48
Sauce, Lemon Butter, 47
Sauce, Mushroom, 50
Sauce, Mushrooms in Home-Style, 217
Sauce, Onion, 50–51
Sauce, Oyster, Braised Broccoli in, 167–68
Sauce, Peanut Supreme, 54
Sauce, Sour Cream, 50
Sauce, Soya Dressing, 134
Sauce, Spanish, 52–53
Sauce, String Beans in Egg, 142
Sauce, Sweet and Sour, 51
Sauce, Tomato, Potatoes in, 235
Sauce, Wine, Onions in, 224
Sauces, 45–58, 112–13
Sauces, Cold, 56–58
Sauces, Hot, 46–51, 52–55
Sauerkraut with Apricots, 176
Sauté à la Crème, Okra, 222
Savory Greens, 200
Savory Mushroom Pancakes, 217
Savory Spinach Croquettes, 201–02
Scallop, Carrot, 106–07
Scallop, Lima Bean, 162
Scallop, Potato #2, 237–38
Scallop, Tomato-Eggplant, 138
Scallop, Winter Squash, 249
Scalloped Potatoes #1, 237
Scalloped Vegetable Casserole, 101–02
Scandia Rutabaga Pudding, 243–44
Scandinavian Beet Salad, 69
Seasoning, 18–22, 32–35, 36–42
Semi-perishables, 12–13
Serbian Mushroom Pudding, 217–18
Sesame, Broccoli, 168
Sesame Seed Dressing, 64
Sesame Seed Dressing, Arabic, 57
Shallots, 9
Shopping, 3–12
Shredded Turnips, Orientale, 243
Simplicity Succotash, 164
Slaw, Cole, 65
Slaw, Hot, 174–75
Slaw, Italian Pepper, 71
Snap Beans (*See also* Green Beans), 5, 12–13, 14, 23–24, 24–25, 26, 27, 28, 36, 129–30, 153–59
Sorrel, 7
Sorrel Soup, Sourgrass or, 97
Soufflé, Basic Vegetable, 113–14

Soufflé, Eggplant, 199
Soufflé, Home-Style Eggplant, 195
Soup, Bean, 85–86, 90
Soup, Chilled Water Cress, 97
Soup, Chinese Hot and Sour, 95
Soup, Cream of Carrot, 87–88
Soup, Cream of Yam, 87–88
Soup, Dutch Pea, 92
Soup, Hearty Tomato, 84
Soup, Lentil-Barley, 85
Soup, Max's Man-in-the-Kitchen, 95
Soup, Mennonite Vegetable, 93
Soup, Old-Fashioned Potato, 88
Soup, Polish Cabbage, 93
Soup, Quickie French Onion, 87
Soup, Scandinavian Root, 91–92
Soup, Sourgrass or Sorrel (Schav), 97
Soup, Spring, 90
Soup, Ten-Minute Different-Ingredient, 96
Soup, Vietnamese Festival, 94
Soups, 78–98
Soups, Cold, 96–98
Soups, East Indian Quick, 92
Soups, Hot, 84–95
Sour Cream Dressing, Sweet and, 64–65
Sour Cream Sauce, 50
Sourgrass or Sorrel Soup, 97
Southern Medley, 244
Soya Sauce Dressing, 134
Spanish Potato Casserole, 105
Spanish Sauce, 52–53
Spanish-Style Eggplant with Eggs, 197
Spanish Vegetables, 28
Spice Guide, Herb and, 29–32
Spicy Greens, 201
Spinach (*See also* Greens), 7, 11, 15, 26, 60, 72, 102–03, 132–33, 163, 200, 201–02, 203, 204, 205, 206
Spinach Cooked in Milk, Country, 205
Spinach, Creamed, 205
Spinach Croquettes, Savory, 201–02
Spinach Custard, 202
Spinach, Mediterranean, 204
Spinach Pastries, 206
Spinach, Rice and Cheese, 203
Spinach Salad Dressing, 132–33
Spinach Salad, French, 72
Spring Soup, 90
Sprouts in Apple Cream, 172

Sprouts in Carrot Cheese, 171
Sprouts, Tomato-Dressed, 172
Squash (*See also* Summer Squash,
Winter Squash, Zucchini), 11,
21, 22, 27, 62, 101, 102–03,
105–06, 129–30, 140, 244–50
Squash, Baked Winter, 249
Squash Festival Pudding, 250
Squash, Hungarian-Style, 247
Squash, Laurie's Summer, 248
Squash-Potato Pie, 105–06
Squash Pudding, 140
Squash Pudding, Flaming, 250
Squash Scallop, Winter, 249
Squash, Simple Summer, 245
Squash, Stuffed Summer, 245
Squash, Stuffings for, 245–46
Staples, 13
Stew, French Cabbage, 173–74
Stew, Onion, 227
Stew, Provincial, 246
Stew, Rutabaga, 242
Stewed Celery, Curried, 135
Stewed Mushrooms, 137
Stewed Tomatoes and Peppers,
254
Stock, 83–84
Stock-pot, 80–81, 82
String Beans in Egg Sauce, 142
Strudel, Cabbage Filling for, 176
Stuffed Baked Artichokes, 147–48
Stuffed Cabbage, 177–78
Stuffed Cabbage, Vegetarian, 177
Stuffed, Celery, with Celery, 186
Stuffed Cucumbers, Baked, 139–
40, 192
Stuffed Eggplant, Confetti, 198
Stuffed Kohlrabi, 206–07
Stuffed, Mushrooms, with Mush-
rooms, 218
Stuffed Onions, 224–25
Stuffed Peppers, 231–33
Stuffed Potato Dumplings, 236
Stuffed Potatoes, Baked, 233–34
Stuffed Sweets, Baked, 239
Stuffed Tomatoes, 251
Stuffed Zucchini, 135
Stuffin' Vegetables, 107–08
Succotash, Simplicity, 164
Summer Squash, 15, 22–23, 23–24,
25–26, 27–28, 42, 66, 101–02,
245, 248
Sweet and Sour Celery, 137, 187
Sweet and Sour Cream Dressing,
64–65
Sweet Onion Pudding Cake, 226
Sweet Pepper Appetizer, 232–33

Sweet Potato Bake, 240
Sweet Potato Balls, 241
Sweet Potato Pie, 239
Sweet Potatoes, 11, 15, 25–26, 42,
53, 55, 233, 239–40, 241
Sweet Potatoes, Baked, 239
Sweets, Baked Stuffed, 239
Sweets, Cranberry, 240
Sweets or Yams, Baked, 240
Swiss Chard (*See also* Greens), 6,
200
Syrian Asparagus, 152

Tomato Aspic, 130
Tomato-Dressed Sprouts, 172
Tomato-Eggplant Scallop, 138
Tomato, Peas with, 230–31
Tomato Pudding, 253–54
Tomato Wine Sauce, 49
Tomatoes, 11, 12, 15, 22–23, 23–
24, 25–26, 27, 28, 49, 60, 65,
104, 130, 134, 138, 170, 172,
192, 207, 230–31, 232, 250 54
Tomatoes and Dill, Cucumbers
with, 192
Tomatoes and Potatoes, Peppers
with, 232
Tomatoes Au Gratin, Potatoes and,
104
Tomatoes, Baked, in Cream, 252
Tomatoes, Braised Kohlrabi and,
207
Tomatoes, Broccoli with, 170
Tomatoes, Grilled, 252–53
Tomatoes, Pan-Fried, 252
Tomatoes, Stuffed, 251
Tomatoes with Cheese, Baked, 134
Tricolor Beans, 159
Turnip Greens (*See also* Greens),
7, 200
Turnip Ring, 243
Turnips (*See also* Rutabagas), 12,
13, 15, 23–24, 24–25, 25–26,
27, 28, 53, 55, 62, 70, 102–03,
137, 138, 241–43
Turnips, Glazed, 241–42
Turnips, Shredded, Orientale, 243
Turnips, Whipped, 138
Turnips with Apple, 242

Vegetable Aspic, 77
Vegetable Casserole, Scalloped,
101–02
Vegetable Cheese Salad, 132
Vegetable Chowder, 86–87
Vegetable Cutlets, Basic, 115
Vegetable Fritters, Basic, 114

Vegetable Gumbo, Baked, 103
Vegetable Loaf, Basic, 114
Vegetable Lover's Diet, 118–42
Vegetable Patties, Basic, 116
Vegetable Pie #1, Basic, 116
Vegetable Pie #2, Basic, 116–17
Vegetable Pudding, Basic, 115
Vegetable Rice, 107
Vegetable Ring, California, 102–03
Vegetable Salad, Chinese Hot, 74
Vegetable Sauce, Devilled, 48
Vegetable seasoning guide, 36–42
Vegetable Soufflé, Basic, 113–14
Vegetable Soup, Mennonite, 93
Vegetable Stuffin', 107–08
Vegetables à la Crème, 101
Vegetables, Cold Sauces for, 56–58
Vegetables, Creole, 23–24
Vegetables, French, 23–24
Vegetables, Hot Sauces for, 46–51, 52–55
Vegetables, Hungarian, 24–25
Vegetables, Indian, 25–26
Vegetables, Italian, 26
Vegetables, Middle-Eastern, 27
Vegetables, Pennsylvania Dutch, 27
Vegetables Polonaise, 102.
Vegetables, Spanish, 28

Vegetarian Liver Pâté, 154
Vietnamese Festival Soup, 94
Vinaigrette, Greens, 201
Vinaigrette, Okra, 221

Water Cress, 7, 12, 60, 97
Water Cress Soup, Chilled, 97
Whip, Carrot and Potato, 181
Whip, Eggplant Potato, 194
Whip, Rhubarb, 140
White Russian Mushrooms, 219
Wine Sauce, Onions in, 224
Winter Squash, 13, 15, 22–23, 24–25, 25–26, 27–28, 42, 53, 55, 129, 249

Yams, Baked Sweets or, 240
Yankee Baked Bean Soup, 90
Yoghurt Dressing, Another, 133
Yoghurt Dressing, Honeyed, 65
Yoghurt Sauce for Hot Vegetables, Cold, 133
Yugoslav Green Beans, 158

Zucchini (*See also* Squash), 24–25, 102, 135, 246, 247, 248–49
Zucchini, Batter Fried, 248–49
Zucchini, Italienne, 247
Zucchini Patties, 248
(Zucchini) Provincial Stew, 246
Zucchini, Stuffed, 135